PRAISE FOR *RESTORING*
THE SOUL OF BUSINESS

"This is a book of wisdom. A book that should be passed down with compassion, care, and grace from CEOs to their teams and from parents to their children. It is not a business book; it is a book full of hope and optimism about the beauty and possibility of the future—tethered to technology but anchored in the "Soul" with empathy and compassion. I loved this book, and am so grateful that Rishad chose to share his brilliance and insights with all of us."
  —Mark Achler, Managing Director, MATH Venture Partners

"We are living in extraordinary times. While our digitally connected world creates remarkable opportunities for businesses, employees are facing tremendous stress from a wide range of sources—a contentious global political climate, concern for the environment, regular reports of mass shootings and natural disasters, the impact of economic inequality, and how the emergence of artificial intelligence will impact our lives and livelihoods, to name just a few. In an era of such broad-based disruption, Rishad Tobaccowala's *Restoring the Soul of Business* and its higher-order thinking on improving the balance of our business communities, enhancing the humanity and generosity of our workplaces, and prioritizing EQ over data in decision-making makes this book essential reading for today's executives."
  —David Carey, Chairman, Hearst Magazines

"A brilliant synthesis by Rishad on how to bring balance to human elements and technology usage in managing a modern enterprise. A must-read for everyone for both personal and professional development and satisfaction."
  —Alok Choudhary, Henry and Isabelle Dever Professor, EECS Department;
    Professor, Kellogg School of Management, Northwestern University

"You know that person who seems to always be ahead of the curve? The one who chooses to zig while zagging is obviously the thing to do? But then, zigging DOES become the thing? What makes Rishad a special man is that he was that person thirty years ago, and he has only gotten better. So, READ THE BOOK, and learn from THAT guy!"
  —Tom Collinger, Executive Director, Medill IMC Spiegel Digital
    & Database Research Center, Northwestern University

"A fantastic guide for leading and succeeding in today's world, Rishad eloquently demonstrates the exponential power in combining math and human connection and provides useful ways to do so."
  —Norman de Greve, Chief Marketing Officer, CVS Health

"With my leadership experience in advertising, I can confidently say that companies and brands whose souls are focused on contributing to peoples' lives with distinct, competitive, groundbreaking ideas and implementation skills have the foundation to build a culture to innovate, disrupt, and eventually lead markets and business categories. Tesla, Nike, Apple, McDonald's, Alphabet, Southwest Airlines, Dove, Walmart, Starbucks, Disney, Netflix, Corona, Johnny Walker, Uber, FedEx, Patagonia, Hallmark, Pixar, *The New Yorker*, Pampers, Foster + Partners, Pentagram, Ideo, Spotify, R/GA, Weiden+Kennedy—all went on creating or leading markets or market segments by passionately building trusted human connections and providing distinct, and often unique, highly inspiring products and services. They have created a human working culture people would kill to join.

By cocreating the Berlin School of Creative Leadership, I've been involved in leadership education for almost two decades. Our curriculum is focused on creative professionals in creative industries to successfully lead their company. To lead toward a distinct, competitive place, to lead clients and partners, to lead product and service excellence, to lead human beings, ethics, humanity, to lead themselves, and to lead the industry they are in—and doing so by getting insightful experience in dealing with complexity, analyses, alternate strategies, decision-making, alignment, and implementation in order to become a trusted person and believable advisor. Rishad Tobaccowala's book provides brilliantly the mortar filling the spaces of our executive MBA architecture, to meet today's artificial and human challenges, building a competitive and truly human enterprise. Especially for industries where creativity is off the norm, not on it.

If you belong to 'The Crazy Ones,' with a deep desire to better our world and our communities, now you have a map to success in your hands: *Restoring the Soul of Business*. Our participants will get this map as well—accompanied by one of those many amazing, long-applauded Rishad Tobaccowala talks given at our school."

—Michael Conrad, President, Berlin School of Creative Leadership; former
    Vice-Chairman and Chief Creative Officer of Leo Burnett Worldwide

"Rishad Tobaccowala is talking my language. This is the cutting-through-the-clutter identification and celebration of humanity, meaning, and soul in business that every industry needs. Rishad has written a book that is not only highly readable and entertaining but also a practical, actionable road map on how to unleash the power and potential of people— threaded throughout with profound and revelatory anecdotes from his personal experience, and shining a light along the way on inspirational figures in our industry who deserve every possible tribute, like Jack Klues and Renetta McCann. Everybody in our industry and every other industry: buy this book now—it will transform the way you see your work, and where you take your business."

—Cindy Gallop, founder & CEO, IfWeRanTheWorld/MakeLoveNotPorn

"Rishad is one of the smartest, most insightful executives in all of Ad Land. Not surprisingly, his book is full of useful thoughts, ideas, and actions for an industry at a crossroads between emotion and technology, data, math, and automation Not only do the souls of business need restoring, but so do its many practitioners. This book is a great place for all of us to start."

—Bob Greenberg, founder and Executive Chairman, R/GA

"If you were to take every time Rishad has been quoted in other books—mine included—you'd have enough for ten books. Now, fortunately, we get to hear it straight from the mouth of a true icon, mentor, role model, and leader. Thank you, Rishad!"
—Joseph Jaffe, author; founder and President, Jaffe LLC

"*Finally!* That was the only word that came to mind when Rishad told me that he would be writing his first book. *Wow!* That was the only word that came to mind when I finished reading *Restoring the Soul of Business*. Rishad has been a mentor and friend to many in the business world, including me. Now he's sharing his sage knowledge and insights with everyone (lucky you!). Many people say things like 'This is a book not to be missed.' This book is more than that. If you're wondering about the state of business today, and where things must go, here is the road map. *Restoring the Soul of Business* is filled with wisdom. It's based on decades of experience and acts as a reminder that technology is great, but humans are greater. Get busy reading *Restoring the Soul of Business* today. This book is your competitive advantage."
—Mitch Joel, founder, Six Pixels Group; author of *Six Pixels of Separation* and *Ctrl Alt Delete*

"Rishad shares his storied career, built on intellectual curiosity and candor, with lessons and insights on how to future-proof your organization. His keen understanding of people and the future of business provides guidance on what individuals and companies need to do to survive and thrive amid the fourth industrial revolution."
—Marla Kaplowitz, President and CEO, 4A's

"*Restoring the Soul of Business* is hard to put down. Rishad offers compelling perspectives and insights on the human elements of management—for companies and careers—with tangible examples and actionable takeaways. Read this book, then read it again."
—Terence Kawaja, CEO, LUMA Partners

"Rishad Tobaccowala's *Restoring the Soul of Business* is a classic, a throwback, and an extraordinarily thoughtful reminder that the fundamentals that most influence a company's fortunes are grounded in humanity.

As we look at our physical world, we can point to the invisible forces of gravity and magnetism for providing order to our universe. In the same way, Rishad establishes his indelible thesis that the order of the business enterprise—its most compelling success factors—reside in the invisible forces of human behavior and culture.

Rishad weaves a fascinating mosaic emphasizing that success is not about what we can see or touch or what we can add or subtract. It is about how we treat our people and energize the enterprise's cultural fabric. The logic of this dissertation is beyond compelling—it is a business imperative. We must all pause and reflect on this—and then embrace this as students of the new company order.

Thank you, Rishad, for showing us the way."
—Bob Liodice, CEO, Association of National Advertisers (ANA)

"Anyone who has had the privilege of hearing Rishad Tobaccowala speak understands his ability to cut through the morass of business hyperbole and zero in on simple, universal truths. What I didn't realize until reading *Restoring the Soul of Business* was his ability to do the same with written prose. Tobaccowala is as gifted a writer as he is a public speaker, and his new book manages to take the rapidly expanding complexities of modern business—technology, increasingly bigger data, and an ever-increasing reliance on screen-based interfaces—and offers practical advice on how to leverage technology to become even more human, albeit more productive ones.

Tobaccowala may be Madison Avenue's greatest living philosopher, reminding marketers, agencies, and the worlds' greatest brands that the most meaningful attributes are human ones. In *Restoring the Soul of Business*, he offers a road map for applying it to any business organization, big or small."
—Joe Mandese, Editor-in-Chief, MediaPost

"In a world that's become increasingly digital and data-driven, the power of creativity and storytelling, and forging a genuine human connection, has never been more important. In this book—a must-read for all leaders—Rishad provides an insightful playbook for balancing the analytical and intuitive sides of business, to create more meaningful connections with customers."
—Shantanu Narayen, Chairman and CEO, Adobe Inc.

"*Restoring the Soul of Business* is a timely reminder that we live in a messy, nuanced world in which respect, empathy, and reflection are of inestimable value. By extension it suggests that we treat ill-conceived incentives, polarizing opinions, and binary conclusions with healthy skepticism."
—Rob Norman, former Global Digital Officer, GroupM, WPP

"*Restoring the Soul of Business* comes at a critical time for an industry that is being turned upside down. With the rules being rewritten, Rishad draws attention to the steps companies, and their executives, need to take to survive and thrive in this age of disruption. I loved the blend of business and practical advice and look forward to applying the learnings in my own attempt to stay on pace with the changes."
—Penry Price, Vice President Marketing Solutions, LinkedIn

"Organizations are already inundated with data, and this is just the beginning. In *Restoring the Soul of Business*, Rishad Tobaccowala offers a guide to business executives on how they should integrate data with business. Rather than putting analytics or profits at the center of the business, he advocates starting with the human. Everything else becomes much simpler then. This very readable book, chockful of examples, is much more than just about how to use data well—it is about doing business with integrity and compassion in an age where these virtues seem handicaps."
—Raghuram Rajan, Katherine Dusak Miller Distinguished Professor of
Finance, University of Chicago Booth School of Business; author of
The Third Pillar, Fault Lines, and *Saving Capitalism from the Capitalists;*
twenty-third Governor of the Reserve Bank of India

"Talk about brilliant timing! Just when the world of business was about to fall into the abyss of numbers, succumbing to the siren call for more data at all costs, along comes this book to remind us that the human element is crucial to the success of any organization. Rishad teaches us that while numbers, data, spreadsheets, and algorithms are important tools for running a business, they are useless unless we exercise our humanity and unleash our creativity.

In one book, Rishad has boiled down and concisely conveyed the wisdom gleaned from his illustrious four-decade career in business. Through his masterful storytelling and narrative, he will provoke you to feel as well as think, provide you with actionable insights you can apply every day at work (as well as in your personal life!), and strengthen your leadership skills in transformative ways. And don't be surprised if, like me, you find your soul lifted as well."
—Geoffrey Ramsey, cofounder and Chief Evangelist, eMarketer

"For thirty years, Rishad Tobaccowala has mentored scores of CEOs, including me, teaching us to be better leaders, bosses, and shareholder stewards. How lucky for our successors that his unparalleled guidance now comes packaged in this one masterful book."
—Randall Rothenberg, CEO, Interactive Advertising Bureau (IAB)

"Humans are increasingly ceding choice and control to machines, and we are at an inflection point where achieving the right balance is going to be critical to our future. Rishad has written a brilliant and timely instruction manual for the workforce in the age of AI, 5G, and quantum computing."
—Vikram Sharma, President, Crisp Thinking; former CEO, Shop
    Local LLC; former President, Data Systems Division of IRI

"In his business career, Rishad has studied more teams, companies, industries, and cultures than most of us can even begin to fathom. Bringing all of that together in a personal, poetic, and practical book is a gift to the rest of us. This courageous and thought-provoking book is a must-read for anyone interested in building better businesses and a better world."
—Shiv Singh, CMO, Eargo; coauthor of *Savvy: Navigating Fake
    Companies, Fake Leaders,* and *Fake News in the Post-Trust Era*

"Advertising is more afflicted by groupthink than almost any other profession I know. Throughout his career, Rishad Tobaccowala has always been the exception to that rule—the ad man as original thinker. In his new book he ranges more widely, to ask what businesses have to do to thrive in the digital future. His surprising answer is that they have to become more humanistic than scientistic. *Restoring the Soul of Business* won't necessarily tell you what to think about data and AI, but it might teach you how to think about them."
—Jacob Weisberg, CEO, Pushkin Industries; former Editor-in-Chief, Slate Group

"Rishad is that rare leader who has deep insights into both the technology revolution and the nature of human beings. He understands the limitations of a data-driven world inhabited by people who, as he says, are analog and are moved by stories and emotion. Everyone who reads this book will learn valuable lessons about how to lead and inspire colleagues in a rapidly evolving landscape. I've had the great honor to be Rishad's friend and colleague since the days of the PIT (referenced in the book), and over the years I have admired his ability to tell compelling stories to illuminate the power of great storytelling. This book is a real page-turner."
—Tony Weisman, Chief Marketing Officer, Dunkin'

RESTORING

the SOUL of

BUSINESS

RESTORING
the SOUL of
BUSINESS

Staying HUMAN in the Age of Data

RISHAD
TOBACCOWALA

HARPERCOLLINS
LEADERSHIP

AN IMPRINT OF HARPERCOLLINS

Published by HarperCollins Leadership, an imprint of HarperCollins Focus LLC.

Any internet addresses, phone numbers, or company or product information printed in this book are offered as a resource and are not intended in any way to be or to imply an endorsement by HarperCollins Leadership, nor does HarperCollins Leadership vouch for the existence, content, or services of these sites, phone numbers, companies, or products beyond the life of this book.

ISBN 978-1-4002-1066-4 (Ebook)
ISBN 978-1-4002-1054-1 (HC)

Library of Congress Cataloging-in-Publication Data

Library of Congress Control Number: 2019945829

Printed in the United States of America
20 21 22 23   LSC   10 9 8 7 6 5 4 3 2 1

For my wife Rekha and my parents—
They keep me rooted and gave me wings

CONTENTS

CONTENTS

SECTION III: FUSING THE STORY AND THE SPREADSHEET: SOUL FOR THE MACHINE AGE

FOREWORD

People react to digital disruption in two ways. Some lean back, feeling helpless and paralyzed, moaning about how awful and unfair it is that they have been victimized by uncaring forces beyond their control. Others lean forward, seeing change as an opportunity, not a problem. These people energetically innovate, constantly trying new approaches to salvage and shape their professions. Rishad Tobaccowala is in the latter group.

I got to know Rishad while working on *Frenemies: The Epic Disruption of the Ad Business (and Everything Else)*, a book that explores the many changes assaulting the advertising and marketing business. Unlike the Candides in that business, who insist this is "the best of all possible worlds" and wallow in familiar ruts, Rishad welcomes change. While conceding that "change sucks," as the longtime futurist for the eighty thousand employees of advertising and marketing giant Publicis, he is determined to treat change as a challenge.

Despite Rishad's background, it would be a mistake to pigeonhole his book as relevant only to those in advertising. With vivid anecdotes he weaves tales, both personal and from his vast business knowledge, of those who have confronted disruption. We see corporate cultures altered; executives who learn how to listen as well as speak; executives who hide problems and don't chase them; qualities that make a boss bad or good; and reasons why mathematicians, with their algorithms and fervid belief that their scientific approach yields Nirvana, turn data into a false God.

This last point is central to Rishad's worldview. He is no Luddite. He is a digital native, as comfortable with data scientists as he is with the yellowed print editions of newspapers. But he understands that while data and algorithms and artificial intelligence have great value, these tools lack the instinct, creativity, and knowledge of humans. In this book, he shows how Facebook's algorithms failed to block fake news or malicious and viral videos, which required Facebook to belatedly hire thousands of human "curators" to mount a defense. A better solution, Rishad writes, marries "math and meaning."

Restoring the Soul of Business is a brilliant how-to book, one that belongs on the shelf next to *In Search of Excellence*. But this book also reaches beyond the business world. It contains more than a few traces of Daniel Kahneman's *Thinking, Fast and Slow*, sharing universal wisdom. And in a book meant to highlight the virtues of humanness, Rishad writes a reader-friendly book that will keep you glued to your seat.

Ken Auletta
Bestselling author and writer, *The New Yorker*

INTRODUCTION

Why This Book?

Time is all we have.

So why should you allocate a part of your most precious asset on engaging with this book?

Because my hope is that it will leave you seeing, thinking, and feeling differently about how to grow and remain relevant in transformative times.

How to grow yourself, grow those around you, and grow your practice, passion, or company.

How to remain relevant by understanding what it takes to make sense and thrive in a world of rapid technological, demographic, and global upheaval.

And it will do so by questioning much of what business takes for granted:

- why data is often not the way forward and we may have too much of it;
- why change sucks;
- why having more—rather than fewer—meetings is better; and
- why it is essential to have a culture and courage that calls out "the turd on the table."

You not only will learn what makes great leaders but also how to deal with, or not become, a bad boss.

You'll discover how to extract meaning from data and see poetry in the plumbing.

This book recognizes that while our world is increasingly filled with digital, silicon-based, computing objects, it is populated by people who remain analog, carbon-based, feeling creatures.

People like you.

And me.

Companies can choose to upgrade the skills of their people and reimagine the way they work or swap out their people and acquire new ways of working.

Often both are necessary.

This book is about upgrading the operating systems of people and companies by remembering the thinking-and-feeling component of the operating system. A central premise is that successful individuals and firms can never forget the importance of people, their emotions, the culture of the organization, and what cannot be measured. I refer to this as the Soul of a Company. This Soul is critical even as individuals and firms reinvent themselves for an increasingly AI-augmented, data-driven, networked and distributed, screen-based future.

As the world becomes more data driven and real-time twitchy, and as financial markets punish companies for failing to meet their goals, I worry that our short-term focus on numbers is destroying the long-term health of business, countries, and people. I worry we are losing our humanity in a world where modern, data-driven economies and cutting-edge technologies are seeping into all of life.

Yes, results, data, speed, and technology are keys for businesses to remain relevant and thrive. But while they're necessary, they're insufficient for long-term success.

Over the past five years, I have seen a significant tilt to the numeric, to the algorithmic, and to the measurable. This causes organizations to think short term, prize individualism, and adopt a mercenary mindset rather than think long term, prize teams, and adopt a meaningful mindset.

Increasingly there is a premium and a dominance on the quantitative, or what I call the *spreadsheet*, and a diminishment of the importance of the culture, humanity, emotion, and complexity of people, or what I refer to as the *story*.

Successful people and companies combine the story and the spreadsheet and by doing so restore the soul of business.

Lest you think I'm an antitech zealot who believes we should go back to a kinder, gentler, analog time, let me tell you a little about myself. I grew up in Bombay, India, receiving a degree in economics and advanced mathematics from the University of Bombay. I then came to the United States and received an MBA in marketing and finance from one of the most quantitative schools in the world: the University of Chicago.

Over a thirty-seven-year career at the companies of the Publicis Groupe, an eighty-thousand-person global marketing and business transformation firm, I helped found or cofound some of the first digital agencies and future-oriented strategic consultancies as well as contributing to the shaping and growth of one of the two largest buyers of digital, data-driven media in the world.

I have served as chairman of major global digital- and e-commerce-oriented firms such as Digitas for Publicis and served as a chief strategist and chief growth officer for Publicis Groupe, while also serving as a trusted advisor to many of our clients' reinventions and reimaginings.

I relate this short history to establish my credentials in the data-driven, digital space. I am obviously someone who believes in digital change. Not so obviously, I also believe in the power of people to make transformation work. As much as I value data, devices, and software, I value empathy, innovation, and relationships.

My career has been about change. Seeing it, managing it, and adapting to it. Change requires adopting the latest technology, but it also requires maximizing the best qualities of people.

My career has also been about reinvention—reinventing companies as well as myself. Reinvention involves implementing state-of-the-art software and digital processes that produce something new, but it also involves getting people to embrace the new and enhance it with their ideas and actions.

I've led transformation efforts both in the US and in countries throughout the world and earned a reputation as a digital pioneer, while also being known as someone who has helped inspire and grow talent. The two roles are not incompatible.

This is a book about the future, fed by the best of the past.

A book about cool data that does not forget warm humanity.

A book that believes business can and should have a soul.

It is nearly forty years of learning distilled into two hundred pages that answer the dozen questions I have consistently been asked in the last few years—regardless of country, industry, or age of the person asking.

Often people asked if there was a book they could buy with the answers. There was not. Until now.

Restoring the Soul of Business has been written to allow you to read any chapter in any order, since no writer can know what will be most relevant to each reader at each stage. You are in control, and in this way I respect your time, since that is all we have.

Hopefully I will get some of yours.

Thank you.

SECTION I

THE CHALLENGE:

Carbon-Based, Analog, Feeling Humans in a

Silicon-Infused, Digital, Data-Driven World

CHAPTER I

TOO MUCH MATH,
TOO LITTLE MEANING

On January 23, 2019, I gave a keynote in New York City to an audience of seven hundred executives who specialized in leveraging data, technology, and algorithms to enhance the effectiveness of their marketing efforts.

I celebrated the great enablement and empowerment that the World Wide Web, search, e-commerce, mobile, and social networks had brought about, and I noted that on that day, the five most valuable companies in America (Amazon, Apple, Google, Facebook, and Microsoft) were pioneers and leaders in leveraging data, algorithms, technology, and networks.

Indeed, with continued advances in artificial intelligence (AI) as well as the increased speed and pervasiveness of connection made possible by 5G, the technological signs were clear: we were about to enter an age of even greater wealth and possibility.

However, something was amiss, and many storm clouds were gathering. The same data-driven technologies giving rise to such wealth and opportunity were increasingly being leveraged in harmful ways, leading to the breakdown of trust, increased polarization, and rising inequality.

As leaders of these companies we needed to acknowledge and address the downside caused in part by our maniacal focus on short-term, data-driven financial and engagement metrics. We saw this all around us.

Amazon had just seemed to overplay its hand by running a beauty contest and insisting on financial breaks to set up a second headquarters, apparently tone-deaf to how such behavior from a trillion-dollar company, led by one of the richest men in the world, would be perceived. A backlash had forced them to retreat from New York as a second headquarters.

Facebook and YouTube were increasingly being leveraged to great harm all over the world, and both firms appeared to be too slow in acknowledging and fixing these problems and were losing public trust.

The challenges went beyond technology firms.

Leaders from Wells Fargo had become so fixated on meeting account-opening goals that they misled their customers in highly troubling ways. Doctors at Sloan Kettering were questioning why some of their colleagues were getting financial stakes in the research the institution had been conducting. Leading consulting firms such as McKinsey were being accused of allegedly helping criminal leaders and pushing unsafe products.[1]

Our wealth and success and the sweet siren call of optimizing numbers had led us to overlook the collateral damage of forgetting, or neglecting to consider, the human side of the equation.

In my speech entitled "It's Time to Optimize for the Citizen," I suggested that we rethink our approach and consider that our customers were not only consumers but citizens. That as Elie Wiesel, Holocaust survivor, had noted, we should "Think Higher. Feel Deeper."

The talk struck a chord. Everywhere, people were realizing that in an age where data and algorithms were upending everything, we need to keep our eyes open and minds alert because sometimes we can have too much math and too little meaning.

The Age of Data

Ninety percent of the data in the world today has been created in the last two years.[2]

Our current output of data is roughly 2.5 quintillion bytes a day.[3]

Companies in the US spent $18 billion on data centers in 2017—double the amount they spent in 2016.[4]

Organizations are expected to spend $203 billion on data analytics in 2020, up from $130 billion in 2016.[5]

And we're just scratching the surface with these numbers. In the dialectic between the spreadsheet and the story, the former is dominating.

Organizations are drawn to data for many reasons, not the least of which is the emergence of incredibly sophisticated technologies that allow us to process and parse information with speed and insight. But here are more reasons why the spreadsheet is dominating the story:

- Data is plentiful.
- Data is not messy or nuanced like feelings.
- Data feels certain, while hunches are uncertain.
- Data is a common language that everyone in a global world can read.
- Data drives wealth creation, as illustrated by the data-driven companies of Google and Facebook, whose algorithms are powerful prediction engines.
- Data can be displayed using stunning graphics.

But just because all things data are dominant doesn't make data a bad thing. In fact, it's a mistake to characterize the spreadsheet as bad and the story as good. Both are crucial for organizations. More to the point, achieving a balance between the two is the hallmark of great companies.

The problem is that data's seductiveness throws the dynamic off balance. Data helps us justify our decisions. It seems to mitigate our risks. It provides insights into consumer behaviors, which can shape our product and service development. It can save us and make us a lot of money.

But it can also seduce us into believing that data is all we need. When that happens, we lose the agility, innovation, and inspiration upon which organizations thrive. Data can and should be meaningful in every sense of that word. We shouldn't use it just to quantify stuff and increase efficiency and productivity, but to gain "softer" insights. What are the ramifications of the employee survey in terms of morale and long-term tenure at the company? What patterns are our algorithms detecting that relate to our vendors, and what do these patterns mean for the ongoing tension and the conflict that flares up routinely?

When thinking about math and meaning, organizations also need to create programs and policies that aren't dictated by the numbers—that might be contraindicated by the data. For instance, the numbers may tell an organization that they need to cut staff by 10 percent to maintain profit levels, but doing so may also demoralize employees. A more meaningful alternative may be to cut other costs proactively and preserve jobs and morale.

Yes, this may be a basic example, but it illustrates the need for an equal distribution of resources between math and meaning. To arrive at this distribution, let's begin by defining and differentiating math and meaning and the need for both.

Different Types of Data: Math and Meaning

Simplistically, math is all the data flowing through organizations and meaning is all the intangible feelings and perceptions surrounding people, products, services, and the companies themselves. Less simplistically, math takes various forms—algorithms, AI, social media data, and so on. Meaning, too, can vary considerably, ranging from organizational purpose to employee beliefs about their companies to brand significance.

Organizations have always used data in various ways—surveys, budgets, focus groups—but because of technological advances, data has now become a ubiquitous presence in every nook and cranny. Consider why data is often talked about as "the new oil" and how it is such a valuable resource for every type of company:

- **Fosters customer insight.** When a Netflix subscriber selects a show to watch, 70 percent of the time it is from the recommendations Netflix serves up. A third of Amazon sales occur through the recommendations of what else other buyers purchased who bought the same product as you.[6] Data reveals opportunities like never before, from maximizing marketing to developing new product ideas.
- **Spurs continuous improvement.** By comparing key metrics against historical performance as well as that of competitors, companies can create benchmarks to improve performance and provide feedback to each individual in objective versus subjective terms.
- **Provides competitive advantage.** In a world where product differentiation is narrowing and price comparison places downward pressure on

margins, data allows for new forms of competitive advantage and monetization. The success of three of the five most valuable companies in America (Amazon, Facebook, and Alphabet/Google) is thanks to their vast swaths of data, which allow them to personalize and customize their services with speed and low cost.[7] Data allows for low cost, speed, and high quality.

Now think about meaning. While it is less tangible than data, it is no less crucial to a company's success. Consider the following forms of meaning and the questions that help elicit it:

- **A brand's reputation.** Is it considered a quality product or a cheap one? Reliable or not? Does the brand connote trust and inspire loyalty or is it seen as utilitarian?
- **Customer service beliefs.** Do customers find servicepeople to be helpful and friendly or cold and bored? Do service representatives and salespeople forge relationships with their best customers or are relationships merely transactional?
- **Company mission/values.** Is the company known for consistent beliefs and principles or is it seen as amoral and fickle? Does the organization try to make its community, its industry, and the world a better place or is it motivated only by profit?
- **Employee perceptions of the enterprise.** Do they perceive the organization as a place where they can learn and grow or one that exploits their hard work and skills? Do they feel they are rewarded fairly or that the company is cheap? Do they feel included and affiliated with the organization or isolated and mercenary?
- **The full significance of the data.** What do all those facts and figures mean beyond the obvious? Yes, profits are up by 12 percent in June, but why? Is this an anomaly or is there an underlying trend to which we must pay attention? Did the new ad we ran have an effect or did our salespeople respond to a new incentive program?

This is just scratching the surface of what's meaningful in organizations. It can take myriad forms—how the vast majority of bosses treat direct reports with respect and demonstrate empathy, for instance. Meaning can also show up in how the CEO speaks to industry analysts and the way bonuses are calculated and handed out. And meaning can emerge when Big Data is analyzed holistically—when diverse experts study it, debate it, and interpret it. Remember the story and the spreadsheet, and how meaning is one part of the story that the organization tells.

The Problem with Being Data-Myopic

Mark Twain said, "There are lies . . . damned lies, and statistics."[8] Perhaps that's overstating the case in a memorably funny way, but organizations make a huge mistake when they become overly focused on the data. Some companies have learned this lesson the hard way.

In 2012, Adobe stopped doing annual performance reviews. These data-driven tools are essentially organizational report cards that measure performance by ranking achievement and improvement in a variety of categories. Donna Morris, Adobe's senior vice president of people and places, likened the review to "annual dentist visits." The company replaced these reviews with much less formal and much more relationship-intensive "check-ins"—one-on-one sessions with a boss where performance evaluation is conducted in a more relaxed and participatory manner.[9]

In an article in *Fast Company* titled "How Too Much Data Can Hurt Our Productivity and Decision-Making," author Bob Nease made the point that "a deep dive into who buys your widget doesn't generate value unless it helps you focus your sales efforts on better prospects and away from people who will never buy your stuff."[10] Nease added that people are unpredictable, meaning that just because you've accumulated lots of great data on a given group doesn't mean that you can use it in a positive way. You may know that a given audience loves the color blue, but when you use it in your packaging, it turns off consumers. Why? Because people, unlike machines, are spontaneous, contradictory, and idiosyncratic.

A 2016 report from consulting firm McKinsey & Company interviewed top executives at leading companies on how they were using big data and analytics. One was Chief Risk Officer Ash Gupta of American Express, and he made an insightful point: "The first change we had to make was just to make our data of higher quality. We have a lot of data, and sometimes we just weren't using that data and we weren't paying as much attention to its quality as we now need to."[11]

Now think back on these examples and the cautionary lessons they teach us:

- Data-centric interactions can be far less effective than human-centric ones.
- People don't always do what data predicts they will do.
- Data is of wide-ranging quality, and if the quality isn't good (or you don't know that it's good), you'll be making decisions on weak foundations.

Despite Its Limitations, Data Will Become More Pervasive

It is critical that we constantly remind ourselves about the challenges of relying on data, since we will likely encounter data more than ever because of a number of factors:

- **Accessibility.** Data is available on a much more real-time, granular, and unified basis than ever before. The easier it is to obtain information—from the demographics of a website to social media friends and followers—the more likely organizations will capitalize on it.
- **Storage and manipulability advances.** It's now possible to measure and store how a single individual interacts with every website component at every moment and link this information to other data about that individual. Lower storage costs combined with powerful computing capabilities make it possible to capitalize on this data and manipulate it in insightful ways. The thinking goes, "We have it, we can shift and shape it, we've got to use it."
- **Leadership tool.** Just about every organization possesses a Bloomberg-like data terminal or dashboard for various levels of management. Data is the spine that holds the organization together and affects every significant decision and communication. Leadership's embrace of data has a trickle-down effect, causing all levels of the organization to buy in.
- **The AI age.** Increasingly powerful computers input huge amounts of

data and "learn" as they process information, getting smarter just as humans get smarter from multiple experiences. But computers, unlike humans, can capitalize on data-driven algorithmic decision-making, and organizations are increasingly relying on algorithms rather than people to make decisions.

How to Extract Meaning from Data by Tapping into People: The 6 I Approach

Over the years I have learned that the best way to gain insights and extract meaning from data is to follow what I call the 6 I Approach: Interpret, Involve, Interconnect, Imagine, Iterate, and Investigate.

INTERPRET THE DATA. Don't just take all those facts and figures at face value. Sometimes, of course, they're exactly what they seem. Other times, they can be misleading. For this reason, view ambiguous data (especially) from multiple perspectives. Develop hypotheses, search for patterns, look for outliers, create alternative scenarios to explain the information you're receiving. Through interpretation you can enrich the data with meaning; you can identify the story it's telling.

INVOLVE DIVERSE PEOPLE. As important as your analytics people are, expand the group that examines the data. When you involve people with various skills and perspectives, you're likely to receive a richer interpretation. The analytics people may say, "The number of followers on our site increased 15 percent in the last month." The marketing people may say, "That increase may be due to the incredibly successful brand licensing program that launched last month." The human resources people might say, "Every time we have a significant increase in followers like this, we have a corresponding increase in job applicants." The importance of diverse people is shown in debacles like the Gucci Instagram ad that resembled black face or the Pepsi ad with Kendall Jenner that misfired at every cultural level.[12]

INTERCONNECT TO LARGER TRENDS AND EVENTS. What does the data mean relative to an emerging trend that's having a profound effect on your industry? How does the information you've gleaned relate to a competitor's new product introduction? Making these types of connections helps you take the data one step further, determining if it's going to have a short-term or long-term impact, if it's suggesting the end of a trend or the beginning of a new one.

IMAGINE AND INSPIRE SOLUTIONS. Too often we look at the data and allow it to set boundaries: "We can't go into Market Z as planned because the numbers indicate sales of our category is starting to fall off." Rather than allowing the data to limit options and actions, explore the solutions it might inspire. If the numbers show that your product category isn't doing as well as it once did in Market Z, is there an emerging opportunity because the market still has potential and competition will be reduced because of this data?

ITERATE. Data can spawn new and better data. Is there a test you might run based on the information you've gathered that can produce more insightful facts and figures? Can you think of fresh ways to generate feedback that might provide multiple perspectives and explain surprising, disturbing, and promising data?

INVESTIGATE PEOPLE'S EXPERIENCES. In a given organization, you have hundreds or thousands of people with data-relevant insights because in the past—whether while part of your organization or with a previous employer—they experienced something applicable to the current information. For instance, someone was part of a company that experienced a huge social media spike because they ran a Super Bowl commercial that went viral. As a result, this employee can relate their experiences to the current data on a similar topic. Tapping into this by seeking out relevant employees and asking about the data may provide ideas that would not otherwise be articulated.

Never forget that data tells a story beyond the facts and figures, but this story can only be told when you find ways to tease out the meaning.

The Need for a Human-Centric Data Policy

Beyond questioning and exploring the data, organizations need to create policies and protocols for it. The tilt toward data wouldn't be so harmful if companies enacted basic rules to mitigate the damage caused by overdependence. Meaning naturally flows back into an environment when companies filter all the facts, figures, and other information through a human lens.

To that end, here are some suggested filters:

DETERMINE WHAT DATA IS WORTH RECEIVING AND ELIMINATE THE REST. This is a simple but very effective step that many companies don't take for fear of missing something. Do you really need to receive five financial reports that essentially provide the same information? Is it necessary to parse the same data through three filters? Do service evaluation reports have to be issued weekly (versus monthly)? Even if something is missed, this type of limit ensures that there will be time for nondata discussion, questioning, and reflection. With apologies to Samuel Taylor Coleridge, here is the mindset that data limits help avoid:

> Data data everywhere,
> So much data I will sink.
> Data data everywhere,
> Pray, who will help me think?

FLAG BAD DATA. Invariably, the increase in data corresponds to the increase in data that is slanted, outdated, or just plain wrong. Without a system to identify suspicious or overly misleading facts and figures, companies will create strategies based on inaccuracies: garbage in means garbage out. Companies need an ombudsman who makes judgments about data, jettisons obviously wrong information, and warns people when data is weak or unreliable.

STOP USING DATA AS A CRUTCH. As I'm sure you're aware, managers justify their decisions by referring to what a report told them. Even when they make a bad choice, they say, "The data made me do it." Don't let people lean on their data or that's exactly what they'll do—it's human nature. Data should inform and enlighten, but it shouldn't be the basis of every decision. Encourage people to justify their decisions based on data plus many other factors—discussion, brainstorming, past experience, creative alternatives, and so on.

ASK QUESTIONS DATA CAN ANSWER, NOT DATA-DRIVEN QUESTIONS. This distinction will help avoid focusing on the wrong things. For instance, companies may focus on how they can reduce time per customer service call to cut costs and increase productivity. This focus stems from the data—it's been proven that reducing customer service calls by thirty seconds results in a 10 percent reduction in costs and a 5 percent increase in productivity (I'm just making up these numbers). So the question—can we reduce costs and increase productivity?—arises from the data. But this may be the wrong question. The real question may be: How can we increase customer satisfaction? It may be that shortening customer service call time alienates people and produces lower customer satisfaction. The key, therefore, is formulating questions independent of existing data.

MEASURE JUDICIOUSLY. Just because you can quantify every aspect of employee performance doesn't mean that you should. Employees often feel as if every task they perform and every keystroke they make is being recorded and assessed. This Big Brother mentality is counterproductive in the long run, even if it may help improve efficiency in the short term. People need the freedom to take risks and sometimes fail. If they believe their every move is being watched and measured, their morale will plummet. Obviously, measurement of some things is necessary. But when it seems like everything is being analyzed and quantified, then people respond poorly.

When It Comes to Data, You Ain't Seen Nothing Yet

It is almost redundant to describe an organization as "data-driven"; it is difficult for any organization to thrive without this as the core organizational driver. In fact, forget thrive. In the algorithmic age, no company can survive without a data strategy. But this is just the beginning, and the coming months and years are going to see data rise to even greater heights. The danger is that the data strategy becomes the only strategy, and everyone's focus becomes building the best algorithm and forgetting the meaning part of the equation.

Each year I attend the Consumer Electronics Show, and in 2018, I was struck by three trends/developments that are going to intensify our data-centric mindset:

1. **Sensing/Senses.** Due to AI and embedded chips, a growing number of devices and technologies can anticipate what we need before we do: cars that not only drive themselves but anticipate accidents, medical systems that trigger warnings or call in for help, and so on. In terms of sensory-intensifying technologies, 4K OLED screens will take our video experiences to another level, while nontethered, mobile, and affordable ($200 to $400) VR systems from Google/Lenovo and Facebook/Xiaomi allow us to sense new worlds and maybe a new level of empathy and presence.

2. **Expansion and Encroachment.** Every technology and every industry is expanding and encroaching out of its category. Here are a few examples regarding AI and voice. New TVs from LG and Samsung embed Amazon or Google into their interface and credit their enhanced pictures less to hardware improvements and more to software driven by AI enhancements. Automobiles can now be driverless due to embedded AI and voice, including a customized new voice interface from Mercedes.[13] And in case you missed it, the Chinese are here and dominating as never before. One out of three exhibitors were Chinese firms; some called it the Chinese Electronics Show. The Chinese are going to encroach and expand into AI, Internet of Things (IoT), and much more at scales that will bewilder.

3. **Augmenting and Accelerating.** We are on the cusp of a quantum jump in technology capability. New chips from Qualcomm and others will now allow for twenty or more hours of mobile phone battery use. A key constraint to phones has been their need to be recharged. Now they will last longer, and with the next generation of wireless charging, they can be recharged faster. While still a couple of years away at that time, we were already seeing demonstrations of 5G technology, which is one thousand times faster than 4G and LTE (Long-Term Evolution)!

Events like the Consumer Electronics Show will affect all organizations, directly or indirectly. Companies are going to be scrambling to find new ways to accelerate customers' experiences through better technologies. They're going to use their technology to encroach on others while defending intrusions onto their turf, as traditional boundaries between companies and categories disappear. And they will be awash in data from sensing systems that "read" people's activities in science fiction–like ways.

What Meaning Looks Like in Action

As the previous section suggests, organizations can redress the balance between math and meaning by enacting data policies that allow people to use their creativity and ideas more effectively. Meaning can also be added in other ways to the numerical thinking that dominates companies. More specifically, organizations can focus a variety of policies and processes to elicit positive employee traits—creativity, empathy, loyalty, and relationship-building.

Costco, for instance, has long enjoyed a reputation for putting its people first. Not only do they pay above the industry norm but they take other, often extraordinary steps to accommodate the requirements of all types of employees. For instance, they offer health insurance and other benefits to part-time employees, a costly policy. They also encourage their employees to think long term—for employees who stay at least one year, the turnover rate is around 5 percent. They also give their managers unprecedented ability to make decisions for their groups independently; they're not hamstrung by ironclad policies and procedures. As a result, managers are able to use their creativity and initiative to make changes that feel right to the people with boots on the ground.

Costco is a hugely successful company, but its operating margin is 3 percent, compared to Walmart's 6 percent. Its labor expenses are 70 percent of its budget, a high percentage. Looking only at these and other numbers, it would seem that Costco couldn't possibly succeed. Yet founder Jim Sinegal figured out early on that if he could free employees to use their considerable strengths as people and provide them with an environment and wages that suited them, these efforts would translate into high customer satisfaction.[14]

In a 2014 *Harvard Business Review* issue, former Netflix Chief Talent Officer Patty McCord wrote "How Netflix Reinvented HR."[15] One of the article's themes is that Netflix chose to rely on common sense and trust their people's desire to do the right thing to guide their HR efforts rather than traditional data-based measures. For instance, instead of the standard vacation policy—employees are limited in how much time they can take off yearly (X number of vacation days, personal days) and must file formal requests through various forms—Netflix created an honor system. Essentially, it leaves vacation time up to individual employees. It's an informal system where common sense, rather than rigid requirements, determines when people take time off and how they report it. While there are general guidelines (e.g., financial people shouldn't schedule vacations when the department is swamped) and more structure for people in call centers, the majority are given a great deal of freedom. Netflix has also freed many of their employees from inflexible policies regarding travel—as McCord writes, the Netflix policy toward travel expenses is summed up in five words: "Act in Netflix's best interests."[16] As a result, they largely eliminated the cumbersome expense account reporting process.

These and other policies help Netflix employees feel respected and trusted—that they're being treated as adults rather than misbehaving children. They want to reciprocate in kind, contributing to the company's profitability and growth. Freed from the reporting requirements and strict parameters that most employees resent, they relish their cultures and find more meaning in them.

Starbucks has developed a system that facilitates their baristas' interactions with customers, allowing them to relate to them as individuals. In retail situations, many salespeople relate to customers in a generic way; they may be polite and friendly, but they treat everyone the same way. Starbucks has a data feedback loop that helps baristas know customers' tendencies, preferences, and idiosyncrasies. One way Starbucks collects customer data is through their rewards programs. Customers gain rewards (e.g., discounted favorite drinks after a certain number of purchases) for specific buying behaviors, and in turn data is collected about these behaviors when customers use the Starbucks app—data about what their favorite drinks are, what days they usually come in to purchase these drinks, and so on.[17]

Armed with this data, baristas can greet customers by name, anticipate their drinks and how they like them, and comment on any deviations from traditional ordering practices. If they usually come in on a Tuesday and arrive on a Friday, the barista can say, "Hey, Joe, I've never seen you here on Friday; something special going on?" In this way, baristas can form a connection to their customers, communicating that they're seeing them as individuals rather than as generic customers. This makes the job more interesting and more of an organic experience for baristas, and it helps customers feel acknowledged as unique individuals. Starbucks is capitalizing on data in a highly human-centric manner.

In January 2018, Lawrence D. Fink, CEO of the huge investment firm BlackRock, took the extraordinary step of writing to the heads of leading organizations and informing them that they needed to do more than be profitable if they wanted BlackRock's support; they had to make contributions to society in some way. In the past, investors like Fink usually cared only about the numbers.

His letter signals a change—a change toward a more meaningful direction. Instructively, Fink noted that profitability was still crucial as an investment factor, but that sustainable organizations must also recognize their responsibilities as world citizens.[18]

But finding the balance between math and meaning isn't limited to philanthropy. As you'll recall, meaning comes in many forms, and organizations need to be aware of all of them. For instance, JPMorgan Chase has had a lot of success with their Sapphire Reserve card, which targets millennials, because card rewards are tailored to what is meaningful to their audience. Based on data, they determined that what was important to millennials was experiences—more specifically, travel and food experiences. To that end, they structured rewards for using the Sapphire Reserve card around these experiences—for every dollar users spend on food and travel, they receive three points (and only one point for nonexperiential expenditures). On top of that, when users spend $4,000 in the first three months of card ownership, they receive up to $750 in travel credit. JPMorgan Chase links users to their own travel agents, and if customers use these agents, their points double.

The card costs $450, which is a lot of money relative to other cards, and the company was criticized when they first introduced it; the critics were convinced the company was going to lose money. But meaning triumphed, and the card has been a significant success.[19]

JAYNE ZENATY SPITTLER

Pioneering with Data and Passion

To some extent, the tension between story and spreadsheet has always existed. Even years ago, numbers possessed power, and people sometimes failed to recognize that story could be equally powerful, especially when balanced with data.

In 1982, when I joined Leo Burnett, I shared a room with other newbies waiting for media-buying openings while we were trained on the basics of media. Jayne Zenaty ran media research and was responsible for what was referred to as the PIT (which we called People In Training but I sense was just a reference to the large room where we all sat like workers in a pit).

Aware of my math undergraduate degree, Jayne had me help her build the case for a new emerging medium called cable television. She had me gather the data demonstrating that cable was spreading geographically and beginning to erode broadcast television in the markets it had most deeply penetrated. Jayne wanted management to start paying attention and prepare our clients for this new media.

The head of our media department at the time grew up in a broadcast television world and took delight in its negotiations and deal making. He was skeptical of anything new and would often throw our numbers back at us as irrelevant, wrongly calculated, or out of context. Each time Jayne would retreat and rethink about how to tighten the math and improve the story. Based on her graduate school experience with a National Science Foundation two-way cable project, she passionately believed that cable was going to be the next big thing and knew the data supported her.

But Jayne also realized she needed to "sell" the data, to breathe life into it with dramatic projections of how people's television viewing habits would change, and how this would transform the entire discipline of media buying. By telling a story that offered hope (unprecedented targeted advertising opportunities) as well as fear (losing clients if the agency didn't transform its media-buying strategy), Jayne prevailed. Not only did she tell the story to our boss—she also lobbied early cable pioneers like Ted Turner to develop the audience data to support buying cable. Cable exploded, and we were early and ready.

Learning from Jayne, who was in many ways my first boss, was something I never forgot. When you believe something new is coming that others resist, combine cool, calculating math with deep passion and persistence to tell a compelling and numerically tight story.

------------------------------ KEY TAKEAWAYS ------------------------------

- We need to pour data through a series of filters that separate the fool's gold of information from the nuggets of wisdom.

- The most successful leaders and organizations will leverage data in ways that extract and amplify meaning and not just math, asking the right questions and involving diverse perspectives when analyzing data.
- We must recognize that human judgment and intuition are often necessary to perceive data's true significance.

CHAPTER 2

MANAGING THE DARK SIDE
OF BRIGHT SCREENS

To paraphrase William Shakespeare, the screens in workplaces are neither good nor bad, but how we use them makes them so.[1]

Or, to paraphrase the '60s science fiction television show *The Outer Limits*, we control the picture.

Unfortunately, organizations don't always capitalize on this ability to take control. Instead, they adopt tech innovation after tech innovation without thinking about the consequences, which may include people—from telemarketers to content moderators to every one of us—who work days or weeks without meaningful human-to-human interaction or managers mistaking digital activity for productivity.

How can we manage ourselves and the cultures of our companies in an increasingly mobile, screen-based, networked world? How can we leverage the magic of modern technologies while retaining the meaning and wisdom of old, but still effective, practices?

Modern technology, from powerful smartphones to increased bandwidth speeds, is making it possible for a growing number of people to work remotely. Since their employees no longer need to be tethered to their offices by their devices, organizations are becoming more receptive to at-home workers, in part because it saves money on office space and in part because it helps them retain employees who would otherwise quit (they require the flexibility of home offices to take care of small children, for instance). Forrester Research's US Telecommuting Forecast predicts that 43 percent of the workforce will soon be at-home employees, and even if that prediction is high, a growing number of people are physically separated from their colleagues because of new technologies.[2]

Even in the office, many employees are screen-locked, failing to travel from their computers to water coolers, coffee machines, and lunchrooms that were previously where a lot of informal business was conducted and relationships were formed.

The increased screen time of employees tilts the balance away from in-person connection and toward machine-mediated interactions. They're empathizing, debating, and reflecting less while streaming, texting, and emailing more. To restore the human-to-technology balance, we need to proactively create screen-use policies and review them continuously. If we take a laissez-faire attitude toward this issue, the natural seductiveness of glowing screens will erode the story in every organization.

In *Deep Work*, author Cal Newport posits the title concept of intense and sustained concentration as the key to innovation and productivity. Newport suggests that in our digital work worlds, we often don't have the opportunity for this sort of deep work, instead spending time sending and responding to emails and texts, being distracted by electronic notifications, and so on.[3]

But we can't return to the past. Organizations would be poorly served by retro policies that forbid electronic devices or impose severe restrictions on their use. We can, however, find a way to integrate story activities with spreadsheet ones. To begin this integration, we need to be aware of the dramatic changes that have taken place in our workplace environments in a relatively short period of time. With this awareness we can see what's being lost, what's being gained, and how we can retain the best of both.

A Contrast Between Then and Now

I first joined Leo Burnett in 1982, when it was located in Chicago's Prudential Building, and we moved to our current location in 1989. From an office space perspective, the two most common complaints about that first building were its lack of sufficient conference rooms and its shortage of corner offices. As a result, our current building was designed with an abundance of conference rooms and twelve corner offices per floor (*corner* being a relative term—the design created additional corners besides the obvious four where building sides connected).

We're about to move again, but this time the offices are being designed with no corner offices and minimal conference room space. The concern now is about mobility—or the lack of it, given how people are addicted to their screens. People complain that their colleagues are "hiding out" in their offices and that they don't see them enough. The new design is supposed to promote human interactions, something that no one had to promote when I was at the old building.

I relate this story because the contrast between 1989 and now is instructive. The proliferation of screens has changed the workplace in ways both obvious and subtle, and it's worth analyzing these changes, since they demonstrate how and why we need to manage our use of screens. The changes fall into three categories:

1. How we access, produce, and share information;
2. Where and how we work; and
3. How we engage with our colleagues and clients or customers.

How We Access, Produce, and Share Information

Then: Obtaining information was a time-consuming, effort-driven task until about twenty years ago. Before then most corporate offices had many rooms and hallways containing black-and-gray filing cabinets, which housed organizational information. In some instances, companies had "librarians" who helped people access this information, but it was usually a haphazard retrieval process. At Burnett, we often had to ask around for the information we needed, sending a written memo to people, requesting them to point us in the direction of someone who might know what we needed to know.

Producing information was a laborious effort. Typically, notes were handwritten, then a secretary typed them (Wite-Out was crucial to correct mistakes), and Xerox machines helped create multiple copies of documents we wanted distributed. Similarly, sharing information was no easy task. For presentations we relied on overhead projectors requiring special acetates. Internal mail was delivered a few times daily throughout the office, and delivering information outside the office relied on the postal service or, when time was of the essence, delivery services. Eventually faxes were introduced, a "miracle" technology that allowed the electronic transfer of information.

Still, looking back, information moved slowly and with a certain amount of difficulty.

Now: Information moves with great speed, ease, and flexibility. Search engines are the real miracle—helping organizations access, collate, produce, and distribute work—and they usually don't require anything except using tools created by Microsoft, Adobe, Slack, and so on. Everything from charts to presentations looks great, and everything can be easily tailored for different audiences. Information is moved instantly both internally and externally, and sharing occurs with a click.

On the downside, the ease and speed of obtaining and sharing information creates an overload. In organizations, most leaders and managers feel like they're failing to keep up with all the knowledge they need to absorb. Documents arrive engorged with links and attachments, and the speed of information renders the latest news dated just seconds, minutes, or hours after it arrives on the screen.

Where and How We Work[4]

Then: The office was the place to be, and everyone was expected to be physically present at least 9:00 a.m. to 5:00 p.m. during weekdays and sometimes on weekends. Conference rooms were so critical to the functioning of organizations that full-time employees were needed to schedule the continuous flow of meetings. People sat in offices or cubicles, and few common areas existed.

Though some worked outside of the office, what they did externally was quite different from today. Back then, this work often involved reading materials that they couldn't get to when they were in the office. Without the connectivity of the internet or widespread use of mobile phones, the ability to work anywhere except the office was severely limited.

Most managers had support staffs of clerical people as well as a number of direct reports to get work done, and to get it done efficiently, people met often in the office, both in groups and one-on-one.

Now: Like many executives, I rarely need to go to my office since most of my interactions are with extended global teams who are networked through email, Dropbox folders, social networks, and Skype. And like many other business people, I'm on the road more, as are my colleagues and clients; various devices become our main form of communication. I have an administrative assistant, but I can perform most work on my own.

Office plans are increasingly open and less space-specific—people are gone so much that having a permanent, private office is far less important than in the past. In fact, armed with a laptop and a mobile phone, even high-level executives no longer need to use the same office daily. Senior managers may rotate between floors and teams based on need, hunkering down in the space of the people with whom they are working; they retreat to phone rooms and other, more secluded spots when they need privacy for calls, thinking, writing, and one-on-one meetings.

How We Engage with Our Colleagues and Clients or Customers

Then: Years ago, our agency, Leo Burnett, created a famous commercial for our client United Airlines. In the spot, a boss tells his team they were just fired by a customer, blaming team members for having lost touch with the customer. He says that they hadn't visited the customer enough, and he is giving them airline tickets so they can start seeing their customers face-to-face more frequently. The boss adds that he is going to fly to see the customer that had just fired them.[5]

As this commercial suggests, engaging meant numerous and regular meetings, lunches, conferences, and so on. People engaged formally through scheduled appointments and informally through lunches, drinks, golf, and other activities. It was assumed that you couldn't build a meaningful business relationship—be it with a colleague, a customer, or a vendor—without these interactions.

Now: We engage in an erratic manner. On the one hand, we're reaching out to people digitally and constantly, connecting via texts, emails, and chats. We communicate with more people more often than ever before. On the other hand, we can go weeks without having a meaningful, in-person interaction or even a one-on-one phone conversation.

So while we're likely to be better informed about what the people in our networks are doing, we're less likely to know what's going on beneath the surface. Distance is the enemy of intimacy, and work intimacy means you feel free to disagree with your boss or suggest a potentially profitable but risky idea. It's tough to be completely open and honest during digital exchanges.

While Google Hangouts and other innovations save organizations time and money and provide forums for thought-provoking discussions, they are inherently limited communications forums. When people meet physically, they don't just have conversations—they have premeeting conversations, side conversations, and rambling, free-form conversations. Ideas emerge in these looser dialogues that rarely surface during nonphysical exchanges. This is the story part of work—spontaneous, provocative, and at times emotive. Literal stories are told—about Jack's feud with Jerry in finance, the yearlong quest to secure the biggest customer in the company's history. But there's also the less formal but no less significant parts of the company story—the evolving relationships, the kind words offered to a colleague going through a tough period, the intellectually stimulating debate in a team meeting. A digital medium is less receptive to story (though as we'll see, organizations can make it more receptive). It is more receptive to fragmented exchanges and data points.

There's a great story about Steve Jobs, who was convinced that unplanned meetings produced great ideas, wanting to build all of Pixar's bathrooms in one corner of the building to facilitate spontaneous interactions between employees. It never happened, perhaps hurting productivity but benefiting those with weak bladders.[6]

What We Gain and What We Lose in a Screen-Dominated Workplace

There are many advantages that today's distributed, networked, tech-enabled, screen-based ways of working bring about. On the bright side:

INCREASED INCLUSIVENESS. Through a wide range of digital tools, organizations foster a participatory environment. People are connected to their peers and their bosses and direct reports in ways that never were possible in an earlier era (because of logistical constraints). There is the opportunity to connect with people not only within one's own office but with people in offices around the world.

ENHANCED SPEED AND COST SAVINGS. It's easier and cheaper to move bits and images and voice and data across screens than it is to move people from place to place. Targeted data is readily accessible on almost any subject, and it arrives with a speed that we could only have dreamed about a few decades ago.

BETTER VISUALS. Modern software and embedding technology lets everyone become a skilled multimedia producer, using deep charts, graphs, and videos. Images have become a primary form of digital communication, and we can manipulate images to do everything from telling a product story to customers to conveying the CEO's organizational vision.

MORE KNOWLEDGE. Screens are portals to the world of information, and today employees know more and know it faster than in the past. They not only can access fixed data sources (e.g., reports, surveys, etc.) but obtain real-time feedback via social media and connections with customers, vendors, and other employees.

There is, however, a dark side:

LACK OF FOCUS. When people look at a screen, they are often distracted by incoming messages, notifications, and the social media reflex to check what's new. Paying attention to the matter at hand—creating a strategy, responding to a quality issue, etc.—is difficult amid continuous visual and aural distractions. In addition, screens make it relatively easy to compile reports, presentations, speeches, memos, and white papers. Before, you had to work hard to gather the research and analyze it; it demanded time and effort and journeys (to libraries, conferences, and interviews) that provided the space to think deeply about what was learned. Now the ease of access eliminates that time and effort. When you can put things together effortlessly, you are less likely to pause, reflect, and analyze in a focused manner.

DIMINISHED COMMUNICATION. While screens can convey far more information than in the past, communication consists of more things than data. Tone of voice, body language, and the context of sharing information all play roles in what is learned. In a screen-dominant environment, these nuances of communication are often lost. As a result, screen conversations feel stilted and prevent the sort of spontaneous, free-flowing dialogues that produce new ideas, fresh perspectives, and productive work. Emojis and clip art can make communication generic and PowerPoint decks are one-way and fixed communication vehicles. A *Harvard Magazine* article titled "The Water Cooler Effect" cited a study by the Harvard Medical School revealing that researchers in close physical proximity produced higher-impact research results than those who worked at greater distances.[7]

WEAKENED RELATIONSHIPS. When people spend a lot of time together—on trips, at conferences, in offices, at lunch—they develop deep relationships where trust and openness exist. This trust and openness creates loyalty, a willingness to provide honest feedback, and other benefits. More superficial relationships are the norm when people work together via screens, tending to make them less-effective collaborators and less willing to be vulnerable, as well as diminishing organizational affiliation and loyalty.

There are many other pros and cons, but here's the takeaway: Screens are a double-edged sword. For every pro, there's a con.

Today, management can be more present than ever before in their employees' work lives using digital communication tools, such as town hall meetings. At the same time, CEOs may come across to employees as nothing more than a moving image, a curated talking-point memo, a CEO avatar.

Rank-and-file workers may be able to make themselves heard and participate more in organizational life, but they also may feel chained to their digital devices, constantly monitored and required to attend a never-ending series of virtual events.

What it comes down to is this: organizations can use screens to filter, project, and separate, or they can turn them into windows that let in the light of learning, diverse viewpoints, and cross-boundary communication.

Seeing Technology from a Human Perspective

We take technology for granted, and that's not a good thing in workplace environments. Being conscious of how technology affects employees, customers, and other stakeholders helps mitigate its negative effects. I have attempted to maintain this consciousness throughout my thirty-seven-year career, a career that has witnessed and been a catalyst of digital transformation. I was one of the first employees in my company to receive a BlackBerry and an IBM ThinkPad, and the first to receive a home ISDN connection. I lobbied our board of directors twenty years ago to adopt a fast T-1 Ethernet to increase the speed of employee internet access.

As I fought to adopt each new technological innovation, I observed the effect it had on people. Over time, I've found that three observations are particularly valuable to organizations, providing them with insights into how the latest device or piece of software will affect employees.

1. Technology is a badge.

Like a Boy Scout merit badge or any positive symbol of achievement, the best technology is something that people feel pride in if they have it and envy if they don't. Technology affects perceptions; judgments are made based on the quality of technology, affecting how outsiders view companies and how insiders view themselves.

When I launched Leo Burnett's interactive marketing group, I insisted that we have a T-1 line brought into the building. I used the fast internet in a mostly dial-up age to prove to clients that we were as "with it" as new digital start-ups and signal to employees that we were serious about the future.

When I helped cofound Giant Step, we had a huge server room with racks of machines behind transparent glass, blinking and beeping for all to see, which created an aura of competence and industrial depth for what was at that time a thirty-person company.

When I started Starcom IP, I insisted that we give every employee (not just senior employees) laptops and pay for all home internet services. This not only allowed employees the flexibility to work from home while feeling the pride of being modernly equipped, it also allowed us to attract the best and the brightest who worked all the time, since they took their laptops home.

This wasn't just about increasing our ability to do good work; it was about perception. I remember clients—some from the largest companies in the world—walking into our office and being both impressed by our technology and jealous that they had nothing like it at their headquarters. More important, it became a point of pride for employees to be on the technological cutting edge. It encouraged them to make use of the technology in the best ways possible—to connect with others, to solicit diverse ideas and opinions, to explore areas of information that they might have ignored in the past.

2. Life, not just work, happens on technology devices.

Organizations are notorious for trying to separate the personal and the professional, but this is not only a futile endeavor but a counterproductive one. People are going to email friends and family, check their stock portfolios, and go on social media sites during the workday. When organizational policies limit or ban these personal activities, they are denying the humanness of their people. Amazon recently sought a patent on a digital wristband designed to monitor employee productivity—it tracks the hand motions of employees in warehouses to determine if they're engaged in "picking and sorting." This seems overly Big Brotherish; most employees want to be treated like responsible human beings, not slackers.

When organizational policies allow life to happen on technology, they empower their people, communicating that they trust them not to take unfair advantage of the freedom they're being given. A minority of employees may abuse this privilege, but the majority will appreciate the trust and respond by being more diligent and productive.

3. Physical gatherings, combined with technology, can turbocharge innovation, productivity, and relationships.

For the past twenty years, my senior executive status has allowed me to insist on, enable, and fund periodic gatherings of team members for in-person meetings that are a combination update and social session. These meetings ideally take place weekly, but at least once a month, at the end of a day. Members in different offices always gather together in someone's room or office, and we dial in other gatherings in other offices. The first half of the call is updates, introducing new members, sharing learning. We then move to the second half, which is someone sharing stories about the craziest client meeting or most embarrassing event, while others discuss either movies or books on a theme. We provide drinks and snacks.

After the meetings, people use technology to share memes on some of the funny topics or to build on the learning. These tech follow-ups often yield nuggets of insight; people think about what was said during the in-person meetings and, after having some time to think and reflect, they use their devices to communicate their thoughts, which often are highly original and perceptive. Without the in-person meetings, however, it's unlikely that they would take the risk of sharing a "different" opinion or a daring concept. Being with other people—getting to know them and letting them know you—encourages taking these types of risks, and technology facilitates the process.

It's instructive that almost all leading tech companies have these all-hands-on-deck meetings. They know they can't live and innovate by tech alone.

The Need for Guidance in Increasingly Screen-Dominant Cultures

The playfield is constantly tilting in the technology direction. In the coming months and years, the IoT and related technologies will turn a growing number of everyday objects into computing devices. Advanced material tech will foster better and more pliable (and even foldable) displays. Augmented and virtual reality will envelop us, and AI will allow us to work faster and more effectively toward solving even the most difficult problems. And we can anticipate machines speaking directly to us all the time; we will have conversations with our intelligent machines like we might have with our colleagues, dialogues designed to tease out issues, obtain information, and formulate strategies. Think of Amazon Echo and Google Home on steroids.

In organizations we're going to be relying on our screens even more in the very near future. In many ways this will be beneficial. As I've suggested, our digital devices and the software inside them can foster better exchanges of information, open us up to new learning, and trigger innovative ideas. The increased portability and powers of devices will increase workplace agility—they will let us work anywhere, and they will encourage us to consider a diversity of options and knowledge.

The danger, though, is that we become so dependent on all the ubiquitous screens and their multiplying capabilities that we lose instinct, relationships, and many other qualities that define us and help us work productively. Therefore, we need guidelines on how to work well in a screen-dominant workplace, and here are the policies I'd suggest.

ALLOW TEAMS AND INDIVIDUALS TO USE TECHNOLOGY ANY WAY THEY CHOOSE. I would add "within reason" to the end of the previous sentence, but it's unnecessary, at least for most employees. Yes, if someone is spending his day visiting porn sites or playing online games, that's not a productive use of his time, but this type of individual is probably not long for the organization. You wouldn't insist that everyone in your group dress alike, write the same way, or adhere to a rigid business philosophy. In an environment where agility is critical, maximize versatility with your technology use policies. Broad guidelines are fine, like minimize use of phones and other devices during in-person meetings to respect the presenter. Restrictive rules, however, will be seen by employees as draconian and alienate them. Give freedom to communicate authentically in the digital space, and it's possible that they'll use their technology to allow who they are and what they believe to come through.

SCHEDULE AT LEAST ONE THIRTY-MINUTE MEETING WEEKLY WITH ONE PERSON OR A FEW PEOPLE. These are opportunities to build relationships, and if you keep the group small and it lasts only thirty minutes, the meetings will help foster meaningful interactions that aren't possible digitally. It really doesn't matter what the meeting topics are, and it's great to veer off work subjects into other matters. The key is offsetting all the digital exchanges with some in-person ones.

FIND WAYS TO USE SCREEN-BASED TECHNOLOGY TO ENHANCE GROUP DYNAMICS. For instance, create team-wide groups on Facebook, WhatsApp, or other social media, or shared folders or fantasy leagues to allow for cross-team communication. This technology personalizes screen time, allowing users to project who they are as individuals. While this isn't a substitute for in-person meetings, it is a supplement representing a way that tech encourages relationship building.

REFRAIN FROM USING TECH TOOLS AS A REFLEX. Many managers can't give a presentation without PowerPoint. Technological tools are great in certain circumstances, but they train people to focus on screens and how things look rather than what is being said. I make all my presentations without any multimedia. I've found that this approach not only helps an audience pay more attention to what I'm trying to communicate, but it helps me pay more attention to them as well. When working on projects, I'll sometimes ask people for ideas or updates in writing (using those ancient tools of paper and pen or pencil). I've found that people are more creative and productive when given the opportunity to respond in this manner—just as artists are more creative when given canvas and brushes (rather than screens), businesspeople often respond better when they have the freedom of a pad of paper and a writing implement.

ENCOURAGE EMPLOYEES TO CREATE SELF-IMPOSED LIMITS ON SCREEN TIME. The best way to encourage this behavior is by modeling it. For instance, I create an oasis of screen-free time for myself daily. For a few hours, I keep my phone on mute and step away from devices so I'm not distracted by notifications and other digital communications. I put my phone away when I'm conversing with others and don't pull it out while waiting in lines. All this helps facilitate daydreaming, reflection, and analysis—activities that make me a more thoughtful and incisive leader.

Similarly, recommend to your people that they restrict their use of social media. As valuable as social media is as a communication and learning tool, continuous streaming can narrow our perception of reality. I carve out fifteen-minute blocks of free time for social media four times daily, and I would suggest to your people that they adopt this practice. It provides just enough of a break without being distracted by continuous notifications, updates, messages, and so on.

Every Screen Can Tell a Story

A device's screen doesn't have to be dominated by the spreadsheet. As much as we associate our screens with numbers and facts, they can also be sources of innovation and inspiration. They can be conduits for the type of stories that foster relationships and provide insights—relationships and insights that can help organizational employees work more effectively on teams and become more innovative in their thinking. But these benefits won't be realized if we leave our devices to their own devices.

Instead of just accepting what appears on our screens, we must be proactive in managing how, why, and when they're used. In 1998, I cofounded a company for digital media called Starcom IP. At the beginning there were just two of us, but over time we grew to more than one hundred employees. In 2018, we decided to hold a reunion for the hundreds of people who had worked at Starcom IP during this twenty-year period. We used Facebook to help spread the word about the reunion and posted photos of employees who had come and gone. We had the reunion in Chicago, and people came from all over the country (including one guy who brought a business card of someone who had visited our offices in 1998, when he was starting his company—the card read, "Sergey Brin, Google").

After the reunion, we followed up with posts summarizing what various alumni and current employees were doing. In response, people commented and told stories about their experiences at Starcom IP. Reading all the posts and seeing all the pictures was a great supplement to the reunion itself; the digital forum on social media allowed a much broader discussion than was possible at the physical reunion, since more people could participate. Using the social media page we created, they participated eagerly and at times eloquently. All the digital exchanges strengthened the sense of affiliation and engagement we all shared.

———————————— KEY TAKEAWAYS ————————————

- Today's mobile and networked workplaces offer many options and greater flexibility to be productive. At the same time, they also create workplace culture challenges: How can you avoid feeling overwhelmed, disconnected, and remote? And how can you encourage your team to avoid this as well?
- Maximizing the best of the screen-based world, while minimizing its downside, means recognizing that technology is not good or bad, but how we use it makes it so.
- Limit the use of screens. Be aware of their ability to colonize our time and minds, and make it a point to have as many in-person interactions as possible.

CHAPTER 3

THE QUEST FOR MEANING IN
THE MODERN WORKPLACE

While existential philosophy has many interpretations, I have a favorite refrain that captures my interpretation: *Life is a journey through reality and time in search of meaning.*

If you think this existential concept is irrelevant to running a business, think again. In the quest to find the balance between the story and the spreadsheet, meaning is what matters. Employees who find work meaningful are highly productive, agile, and committed. They possess a positive story they tell themselves and others about their work, and even if they're up to their eyeballs in data, they are not ruled by it.

As always, the key is finding the balance point between the human story and the data-laden spreadsheet. To understand what we're balancing, though, we need to grasp what is meaningful about work.

People Work for More than Money, Titles, Perks, and Power

Most employees value money, titles, perks, and power, but it's a mistake to believe that these are the only, or the most important, things they look for at work. Consider that as adults, we spend more than half our hours working. Consider, too, that time is the only real resource we possess, and it is limited and unrecoverable.

While some of us find meaning outside of work and settle for jobs that pay well (or not) but aren't particularly rewarding, most people want fulfilling, satisfying work, especially given the amount of time they devote to it. Meaningful work offers purpose, self-improvement, and connection. The challenge today is how to find that meaning.

Our story is the path to meaning. The writer Joan Didion talked about how "we tell ourselves stories in order to live," and that our biggest story is our interior narrative.[1] At work, is our story one of tedium and rule following? Is it one where we do our jobs competently and receive regular raises and promotions, but we constantly dream of doing something else?

Or is the story about a journey of learning and growth, of stretch assignments and camaraderie, of temporal experiences—time passes without notice because you're so wrapped up in what you're doing?

Employees want to tell themselves these types of meaningful stories, but in our workplaces, the myopic emphasis on spreadsheets can get in the way. To a certain extent, this emphasis has existed for years—organizations have always wanted employees to produce as much as possible in the shortest time possible with the lowest costs.

What's different today is our ability to measure input and output. We have become brilliant at measurement because of technology, and while this has critical benefits, it also (inadvertently) diminishes the importance of story. If you drive a vehicle for a living, sensors in the vehicle track every aspect of your route from speed to brakes. Your passengers use apps to rate you. All this data is collated and compared against the norm. At a certain point, you may feel like a cog in a machine, and that is not an existential experience by any stretch of the imagination.[2]

Different Ways Measurement Diminishes Meaning

If you write, the quality and quantity of your words are measured, but so is the number of interactions your article or blog generates. The number of readers, whether a post is shared and discussed, if a given piece makes the popular list—all this and more are often shared on screens. Interestingly, the most popular way to navigate the *New York Times* online is via the most shared list rather than through the home page. The numerical wisdom of the crowd is perceived to be a better guide than what the home page professionals feature.

As medical practices focus on business efficiencies and legal issues, we see data-driven medicine move from just the efficacy of drugs and procedures to how long a doctor takes to see a patient or whether protocols and checklists are followed. A number of hospitals have initiated a new way to measure doctors, called "relative value units," as explained in an article in the *Post and Courier*:

> The committee proposed a new plan, which would tie a percentage of each doctor's salary to the amount of work each doctor does. Moving forward, their productivity would be measured in "relative value units," or RVUs. More patients, more tests, and more procedures generate more RVUs.
>
> But RVU targets aren't universally popular, either.
>
> Some patients argue that RVU goals force physicians to work more quickly, thereby spending less time with each patient and opening a window for mistakes. Doctors, particularly those employed by academic medical centers, worry that productivity targets offer no incentive for physicians to teach or to conduct research if they're not generating RVUs in the classroom or lab.[3]

Meaning is necessary not just for the well-being of employees but to maintain healthy cultures and companies. A case in point is Wells Fargo, which has received a lot of bad publicity in recent years because of its "fake accounts" scandal. The company had a culture that rewarded volume-based outcomes, which were good for the bank but not for its customers. According to a Bloomberg report detailing the company's problems,

> The bank is seeking a federal judge's final approval of a $142 million settlement with some 3.5 million consumers over its practice of "cross selling," which pushed staff to open multiple accounts per customer. Some employees tried to meet sales goals by opening up bogus accounts. More than 5,000 employees were fired, and John Stumpf resigned as chief executive officer. That settlement, even if approved, won't resolve claims by shareholders

who say the bank touted the cross-selling program even after realizing it was a problem. Other investors filed derivative suits, on behalf of the company, against managers and directors of Wells Fargo, claiming they were responsible for the aggressive sales culture. Wells Fargo employees have filed an action for losses in their 401(k) plan, and some former employees say they were wrongfully fired.[4]

Too often, work is benchmarked against a norm: a row on a spreadsheet. What's valued is your economic productivity—your ability to work faster, cheaper, and in high volume—and ethics aren't valued because they're so difficult to measure from a productivity standpoint.

It's one of many intangibles—how innovative you are, your empathy, or why you're doing what you're doing. Purpose, self-improvement, and connection, especially, are not conducive to measurement. As a result, very little time or effort is devoted to ensuring that employees are learning and growing, are committed to organizational goals, or are enjoying a sense of affiliation and inclusion.

While human resources (HR) departments aren't the cause of this problem, they contribute to it. Traditionally, HR has been in charge of data-driven processes. They ensure that evaluations are conducted, employee pay is managed and benchmarked, and the proper verbiage (from a legal standpoint) is used when appraising and terminating employees.

Today, HR receives a steady stream of employee data related to productivity, social media interactions, and much more. They use this data to define, categorize, and measure people. Rarely do they spend time trying to understand the people behind the data.

I'm not beating up on HR; they serve an important and necessary function. Ideally, however, they should serve two functions. The first is to ensure processes, laws, and systems are followed. This is a rigid, legal, and scalable function. The second is to help teach, grow, and retain talent. This is a fluid, flexible, and customized function.

In too many companies, HR devotes the lion's share of their time to the former. Along with incentives that drive specific behaviors—faster, cheaper, more—HR contributes unintentionally to reducing meaningful work experiences.

The Link Between Meaning and Highly Productive People

People who feel valued by, proud of, and affiliated with their organizations perform better than those who don't. This is a tough statement to prove with hard data, but it's one that I and most leaders I've talked to would stand behind. Empirically, we know that the people who have contributed the most to our organizations are those who find their work to be meaningful. While I can cite many examples to illustrate this point, forgive a little civic boosterism and let me tout the culture of the Chicago Cubs.

As most people know, they won the World Series in 2016 and many observers attributed this victory after a century-long drought to the culture and character instilled by president of baseball operations Theo Epstein and his colleagues. While they were smart about developing players in their system, they also have been able to attract free agent talent and keep existing players because of the culture they established.

In a *Wall Street Journal* article, Jared Diamond examined the Cubs' success in attracting free agents:

Tyler Chatwood thought he knew what to expect when he met with the Chicago Cubs this offseason to discuss the possibility of joining them as a free agent. He assumed he would hear plenty about the Cubs' recent on-field success, their plan for him in the starting rotation and, of course, the boatload of money they could offer to lure him.

Instead, president of baseball operations Theo Epstein and general manager Jed Hoyer took the conversation in a direction that surprised and disarmed him: They recommended the best physicians and hospitals in the area for his pregnant wife.

"They had never met me or my wife, and they were giving me doctors' names," said Chatwood, a twenty-eight-year-old right-hander. "They were already going to put us in contact with the OB/GYN over there."

He signed a three-year, $38 million contract with the Cubs shortly thereafter.

This is the secret weapon that enables the Cubs to practically hand-select talent: a compelling personal touch that goes beyond players' value on the field. In many cases, that means appealing to the people most important in their lives—their families.

"We feel like all of those things are exceptionally important," Hoyer said. "There's more than just playing. There's a whole life outside baseball."

They are once again the favorites in the NL Central. As Hoyer put it, "We have something that we're proud of here to sell."

More often than not, players buy it, rushing to join an organization where they believe they'll be happy.

"Money can't buy that," Heyward said.[5]

The Four Keys to Retaining and Motivating the Best Talent

In decades of working with some of the most talented people across a spectrum of situations—from small to large companies, as well as staff and operational roles—I have extracted four keys to retention and development of talent.

A CARING, DEVELOPMENT-ORIENTED BOSS. Bosses foster meaningful work experiences. In fact, a great boss supervising someone who isn't paid particularly well and has a mediocre job drives more employee happiness and growth than a bad boss supervising someone in a high-growth, high-paying position. Who is a great boss? While the personalities and abilities vary, most who fit this definition have the following traits in common: they celebrate the team more than themselves, possess integrity, are approachable, and recognize that their people have lives and pressures outside of work.[6]

If bosses use a spreadsheet-only mentality to manage people, they are unlikely to exhibit these traits. They focus on individuals rather than teams because it's easier to measure the performance of the former rather than the latter; integrity and approachability are "soft" characteristics that aren't measured or rewarded by most companies, and outside pressures don't compute in a work- and data-driven universe.

Perhaps you've heard the saying, "People leave bosses more than they leave companies." Bad bosses suck the meaning out of the work environment, and people who work for them can't wait to get out of their jobs, no matter how well they might be paid.

COMPANY AND TEAM PRIDE. People care a lot about working for organizations with mission, purpose, and values to which they resonate. The litmus test is whether, in social situations, they are happy to tell others about where they work and why they work there versus shying away from mentioning their companies. They believe they have found the right company for themselves, that the company is a reflection of them and they are a reflection of the company. In many cases they also believe they work in special and elite teams.

Whenever I built teams I'd do everything possible to make people believe they were extraordinary—even in situations when people considered what we were doing as less important to the organization than what others were doing (e.g., direct marketing in a large advertising agency). A criticism I would get is that I was creating elitist teams. My answer? From the Marines to McKinsey to Goldman Sachs, everybody wants to be special and world-class. Why should I breed mediocrity?

QUALITY COLLEAGUES. This is analogous to why people like or dislike their colleges. Studies show that what makes students happy at universities are the quality of the professors and the quality of other students. Bosses and fellow employees are the organizational equivalents. What many employees find meaningful are the work relationships they make and sustain over time. Developing a sense of camaraderie and a belief that your team is smart, fun to work with, and successful means a lot to people, especially in increasingly team-oriented work environments.

Over the course of my career, I have cofounded three different companies within Publicis—Giant Step, Starcom IP, and Denuo—and each has enjoyed a great deal of success, primarily because we attracted high-quality people using the following criteria:

- Be careful of the first few hires since they will make (or break) the culture of the company.
- Ensure that nobody is hired without at least eight to ten folks in the company meeting and agreeing to the hire since, until the company grows past fifty people, that one hire can represent at least 2 percent of the workforce.
- Communicate your mission, vision, and values clearly. Even if these

elements strike you as daunting, let people know. The individuals who are right for the job will self-select, embracing the challenge.

OPPORTUNITY TO ACQUIRE NEW SKILLS AND GROW. In a rapidly changing world, the ability to learn and grow is more meaningful than ever before—it helps people retain their marketability and it allows them to keep their skills current. I was able to retain the best talent—talent that could have been paid a lot more elsewhere—by leveraging their higher external offers as positive proof that they had the best job. I said, "This is proof that you have skills that are sought after and you are well-known outside." I would then suggest, "Check in six months and you will be worth even more. Why? Because you are learning and growing new skills. The day you are not worth much more outside, you should leave. Until then, keep growing, and you can always monetize that in the future."

Again, this doesn't negate the importance of a good salary and various perks. To a certain extent, this is the ante to get in the talent acquisition and retention game. But meaning doesn't come from the compensation data. It comes from the human story: the story of skills and growth, the story of great colleagues and bosses, the story of organizational pride.

The Danger of Measurement Imbalance

In some ways the common performance-measurement and rewards system brings out the worst in employees. Rather than encourage them to discover and pursue existentially satisfying work, the system pushes them toward short-term, superficial satisfaction.

Typically, organizations build their incentives around numerical goals such as sales and profits. Salespeople are still rewarded primarily for meeting or exceeding their quotas; other employees are rewarded when they achieve numbers-related objectives, such as finishing a project by a deadline or decreasing costs in their unit by X percent.

I'm not minimizing the importance of achieving these short-term numbers.

I am suggesting that when they become the dominant or only incentives, employees become unbalanced—they are working only for the spreadsheet and are ignoring the story.

There is no question that organizations attempt to integrate team and long-term goals into incentive plans. Unfortunately, it is much more difficult to measure group dynamics and results over a period of years, so short-term, immediate results become the de facto, dominant measure, encouraging one-sided behaviors.

Having a lot of these unbalanced employees is toxic to organizations in the following ways:

- **Breaks down teamwork.** Teams require high levels of trust, cooperation, and sharing; they also need to prioritize company and customer goals over individual goals. When people are being measured primarily on quarterly, individual performance, however, they are dissuaded from adopting team behaviors. They develop a false idea of what's meaningful.
- **Loses the best talent.** The employees who value meaningful work— who relish team interactions, honest conversations, and learning and developing—are alienated by how companies reward short-term results-producers and individual achievement. They feel their ability to grow is compromised and look for employment at companies that value meaningful work.
- **Hurts company reputation.** Glassdoor and other social media sites allow employees to tell the world how their companies are short-term thinkers unconcerned with helping people grow and develop. The word spreads quickly that if you are looking for a caring company that values development, you should look elsewhere.

Admittedly, it's difficult for organizations to change their measurement methods, in part because of the previously stated point that short-term individual performance is easy to measure, and long-term team performance is not. But there's also the question of whether organizations want to create a balanced measurement/rewards process. Public companies are under intense pressure for quarterly earnings, so they value people who can deliver great, individual results quarter by quarter. It's tough to risk reducing individual results, and it's even tougher to have a conversation with high performers and ask them to balance their outstanding individual work with teamwork.

Ideally, organizations will create a recruitment/hiring process that looks for people who have an inherently balanced approach to work and weeds out those who are just in it for the money. I absolutely believe you can recruit with an eye for people who value meaningful work. In fact, I've done so by asking the following two questions of job candidates:

1. How many of the people who used to work for you believe you aided and built their success?
2. Would your ex-bosses and ex-direct reports (not current ones who are unlikely to speak the truth) want to work with you again?

Finding Meaning:
The Opportunity for Improvement

The first self-help book, *Manual for Living*, was written by Epictetus more than two thousand years ago. The desire for improvement is not only ancient but it's hardwired into us. We want to lose weight, create better relationships, become more successful. Companies, too, mirror this desire for self-improvement. They live and die by their growth rates and comparable metrics—comparable to the previous year and competitors.

Through investment and incentives, companies try to help their people and their organizations improve. They make huge investments in training—$150 billion annually in the US—and incentivize improvement by offering promotions and financial rewards for those who meet sales quotas, generate revenue, and achieve other desirable outcomes that represent increases.[7]

Given this book's theme, you probably can guess where all this is heading. The training and incentives are all spreadsheet-based, numerical, and quantifiable. While numerical measures of improvement can have organizational value, they're also flawed in three ways:[8]

1. **They may no longer be relevant.** Measuring against past competitors or oneself tends to be insular and backward-looking; it's often the

wrong measure in a world of change. Improvement against the past or oneself might seem like a positive barometer, but what if other competitors are improving faster? Gillette may have benchmarked against Schick, but the real competitors were Harry's and Dollar Shave Club. I once told General Mills that they were not behind their competitors but behind their consumers, and benchmarking and being slightly better than other pathetic competitors did not make one world-class. They didn't forget that meeting for years.

2. **They can be gamed.** Once incentives are linked to outcomes, individuals and organizations may manipulate budgets, goals, and metrics to ensure they exceed the numbers they have to hit. The telemarketers at Navient who were supposed to help people who had taken out student loans had a "seven-minute rule": they needed to complete a call in seven minutes. So guess what they did? They did not answer questions but said they would mail out information, and in many cases when the calls were going long they hung up, pretending the call had been dropped. The customers were irate, but the seven-minute rule—and the telemarketers' incentives—had been met.

3. **They rarely measure the intangibles.** For growth, expertise, depth, and soft skills, most companies measure what's been done but not the quality or service or experience delivered.

Meaningful improvement, however, can be measured in stories—the stories people tell within organizations about improvements in service, skills, and growth. When employees and their bosses share stories about how Eduardo solved problem X or how Maya capitalized on opportunity X, they usually are tales not of productivity speed but of depth of knowledge. More specifically, meaningful improvement stories usually are about the following:

ABILITY TO INCREASE SKILLS AND COMPETENCE THROUGH CONTINUOUS LEARNING. As the world changes, we have a reflexive desire to keep up, to remain on the cutting edge. As we learn and translate that learning into on-the-job achievement, we feel good about ourselves. We tell our colleagues about all the great knowledge we acquired at a workshop or how an off-site retreat really changed our thinking.

THE CHANCE TO INNOVATE. We can improve by connecting the dots in new ways. Out of these fresh connections come new realities and opportunities. People are amazing in their facility to link things in new ways—e.g., Lyft and Uber, where the traditional concept of taxis was linked with new technology and entrepreneurial individuals. Creating something innovative is tremendously meaningful; it feels like we're using our brains productively.

BECOMING BETTER COMMUNICATORS. Perhaps more accurately, there's room for improvement in emotional communication. Machines are great at reading data and terrible at reading human emotion. We need employees who can motivate and empathize, and there's always room for improvement here. People who can make diverse, sometimes contentious teams work better together through emotional intelligence feel a great sense of satisfaction, especially in cultures that increasingly value collaboration.

As AI becomes a greater force in organizations, and the spreadsheet side of things becomes more effective and dominant, we'll need improvement in the aforementioned three areas more than ever. Learning, innovating, and communicating will take all the great data machines produce and maximize their value. People will find exercising these three very human abilities highly satisfying in an era where AI will become a growing organizational force.

Finding Meaning: Self-Actualization[9]

This pop psych term probably isn't the best descriptor of meaning in the workplace, but it does capture the idea of doing work in a way that is true to who you are. It has been said, "It's never too late to become what you might have been." You probably know people who have found jobs that allow them to be their best work selves (and perhaps you're one of those lucky ones). These individuals experience what psychologist Mihaly Csikszentmihalyi termed "flow,"[10] a mental and emotional state that is equivalent to the sports term "the zone"—for example, basketball player Michael Jordan had games where it seemed he was making every shot he took. At work, flow means that you're highly productive, innovative, and agile, and that you're doing the work you were meant to do at the peak of your powers.

In spreadsheet-dominated organizations, self-actualization isn't a big priority. Numbers can't measure flow. They can measure the output of someone experiencing flow, but there's little concern about creating work conditions that facilitate achievement of this state.

In companies where a good balance exists between the spreadsheet and the story, people are allowed, encouraged, and helped to align their passions and skills. They are then motivated to learn, take chances, grow, and communicate in ways that benefit not only their careers but their organizations—they become experts at what they love to do.

I am a good case in point. My company's focus is marketing and communications, and we develop creative, media, and technology solutions for our clients. While I am familiar with these areas of expertise, I am not an expert at any of them. Instead, my success in the company is due to combining my skills and passion for foreseeing, forecasting, and forging change. I became the company's futurist, change enabler, and reinventor, a role critical to our company's and clients' growth in a transformative age.

Not every organization would have allowed me to self-actualize. Mine did so because the culture and talent-development approach fostered the following behaviors:

- **Live and work in your own mind, not in the minds of others.** In many companies, people try to anticipate what their bosses want or what will impress their colleagues rather than what matters most to themselves. In highly politicized cultures this is especially true, as it is in companies where promotions and bonuses are basely solely on traditional productivity measures. Cultures that encourage authenticity help people work in their own minds. It may take them longer to be major contributors, but their passion for work motivates them to become experts in the long run.
- **Experiment and iterate to find a fit.** After some time in the workforce, people have a sense of what they like and their area of talent. They recognize that they are better than others in a given space. Companies should be aware of this intersection of passion and comparative advantage and funnel people into jobs and tasks that place them in this intersection. They should give them stretch assignments and incentivize them to take risks and develop their abilities.

I should also point out that self-actualization occurs increasingly within teams. When team members are aligned with each other as well as with themselves, they function at peak levels. Here's how to foster this alignment:

- **Ensure receptivity to diverse skills and perspectives.** It takes a village to raise a child, and it takes a range of individuals and talents to raise a great idea. Teams receptive to a range of employees' voices provide them opportunity to be heard. Too often, participation on teams is an exercise in futility and frustration—the team leader or one member dominates the discussion and decisions. When people feel listened to and appreciated on teams—and when they manage to reach consensus after stimulating debate—the results are truly satisfying to all participants.
- **Compensate and appraise based on team performance.** Some companies persist in linking compensation only to individual performance. As a result, people who shine in team settings feel devalued, no matter how much they contribute to the team success. People need to know that their ability to support team members, manage conflict, and move the group to consensus is esteemed by their organizations. In this way, they see their team talents and participation as increasingly meaningful.

Finding Meaning: Deeper Connections

As everyone knows, we are living in a connected age because of technology: mobile devices, social media, group collaboration platforms, video sharing, and so on. These connections can be shallow and superficial, but just because they're made by screens doesn't have to preclude deep connections. Again, it's all a question of how we use the technology. While Facebook is often seen as a platform for weak and trivial connections, it can foster thoughtful and emotional exchanges that influence behavior in profound ways. People come away from these tech interactions with a fresh understanding of issues such as white privilege and are more cognizant of the problems minorities encounter in some workplaces.

We should use all the means at our disposal—both digital and analog—to deepen our connections. Our relationships with bosses, direct reports, peers, customers, and vendors are what contribute to a meaningful workplace. More specifically, when we give and receive empathy and trust, we feel good about ourselves and our place within the organization. We relish being part of a culture that fosters these qualities, especially when we've had previous experiences in companies that were cold and distrustful.

When a boss empathizes when we make a mistake or struggle to meet a tough objective, we relish that empathy, even though we might beat ourselves up for falling short. Empathy makes failures and mistakes palatable. More important, it motivates employees to try harder, to learn more, to develop knowledge and skills that will help them succeed the next time they face a similar challenge. Tim Harris, who once worked with me, told me the story of when he was a newbie and he made a trafficking error that would cost the company a few thousand dollars. After berating himself up over the weekend, he went to his boss to tell her of the mistake, and he expected to be fired. Instead she laughed at him and said, "Don't be a drama queen and think you are so special. We all make mistakes like that when we start. Now, be careful and get out of my office." His then boss, Lisa Donohue, earned his lifelong allegiance and in time she became the CEO of the company.

Similarly, trust gives us the freedom to fail gracefully. When we trust that our boss won't fire us if we make a mistake, we're more willing to take a chance on a fresh approach or an innovative idea. As managers, when we demonstrate that we trust our teams, they are more willing to share diverse ideas and opinions that may run counter to the company's (or the boss's).

Trust and empathy are the glue of solid relationships—of relationships that make us look forward to coming to the office, to working with our colleagues on teams, to proposing ideas to our boss.

To create an environment of trust and empathy where connections are strong and deep, organizations should focus on motivating managers to display the following three traits and create "tattoo moments":

INTEGRITY. Bosses earn trust when they are authentic, transparent about their intent, and open to feedback. People love working for and with executives who possess integrity. They feel they will be treated fairly and respected, which are meaning-creating qualities in business environments. This isn't something you can fake or ignore. In a networked age, people are sharing things about you constantly, so if you lack integrity, everyone will know it. And in an age of #MeToo and corporate social responsibility, organizations are increasingly eager for their leaders to be honest, ethical, and fair.[11] Integrity was always critical, but today leaders who lack it or lose it often take down their companies and not just themselves.

HUMOR. Meaning isn't always associated with serious stuff, and connections don't deepen just when you share your most heartfelt emotions and secrets. When leaders and managers use humor regularly to diminish tension when dealing with tough issues or to create a relaxed, friendly atmosphere, they add to the story side of the equation. Environments filled with laughter and smiles encourage expressiveness and risk taking. It shifts the perspective on negative events, making them seem less like the end of the world and more like a bump in the road. And it helps people relate to each other in a way that's highly enjoyable.

At a major industry conference a few years ago, when everybody was calling advertising agencies dinosaurs, I said that we were not dinosaurs but cockroaches. For like cockroaches, we may be looked down on with disdain, but we scurried around and found ways to survive and outlast everyone else. Everybody laughed, and rarely did people call us dinosaurs after that. Rather, industry analysts noted we would thrive like cockroaches!

VULNERABILITY. To understand someone, you must be able to be understood. If you want your people to share their feelings and challenges, you must share your own. This doesn't mean just saying to an anxious employee, "Sometimes, I get anxious too." You have to tell the story of your anxiety, to make it come alive in ways to which people can relate. Personal stories about vulnerabilities resonate a lot more than facts and figures. If you're trying to encourage someone to take a risk, don't send them a study about the benefits of risk-taking; talk about a risk you took in your career and how it paid off. This is how you build meaningful relationships.

I often told the story of when I had started the Interactive Marketing Group and we had a single client, McDonald's, who had hired us for one project: a test of Time Warner's Full Service Interactive Television in Orlando. I soon determined the technology underlying the project would not work, and the project would therefore fail. I went to the client to tell them not to move forward, knowing that the only revenue—and therefore my job—was dependent on what I was recommending we shut down. The client looked at me and said, "Don't you feel vulnerable for your career?" I said yes, but I was sure the test would not work, even though Time Warner said it would and other clients were signing up. The client decided to withdraw from the test and continue paying my team the fees to help them come up with other ways to do interactive. Some months later McDonald's began working with America Online at our recommendation, and McDonald's became a very large client.

TATTOO MOMENTS. Deep connections occur because of all the previous factors, but emotion is a key component. Typically, a leader or manager reaches out to an employee with a gesture or words that imprint themselves, not just cognitively but affectively. I call them tattoo moments because they are indelibly marked in our memories like a tattoo is on the skin. They become part of our identity and mark our future days.

Years ago, I worked for a man named Jack Klues, who oversaw billions of dollars of business, was a member of Publicis's board, and was the number two executive in the entire organization. We were working together on a new business pitch, and because of bad weather, I was forced to take a train to Urbana, Illinois, where I would meet with Jack the next morning and then fly to our destination. I had never been to this city before, and I arrived at midnight, disembarking into a gloomy, near-deserted station. This was before Uber and smartphones, and I had no idea how I was going to find my way to a hotel.

But then I saw Jack, seated by himself on a bench. "Welcome to Urbana," he said. "I thought you might need someone to drive you to the hotel."

That a leader of a huge organization would do this for me was astonishing. I never forgot his gesture, and I worked for Jack until he retired. I would have done anything for him. That one gesture was far more motivating than any bonus or other perk he might have offered. I loved working with him and helping achieve goals—our deep connection made all our work together meaningful.

―――――――――――― KEY TAKEAWAYS ――――――――――――

- We spend a significant part of our lives at work, and to be productive and happy we seek relevance, affiliation, and purpose in our jobs.
- Meaning is found in some combination of growing and building new skills, finding work that resonates with oneself, and establishing nourishing human relationships.
- The best workplaces foster self-resonant, relationship-rich environments and prevent math, machine, and motion from diluting these healthy attributes.

COUNTERBALANCING MACHINES, SCREENS, AND DATA:

Seven Keys to Staying Human

CHAPTER 4

TALK ABOUT THE
TURD ON THE TABLE

While the first two chapters talk about the dominance of machines, screens, and data, the third suggests that (1) opportunities exist to counteract this dominance and restore the balance between the story and the spreadsheet, and (2) restoring this balance isn't only good for employees but for organizations as a whole. Once companies understand what constitutes meaningful work, they can design programs and policies to promote it.

In this section I suggest actions every organization can take to restore balance. The good news is that there's a lot companies can do; I've already made a number of recommendations, such as humanizing the data (chapter 1), limiting screen time (chapter 2), and infusing meaning (chapter 3).

Here I will provide seven overarching steps corresponding to each chapter in this section—steps that can take companies closer to the story-spreadsheet ideal. These steps can be adopted by anyone wanting to be more successful in this endeavor, whether they're a new employee, manager, or CEO.

You probably can't anticipate what I'm going to suggest. They go beyond the obvious advice. Some are idealistic. Some are iconoclastic. And some are provocative, as the title of this chapter suggests. All of them, though, are user-friendly, and I strongly recommend you start putting them to use in your own organization.

Talking about It Before the S*** Hits the Fan

This chapter's title has its origin in a meeting I had many years ago with Shantanu Narayen, the CEO of Adobe.[1] We were discussing how our two organizations might work together. I knew that we were facing a big obstacle to partnering: at the time we were fringe competitors, but our future growth paths would intensify the competition. Though we avoided this touchy subject initially, it loomed increasingly large in my mind. Finally, I couldn't stand it any longer.

"We need to address the turd on the table," I said.

I wasn't sure how Shantanu would react, but fortunately he said, "I am so glad you brought up what I was thinking about, and you brought it up so elegantly."

The meeting became highly productive after that; we were free to speak openly and honestly about subjects of mutual interest without holding back ideas, information, and opinions.

Pardon the distasteful metaphor, but as I think you'll see, it's apt. Instinctively, you may know the turd on the table that is confronting your organization or team—it's an unpleasant but highly significant subject that everyone would prefer to pretend doesn't exist.[2] It can take many forms:

- **Mismanagement.** For instance, management (particular leaders or leadership teams) is disconnected from reality and refusing to acknowledge the facts—or they're guilty of bullying, discrimination, or harassment. These are incredibly touchy issues, since the former means confronting powerful people in denial and the latter means addressing an individual's unethical or immoral behaviors.
- **Toxic cultures.** Organizations are highly defensive about their cultures, even when they become cultlike and inflexible or fear-driven. Telling a leader that the culture has become poisoned requires courage.
- **Financial improprieties.** Here, the problem may be a company overinflating revenue, such as Enron, or one that takes short-term measures to goose the numbers, such as Wells Fargo. Confronting these improprieties that have major short-term benefits and may involve illegal or unethical actions is a challenge.
- **Major industry shifts.** A leader may refuse to address big changes in customer behavior, or the competitive landscape, or mammoth

technology changes requiring tough decisions (such as Kodak and digital emergence). It's easier to rationalize or deny shifts than articulate the business-altering trend and the need for rethinking everything.

- **People problems.** The boss or some person with influence is acting like a jerk, or is playing favorites, or is blind to internal or external developments. In many ways, this is the biggest turd on the table, in that it requires confronting a powerful individual about his or her issues.

Leaders can also address the turd on the table externally rather than internally. A small minority of leaders are willing to be outspoken and raise what Al Gore has termed "inconvenient truth." I like to count myself among these leaders. For instance, I recently told a meeting of advertising industry executives that advertising spending would decline between 20 percent and 30 percent over the next five years.[3] This prediction was pounced on by print and digital media, and a MediaPost reporter noted that I was making an "ironic prediction for an ad executive whose title is chief growth officer."[4]

I suppose it was ironic, but more than that, it was a provocation designed to surface a huge issue in the industry that few wanted to confront. My intent was to disabuse marketers of their long-held belief that they could depend on mass advertising to build brands. The whole point of calling attention to the turd on the table, whether it's inside or outside a company, is to stimulate frank discussions and fresh thinking about how to deal with the issue. The initial articulation of the unpleasant subject can evoke a negative, defensive reaction, but in most cases, it will produce positive results eventually.

The Reluctance to Verbalize Tough Truths

In spreadsheet-dominant organizations, people are often less than forthright. These types of companies don't just program with code, they speak in code— they qualify their statements, sugarcoat their words, fail to disclose because of paranoia about "security." In these cultures, leaders are always worried that a competitor is using sophisticated technology to spy on them, that hackers are going to breach their firewalls.

It's not that all leaders of these companies consciously avoid confronting and talking about difficult issues. It's simply that, like the stereotypical accountant or tech geek, they gravitate toward safer subjects that can be discussed factually rather than emotionally. A spreadsheet-focused mentality promotes fear and magical thinking.

Common Fears

BEING PUNISHED. You've heard the phrase "Don't kill the messenger"? In spreadsheet cultures, people who bring up messy, problematic subjects tend to draw the ire of others in the room. If it can't be dealt with logically and analytically—if it causes people to feel upset, embarrassed, or confused—then raising these issues creates consternation. And sometimes it creates condemnation. People are afraid of being punished—verbally reprimanded or worse—for talking about difficult subjects. For instance, they don't want to address how the CEO intimidates everyone or how the CIO's tendency to play favorites is lowering morale.

BEING WRONG. In a data-driven world, people like accuracy and correct decisions. The reasoning goes, if you follow the data, you'll get it right. Of course, that's not always true. In these cultures employees are often plagued by self-doubt: Am I reading the situation right? Is there a subject flaw in my thinking? Have I analyzed the situation incorrectly? Self-doubt is a highly effective censor.

BEING ASKED TO DO MORE WORK. Or, as they warn you in some stores, "If you break it, you buy it." People fear that if they raise problems or difficult issues, they will be asked to deal with them.

BEING DISLIKED. Truth tellers aren't popular in spreadsheet companies, especially when they're telling hard truths. Most employees want to be liked by their colleagues and bosses, and articulating troubling issues will get them branded as troublemakers. This is especially true if they don't have facts and figures to back up their insights and opinions.

Magical Thinking (or the "Turd Is a Brownie" Phenomenon)

INABILITY TO SEE A TURD. When you're viewing the data constantly and thinking about it endlessly, you're viewing the turd through distorting, rose-colored glasses. I've worked with managers like this, people who are insulated by all their software and systems and benchmark developments in a formulaic manner—i.e., they always compare their performance with traditional competitors or use other established measures. As a result, they miss untraditional competitors or unmeasured innovations. They see only what their screens show them. Thus, they fail to raise problematic issues because they can't see them clearly. At first the music industry did not see—and then did not understand— the impact of the iPod and iTunes on wresting away control of the industry; what did a technology company understand about music?

ACCEPTING DATA WITHOUT QUESTION. We take refuge in the data, believing it to be holy. We accept whatever the machine spits out and forget to ask how the data was collected and compiled, or what biases were in the algorithm. Even if our instincts are prompting us to call a turd a turd, we don't because the data says it's actually a brownie. Today many marketers tell me how well their online campaigns are doing and how they wish to allocate more money to these programs, despite no overall gain and often a decline in their total business. I let them know that they remind me of a patient who is getting sicker and sicker but believes the vital signs on the monitor, which seem to be glowing healthily. Could it be that they are not measuring the right thing or the measurement is wrong?

MYTHMAKING AND HERO CULTURES. Magical thinking prevents people from stating unpleasant truths for subtler reasons than the previous two factors. In tech start-ups, especially, cultural success myths are powerful, and they often relate to formulas or other numerical concepts that helped the company achieve success. Obviously there's validity in these cultural stories, but at times the stories become sacrosanct and that's when they become a problem (e.g., it's heresy to speak against the company ethos or its leaders and founders).

When I joined Leo Burnett decades ago, I found an admirable culture of excellence, humility, and achievement reinforced by stories and symbols. Our logo had a hand reaching for the stars, accompanied by the founder's statement, "When you reach for the stars you may not touch one, but you will not come up with a handful of mud either." The logo and other symbols had an almost religious significance, and few would have spoken against this message; no one would have said we need to set realistic goals rather than reach for the stars.

I'm not criticizing these symbols and stories, only suggesting that they can have the unintended effect of inhibiting straight talk. At Apple, for instance, they still ask, "What would Steve Jobs do?" That may not be the right question today or in the years ahead because things change. Data-centric companies that have been highly successful are especially vulnerable to drinking the Kool-Aid, since people who work in these companies often have fierce beliefs in their technology, and they have trouble violating their sacred beliefs.[5]

The Value of Straight Talk

Before I offer some advice on how to put this first step into action, let me take a moment to note three organizational benefits of calling a turd a turd.

First, *it increases the effectiveness of teams.* Teams function best when they possess a sense of connectedness—a sense that often comes from trust and empathy. Straight talk fosters trust and empathy. When teams can't confront problems or talk about sensitive subjects, they are engaged in a charade. Their members won't be honest with each other or genuine about themselves. They may be smart and skilled as individuals, but they never generate the synergies that foster great ideas and great execution.

Second, *it gets to the root of problems.* Discerning problems in organizations requires developing and testing hypotheses, from realistic to speculative. This means taking risks, shooting down bad ideas, identifying who or what is caus-ing problems. In other words, difficult topics must be brought to light. Toes may be stepped on in these activities. But this is the best way to figure out why something went wrong and start on the path to fixing it.

Third, *it fosters creativity and innovation.* When organizations are overly politically correct, when there's fear of telling bosses the truth, when employees are so polite that no one is ever wrong, then no one wants to rock the boat. We've learned that disruptors are valuable, and when no one ever points out the turd on the table, disruption is rare to nonexistent.

For great ideas to soar, we need trampolines of trust—we need to know that even if we say something that is wrong or upsetting, we can bounce back. If these trampolines are not there, then no one is going to risk saying anything that might cause them to splatter on the ground.

If organizations need a model for turd-talking, they should look to their brainstorming and off-site meetings. At these meetings, people are usually told that there are no wrong answers and that they should not put down colleagues who say things they perceive to be off-point or dumb. They are also told that they can level with anyone and everyone, no matter what their titles may be.

Why do we segregate our ability to generate ideas and look at issues with piercing clarity to these off-sites? Why do we need inspirational speakers and role-playing to generate straight talk? It seems to me that organizations would benefit enormously if these were organizational policy rather than limited to a few special occasions annually.

Three Magic Words

My colleague Michael Donahue, who is a high-level, senior executive at the Association of National Advertisers, shared his belief that the most valuable assets in communicating were the following four-, five-, and six-letter words: *data, trust,* and *intent* (DTI).[6]

Do you have good *data* that supports your point of view? If not, why do you feel so strongly about surfacing an issue? Is it a combination of your experience and instinct (which can be forms of data)?

Can you be or are you *trusted*? Are you someone people believe is open and honest?

What is your intent?—i.e., why are you saying what you're saying? Is it because you believe what you have to say will benefit an individual, team, or the company as a whole?

People who have all three assets are usually seen as possessing candor; they are willing to address uncomfortable or difficult issues. More to the point, they address issues with relevant facts and figures, are taken seriously because they're trusted, and are perceived to have positive intentions (i.e., to solve a problem confronting a team rather than working from a political agenda).

Organizations must encourage trusted, well-intentioned, well-informed people to display this type of candor, no matter what their titles are. They can perform a vital role for organizations, whether it's speaking up and stopping a problem that's about to explode or disrupting business as usual with their candor. And even if they're wrong—if a turd is not really a turd—they can clear the air by catalyzing a discussion of the touchy issue and flush it away if it proves to be unsubstantiated.[7]

Here are four ways organizations can encourage people to display candor:

1. **Ask, "What if the opposite were true?"** Leo Burnett originally hired me in 1982, after I wrote an essay as part of the job interview process, titled, "What If the Opposite Was True?" My premise was that unless someone can build a strong case for the opposite of what they say or believe to be true, they lack credibility; they've failed to analyze a given situation thoroughly. Similarly, I've always asked this question of myself before making an important statement or decision.

   Organizations should train their people to factor oppositional thinking into their mindsets. When they consider the opposite of what they believe, they can surface all sorts of possibilities and risks that they may have never considered previously. When these opposites become conscious, they will more likely be articulated during discussions.

2. **Model straight-talk behavior.** When leaders and managers are willing to be consistently and sometimes brutally honest in their communication, their people are likely to follow suit.

3. **Celebrate and incentivize turd-identification behaviors (rather than discouraging or punishing people).** Give bonuses to those who display the most courage in identifying dicey problems or challenging their bosses with hard truths and disruptive perspectives. Recognize, too, that in most organizations, these behaviors aren't incentivized unless an individual can provide irrefutable data to back up his or her point of view (and while irrefutable data is great, it's often not available).

4. **Discuss and use the DTI filter.** Is there data to support the point of view (not irrefutable, but compelling)? Is the speaker generally trustworthy? Is the intent to help the team or the organization (rather than the individual)?

Today we're living in a connected world, and innovation emerges from fresh insights. These insights need to be incubated in a safe, nurturing environment, and that environment is created when people feel free to say exactly what's on their minds. They especially need to feel they have permission to challenge the conventional data wisdom—the statistical "truths" like who the company's market is, the strengths of competitors, the economic trends, the software preferences, and so on.

Integrate Judgment and Savvy into the Data

As the previous paragraphs suggest, people are often unwilling to go with their gut—or even their experience—in data-dominant cultures. Consider how close many companies are to having AI make decisions for them. The attitude often is that "machines know best," and so we allow data to connect to other data and come up with the answer. This is happening in every area of organizations.

In marketing, especially, analytics determine the look and content of advertising.

In finance, budgets are based on highly sophisticated numerical projections.

In human resources, everything from training to downsizing decisions emanate from statistical analysis of the value of each activity to the organization.[8]

Again, it's not that these numbers are bad; they are crucial to companies today. But numbers have become omnipresent and in some cases are perceived as omniscient. There are social media numbers, financial data, website usage figures, algorithms that influence search results. They are embedded in strategies and cultures and policies and procedures, and they become stubborn things.

All employees need to wrestle with stubborn information rather than accept it as gospel. Why? Because as Plato said, "A good decision is based on knowledge and not on numbers."

I'd amend the philosopher's statement to, "A good decision is based on knowledge and not *solely* on the numbers."[9]

People won't talk about the turd on the table if the numbers tell them that it's a delicious brownie. Even if their instinct and experience are screaming that they should insist the brownie will not go down well, they will withhold this truth because their beliefs are nothing compared to the data.

Consider these two examples where leaders at Costco and Apple must have defied the data and relied on their gut to make decisions crucial to their companies—decisions in which someone identified the turd and moved their companies in directions that ran counter to the prevailing data-based wisdom.

If Costco paid its employees only by the numbers, those employees would receive less than they are paid today. To maximize profit, Costco could have paid closer to minimum wage; it was the spreadsheet thing to do, and it certainly helped Walmart achieve maximum profitability—for a while. But by paying higher wages, Costco ensured that its workforce would be happier and feel more valued; that in turn motivated them to go out of their way to help shoppers and to be more productive.

I don't have the inside story of who made this decision at Costco, but I would bet this leader or team of executives decided to rely on their experience and instinct rather than just the numbers. Someone was brave enough to talk about the turd on the table—that paying employees less may be great for the bottom line in the short run but could hurt the company over the long haul.

Similarly, Apple made the costly decision to create their own stores at a time when direct-selling computer companies Dell and Gateway were industry leaders. From a spreadsheet perspective, this looked like a bad decision—retailers have a lot more costs than direct sellers. Again, I have no personal knowledge of the conversations that took place at Apple, but I would bet someone said something to the effect of, "Look, I know you don't want to hear this, but we need to build our brand, not just sell a hardware product. And my experience tells me the best way to build our brand is by giving people the opportunity to see and use our product, to create an environment reflective of the values we espouse. This means building stores—really nice stores—and that isn't going to be cheap."

How do you encourage people to combine their experience and instinct with the numbers to say what's on their mind? By using what I refer to as the Three Limits Method:

ENCOURAGE DATA COLLECTION WITH LIMITS. In our data-rich world, people often refuse to make a decision or even venture an opinion until they've collected a "sufficient" amount of data. This focus on accumulating all available facts and figures is counterproductive in two ways. First, leaders and managers refuse to act quickly and instead procrastinate to the detriment of their organizations. Second, it discourages people from drawing on empirical evidence or playing hunches; they believe that experience and instinct aren't scientific, and that if they just have sufficient data, they can make the right choices.

My advice: Collect often. Collect more. But collect fast. Set a time limit on gathering information. Don't dither. Look at the data and then filter it through your own experiences and the experiences of other savvy veterans. Recognize, too, that you may as well impose limits since so much new information is pouring through screens daily that you're never going to be able to accumulate all the evidence you desire for a decision.

REMIND EVERYONE THAT DATA IS INHERENTLY LIMITED. We tend to apotheosize data. As valuable as it is, if you treat it like the holy grail, you'll become overly dependent on it. Perspective, context, theory, instinct, experience, and many other factors exist outside of the data, and you need to recognize them. When you receive that survey that spotlights an emerging trend or you're studying the latest social media numbers, tell yourself that, as compelling as the data is, it's not the whole story. View it as limited and you'll be in the best position to use it effectively. Remind your people who rush in with the latest numbers that they need to take a breath and use their ability to interpret what these numbers might mean.

COMMUNICATE THAT PEOPLE WHO DEPEND ONLY ON DATA WILL LIMIT THEIR CAREERS. This limit is personal and serves as fair warning that they need to use their creativity, agility, and savvy if they want to prosper in an organization. When someone comes into my office and informs me they made a decision solely or primarily based on what a spreadsheet or other data source told them, I suggest they start looking for a new job since they'll soon be unemployed as the age of algorithmic machines dawns. In this age, it's imperative that people discern what a machine cannot do and augment it with their own analytical abilities. Machines will have more decision-making power in an AI world, but they are fallible and in great need of humans who point out errors, suggest alternatives, and communicate possibilities.

Five Best Practices to Encourage Table Talk

While organizations are quick to endorse the concept of disruptive thinking, they are not always so quick to encourage the practice of it. It's a conundrum for leaders. As much as they value disruptors and know they are crucial for growth and innovation, many leaders also have been raised in the old paradigm where the status quo was maintained, the chain of command was observed, and teams in the trenches were seen but not heard.

As a result, cultures are not as receptive to people pointing out turds on the table as you might think (since turds are nothing if not disruptive). Challenging the status quo or the conventional wisdom takes bravery, and it's tough to be brave if you think you might be punished or branded as not a team player.

For years newspapers did not see the impact of Google. They then refused to face the fact that online advertising dollars would never replace the offline dollars and that giving away the news for free, and therefore making people drop their offline subscriptions, was doubly tragic.

Smart companies that created amazing content, like Condé Nast, believed the shibboleth that content was king—despite the fact that in a world of social media and search engines, content was being commoditized. It was not the content owners but the people who pointed to content, like Facebook and Google, who were making money. Today Instagram is what Condé Nast could be. For years the incentive systems and cultures of these fine organizations were skewed to the past, and they lit and scented the turd to look like a brownie.

You would think organizations would understand that if someone does not speak truth to power, this truth will arrive via competitors who take away market share, or through a newspaper article, or through social media that spreads the rumor about the company's unfair practices. Truth has a habit of breaking through whatever barriers companies erect, especially in a digital age. It's better that the company facilitates the emergence of truths internally rather than externally.

Here are five ways to do so:

1. **Anonymous tip lines or suggestion boxes.** This is like training wheels for turd table talk. Yes, it's old-fashioned, and employees may be skeptical at first about whether their suggestions will be read or acted upon, but it provides a starting point for people to voice their truths.

2. **Leadership modeling of truth-talking.** This is a simple but effective way to integrate truth-telling into the culture. At the end of every important meeting, meeting leaders should ask the following two questions: (1) Is there something that has not been said that should have been said? (2) Can someone please say why what we discussed or agreed on today might be wrong?

   The Navy SEALs have a practice that after every operation, they have a debrief where everybody leaves their titles at the door. It does not matter if you are a newbie or a commander; everyone is asked to talk about what they and everybody else in the team could have done better.

3. **Truth-telling incentives.** Nothing aligns values and behaviors like incentives. Rewarding rather than punishing people who challenge

the status quo with financial benefits, promotions, and verbal approval sends a powerful message. If you want people to take risks and challenge the status quo, you need to reward such people and such behavior. When I ran new small units for my company, they did not reward me on the size of the team or client or revenue we added but on other metrics more in keeping with our focus on tomorrow.

4. **Admitting wrong.** Bosses hate to say, "I made a mistake," or "That was a dumb decision." When bosses admit they were wrong, especially when they do so with humor and vulnerability, they convey it's okay to admit mistakes and point out what didn't work. Sometimes the turd on the table is a bad leadership choice, and when the leader points it out, it signals to others that it's okay not only to admit mistakes but to note when bosses do something wrong. Every CEO I know has overcome significant boo-boos. They survived and thrived because they realized they were wrong and rectified their mistakes.

5. **Storytelling.** Dramatize the positives of identifying the turd on the table. Bring in outside speakers who can lay out scenarios in which organizations benefited when people started telling the truth.

KEY TAKEAWAYS

- Successful organizations and people ensure that diverse points of views are heard, even if they challenge the status quo or are disturbing in other ways. Many companies, from Wells Fargo to Boeing, could have avoided billions of dollars of damage had they allowed and listened to dissenting, disturbing viewpoints.
- Speaking truth to power requires both courage to speak and willingness to listen. Companies that foster these behaviors have trust- and relationship-building cultures—they create environments conducive to tough talk and hard listening.
- By asking for dissenting opinions, encouraging opposing points of views, and celebrating those who speak out even if they are wrong, organizations can facilitate talk about the turd on the table.

CHAPTER 5

ADDRESS THE REALITY
THAT CHANGE SUCKS

C hange sucks.

When people insist that change is good, I tell them that I'm fine, but if they wish to change, go ahead.

Similarly, when organizations talk hyperbolically about all the benefits that will accrue when they change their structure, culture, software, and so on, I don't doubt their sincerity but I question their perception. Organizational change can be brutal. People lose jobs and friends. They have to adapt to new ways of working. They must adjust to new leaders and styles of leadership. Many times, they feel that the company has changed for the worse—that the organization and culture they once loved no longer exist.

More succinctly, let me repeat: change sucks. It takes us to places unknown and requires us to learn new things. In the process of learning we often fail, embarrass ourselves, and suffer discomfort as we leave familiar routines and beliefs behind.

Dealing with change, then, is emotional. Too often organizations approach change from a spreadsheet perspective. The numbers say cut staff, the cuts are quickly made, and people who have been with companies for years find themselves suddenly out of work. Organizations may believe they're handling downsizing as humanely as possible, but in reality, it is often done impersonally with little regard for feelings—the feelings of those being let go and the friends of the departed who remain.

Change is necessary and can be enormously beneficial, but it should be undertaken with the story in mind. This is the only way to mitigate change's harsh realities.

Leaders tend to be myopic about the numbers, especially when those numbers go up or down in major ways or when a significant pattern is detected. They analyze them every way possible and then create a change strategy that addresses numerical priorities.

But there are stories associated with these numbers that also must be addressed. Some of the stories are related to what I've already alluded to—the effect a given change will have on people. Other stories are related to interpreting what the data suggests. People possess a combination of deep knowledge and broad experience that helps them talk about the data in illuminating ways. They can relate stories about similar data-based trends in the past, about how a given leader failed or succeeded to address problems and opportunities. These stories create a context that is crucial in helping management make the right decisions.

Thus, as we contemplate change, we need to obtain the story behind the spreadsheet.

Money, Influence, and Fame

Changing by numbers is like painting by numbers. You'll end up with something that looks good on paper but doesn't deliver on its promise. Contrary to what some organizations believe, change is about more than percentages: downsizing by 15 percent, moving 25 percent of the workforce onto teams, growing by 18 percent, transferring 12 percent of human functions to machines.

Organizations often embark on change strategies with target percentages in mind, but they fail to achieve lasting and impactful results unless the people issues are integrated into the planning. These issues are diverse and multifaceted, but before getting to them, let me share a story about why organizations may recognize the need to change, may create programs to facilitate this change, may talk a lot about the need to change, but they don't achieve their goals.

By 2005, the effect of digital on the newspaper business was clear. Craigslist, Google, and many other sites were siphoning away advertising revenue, making the traditional model untenable sooner rather than later. Three years earlier, at a newspaper industry convention, I forecasted this likelihood and suggested a number of initiatives, including investing in technology, purchasing digital start-ups, rethinking their business model, and putting their best minds to solving for the future versus milking the cash cows of the past. Years later a senior executive at the *Chicago Tribune*, who had been at the convention, told me he wished they had listened.

In 2010, I spoke with a major magazine publisher, telling them they were no longer in the print business where they made money from advertising but in the multimedia business where they had to make money from advertising, commerce, subscriptions, and services. Seven years later after seeing revenues halved, the closing of many magazines, and their loss of relevance, the company began to reinvent with positive effect. Imagine how much more successful they would have been if they had moved early. Why didn't they change when the evidence was so clear that they had to transform themselves?[1]

Because change is hard. You can't change an organization just by talking about why change is necessary and providing a blueprint for that change. You have to integrate people's desire for money, influence, and power into the mix, and you have to incentivize them in ways that are aligned with future change goals rather than goals from the past.

Data Can Be Strong, but the Will Is Weak

It is key to recognize that everyone looks at change through the lens of what it means for them. How do they fit in, what role do they serve, and do they agree with the change?

In 1999, Leo Burnett's Jack Klues began the effort to create Starcom, a separate media operation from the main ad agency. This move represented a radical change, but one that was critical since media tools and technologies were becoming increasingly complex and required a significant development investment—an investment that wouldn't have been possible if the media operations remained an integral and profitable part of the parent company.

Later, Jack recognized the need to create more change—a new division of Starcom that focused on internet media planning and buying. As a cofounder of Giant Step, the digital arm of Leo Burnett, Jack asked me to help launch this digital group, called Starcom IP. To implement this change, Jack and his management team incorporated the following people-centric principles:

1. Starcom IP would report directly to the global CEO and not to Starcom management, even though initially it consisted of only two people to Starcom's five hundred.
2. The leadership of Starcom IP would be on the board of Starcom to help influence the overall company and also be aligned with Starcom's overall goals.
3. The best talent hired for Starcom would be given an option to work for Starcom IP.
4. Both Starcom and Starcom IP were given financial goals, but they were different goals. Starcom focused on growth and profitability while Starcom IP focused on generating clients and credibility. Both management groups were incentivized to help each other through revenue recognition and benefits.

Starcom IP was quickly and sustainably profitable, and it grew quickly. Why? Because the needs of the new company's people were addressed right from the start. Its leaders were given a great deal of independence as well as power (board membership), provided with talent and not just financial resources, and encouraged to build credibility and depth of expertise first and make money second. Everyone at Starcom IP felt their concerns were addressed and their goals clear and appropriate. With everyone aligned, the company was able to change its approach to media quickly and effectively.

RENETTA MCCANN

Never Forget Your Roots When You Get Wings

When a company has soul, it's not just big-hearted but big picture. It refuses to be myopic about delivering short-term results, recognizing that sometimes the short term isn't as important as long-term objectives. A soulful company also encourages its leaders to sacrifice—to pass on plum projects when they believe another team can do the project better.

Over the years at Burnett, the evolving culture encouraged leaders to find a balance between short-term and long-term goals, to view other teams and functions as collaborative rather than competitive. Here's an example of one leader who exemplified these soulful attributes.

In the mid '80s I would take the Number 6 "Jeffrey" Bus from the Leo Burnett building downtown to my home in Chicago's Hyde Park neighborhood.

Renetta McCann often waited at my stop and rode the bus to work with me. She was a couple of years my senior at Burnett, but we were both in the lower echelons of the company and we commiserated and complained about senior management. We vowed that if we ever occupied leadership positions, we would not become political but keep the good of the company and the people who got the work done paramount.

By 1999 Renetta McCann was the CEO of Starcom in the United States. Starcom was one of the two biggest media and buying companies, placing billions of dollars, and Renetta was one of the most powerful African American women in the nation.

As mentioned, I had been invited by Jack Klues, who was the global CEO of Starcom and Renetta's boss, to help him launch a digital media buying-and-planning unit called Starcom IP. Renetta would run all the nondigital revenue, which was in the hundreds of millions of dollars, and I would run all the digital revenue, which at the time of our launch was barely above zero.

Within three years and despite the dot-com implosion, Starcom IP grew to over one hundred employees and multiple millions of dollars of revenue at a healthy profit margin. In addition to the amazing team of Tim Harris, Jeff Marshall, Christian Kugel, Chandra Panley, and other early Starcom IP leadership, the driving reason for our success was Renetta McCann.

Though I did not report to her—I ran a separate profit and loss statement, and was aligned with the cool digital future while she worked on the meat and potatoes of mainline media—Renetta moved heaven and earth for Starcom IP to succeed.

She allowed me to poach some of her best talent (after getting her okay), provided me with client leads, and supported us and our different pricing structure with them. Most important, she let me operate a variant culture where the employees at Starcom IP were given better technology and wages that benchmarked against the outside world for digital talent. She recognized that Starcom IP was not competing with Starcom but with Modem Media, Avenue A, and Digitas for talent and credibility. She also recognized that she and I were aligned on how well Starcom would thrive in the future, and in time Starcom IP could be folded back into Starcom.

Change Is Hard, People Are Soft

By saying people are "soft," I don't mean weak or fragile; they are vulnerable and anxious, and they can't be treated like metallic cogs in the machine. When the organization announces that their group is being spun off and restructured, or that they're going to be asked to move halfway across the country, or that they will need to learn how to work within a matrix rather than a pyramid, they are understandably concerned.

People won't support and further change unless they perceive how they and their skills fit. Financial incentives aren't sufficient to motivate people to become deeply involved in making a change happen. Instead, organizations need to mirror their organizational goals with individual ones. The growth, relevance, and transformation they seek for the company should be reflected in similar programs for individuals.

Employees need to see how the change strategy helps them grow, not just the organization.

They need to understand how their skills and knowledge will be more relevant to the company, just as the company hopes to be more relevant to its customers.

They need to recognize how they may transform themselves through learning and training, just as the company hopes to transform its practices and place in its industry.

These needs are especially compelling given that many employees experience negative financial outcomes as the company embarks on change. Many companies reduce bonuses and freeze raises (to conserve funds required for a costly change) while the workload remains the same or increases. Organizations may also ask their people to move into situations where opportunities for advancement and higher salaries are less likely in the short term.

As I noted at the start of the chapter, change sucks.

To offset this negative, organizations have to tell a better story than the one the spreadsheet dictates. They must focus on people's concerns using the following three approaches:[2]

STRAIGHT TALK. Be truthful about the challenges ahead and the pain that will be faced in the short term. Truth includes admitting the pain might have been avoided if the company had acted faster or was more prescient about the changes. Truth also includes recognizing that success is not a given and enumerating the risks and pitfalls ahead. While organizations are often reluctant to be anything but hyperbolic and grandiose in their description of the change effort, most employees are savvy about the odds of succeeding. If management fails to be honest, they will respond cynically at best and with little effort or enthusiasm at worst.

ONE STANDARD. When change is being wrestled with, the entire team or organization must be treated with one standard. If there is to be a cutback of benefits, everyone must suffer the cut or, at minimum, the more senior folks should bear the brunt of it. Organizations that preach belt-tightening and increased workloads to make it through transformational times but ask the rank and file to sacrifice are asking for trouble.

GUARANTEED FUTURE BENEFITS OF SOME TYPE. People need hope and a powerful reason to navigate the change. They must envision a future benefit that they will gain regardless of the outcome of the transformation journey. I recognize that it's difficult to make a specific financial promise—for example, you'll make 25 percent more in five years if the change is successful. But organizations can make other promises in the following areas:

- **A pioneering credential.** Companies are looking for people who have gone through the leading edge of change; they want to recruit people who have been there, done that. By being part of a transformational effort, they have a marketable experience to put on their résumés.
- **Growth and skills.** Being part of organizational change means learning and growth—employees can't survive without both. They will acquire

new skills and learn how to adapt to a new environment, becoming more agile, innovative, and effective. All this makes them more marketable.

Obviously, companies must tailor these benefits to specific circumstances—the value can range from learning how to manipulate a new piece of software to the chance to work on cross-cultural teams or gain cross-cultural experience in India, China, or another emerging power. When people can see legitimate benefits to a change program, they believe there's something in it for them, not just for the company or its management.[3]

Coaching Slow and Fast

Theoretically, coaching is all about people. But some coaches go about their business with organizational objectives spotlighted and individual requirements subordinated. They fail to recognize that there are different types of change and that they affect people differently. Instead, they focus on assessment: Can this individual contributor make the transition to a team culture? Or they coach them like propagandists, trying to convince people that a change initiative will be wonderful for everyone. Or they coach everyone the same way, failing to account for individual concerns, strengths, and goals.

It shouldn't be surprising, therefore, to hear the conclusions of authors John L. Bennett and Mary Wayne Bush in *Coaching for Change*: "Research indicates that approximately 70 percent of all organizational change initiatives fail . . . including mergers and acquisitions, introductions of new technologies, and changes in business processes. This statistic emphasizes the need to leverage any and all organizational resources to make change work. . . . Change coaching is an ideal way to ensure that change is supported at the individual and group levels for the benefit of the entire organization."[4]

While other types of coaching exist, transformational coaching is the most challenging since it isn't just about getting people to do things differently but to think and be different as well. To motivate people to embrace a new way of thinking and being doesn't happen with a cookie-cutter approach or in a single coaching session.

Complicating matters is the concept of "pace layers of change," articulated years ago by Stewart Brand and Paul Saffo. Their thesis was that some things change at a different rate than others: fashion, commerce, and infrastructure change faster; governance, culture, and nature change slower. They suggested that each type of change has different traits, and that change works best when conversations are held about each type.[5]

I'm not going to cite all the various change theorists and contrast all the different approaches. Suffice it to say that change is complex, and that to make it work organizations and individuals must rewire their thinking and then twist themselves (behaviors, being) into shapes aligned with change.

To help your organization and people rewire and twist, here are three suggestions:

COMMUNICATE AND REPEAT. Why is the organization changing? Why is it critical that it change both for itself and its employees? Clarity and repetition are essential here, not because employees are dumb but because the issues can be complex and can evolve and need updating over time. The communication should be succinct, but it needs to occur regularly. Transformation is often a slow process, and people need to be reminded why change is occurring and why tweaks are being made to the original plan. Employees are all different, and while some might "get it" immediately, others need inspiration, motivation, and a variety of explanations to secure their buy-in.

REWARD BEHAVIOR, NOT JUST OUTCOMES. Remember, a key to transformation is rewiring. This means it's not enough to achieve specific benchmarks through change—a temporary goal. Organizations can achieve outcomes via short-term moves such as cutting costs, downsizing, introducing new products, or acquiring other companies. But to change how people think and act within a long-term context, organizations must commit to rewarding behaviors that may not have a short-term impact but will dovetail with long-term transformational goals. For instance, rewarding contributions to a team rather than individual achievement. Or rewarding a willingness to take risks and fail rather than playing it safe and achieving management objectives.

DISCUSS THE COLON. Not the punctuation mark, but the body part. Given my previous metaphor ("turd on the table"), you may think I'm digestive system obsessed, but this is too good a related metaphor to pass up. The temptation is to focus on positive outcomes of transformation—the cost savings, the gain in market share, the increased speed of digital tools. In other words, the cool stuff that emerges from the change. But savvy transformers recognize that employees require a discussion of the unattractive process that eventually produces great outcomes. This discussion demonstrates that management understands and empathizes with the difficulties accompanying change. Discussing the colon means looking at the journey of transformation from start to finish, setting up signposts, and marking progress. Pardon the pun, but people are much more willing to go along with change when they're reassured that things will work out in the end.

Don'ts: Common Spreadsheet Mistakes

When you're operating with a spreadsheet-only mentality, you think in absolutes. Numbers are clear and unambiguous, and data is scientific. Therefore, from this perspective, it makes sense to see change as an either-or proposition. For instance, believing that there are only two ways to change an organization— either you change the people or you change the mindsets.

As a result of this perspective, some companies commit the error of believing that by downsizing 18 percent of the people who lack the right skills or attitude for the change and bringing in 18 percent new people who do, the change effort will be successful. Other companies believe that if they commit to changing mindsets—if they try to teach existing employees a new way of working—they will transform their people.

The story perspective holds that things aren't that simple—ambiguities, uncertainties, and complexities are all part of the human experience. Change requires changing people's mindsets in relation to many different factors—the change objective, the current skills and attitudes of employees, the obstacles to change, and so on.

Admittedly, the spreadsheet perspective is more attractive—it's simpler and easier. That's why companies make so many mistakes when it comes to change strategies. Here are three common ones to avoid:

Mistake 1: Giving up on existing talent and conducting massive layoffs

It's not that everyone can or should make the transition, but that when too many people are downsized, and good talent is thrown out with the bad, organizations suffer. In fact, massive layoffs create an antichange environment.

First, *it discourages risk-taking.* When people see their jobs at risk—a common belief among the survivors of these layoffs—they are loath to take any chances that might cause them to be on the next layoff list.

Second, *it kills resistance.* You want to have a certain level of opposition to the change—not outright rebellion or sabotage, but people who engage in debate and help correct the missteps.

Third, *it harms relationships that are crucial for transformation.* Inevitably, people start talking about the old guard (veterans) and new guard (recent hires) in the wake of downsizing. This creates tensions between both groups—tensions that hurt the teamwork crucial to most transformations.

Mistake 2: Condoning behavior of veteran managers who undermine change

Yes, some pushback on change is good. A difference exists, though, between initial pushback and ongoing sabotage. Organizations may allow senior people to be out of alignment with the change effort. They may insist that everyone participate on teams, but then they allow a highly productive manager to avoid teams and continue as an individual contributor. They may allow one or more people to remain as command-and-control leaders, even as the company is moving toward a more participatory, flatter structure. And they may permit some people to verbally mock the change effort, giving them a pass because they possess sufficient influence to cause trouble.

These individuals usually receive a pass because they're producers—they contribute to the numbers that look good on spreadsheets. Allowing them to undermine change, however, creates misalignment. Other employees say, "They don't have to transform. Why do we?"

Mistake 3: Underestimating the difficulty of change

Again, this mistake is made when you have a numbers focus. Change becomes just another program to implement with budgets and timelines and measured outcomes. But it's difficult to measure whether a change initiative has won the hearts and minds of people or whether they possess the ability or motivation to put it into practice effectively. Remember, you're asking people to twist into a new shape. A commitment to training is necessary—training that will facilitate understanding, accepting, and adapting their work to whatever change is necessary.

Talking about Tech in Human Terms

I would be remiss if I didn't mention something about technological change. As a digital transformer, I'm all too familiar with the problems that can occur when organizations ask people to make significant digital shifts. It doesn't matter whether the company is introducing new software or integrating AI into a process or rolling out a disruptive technology as part of a new business strategy. It requires more than teaching people how to use the new technological tools or convincing them that it will make their jobs easier.

In a moment, I'll suggest three ways to facilitate managers' and employees' transitions to new technologies. First, though, I'd like to focus on the concept of connections and how organizations should think about this concept from both spreadsheet and story perspectives.

We are living in an increasingly digitally driven, screen- (and voice- and gesture-) mediated, algorithmic, AI-driven age where we interact with each other and stimuli across the internet via screens and devices. We leave a trail of data exhaust, which is refined and fed back to us to breathe in customized, relevant, and addictive stimuli. Our reactions create another virtual cycle of signals that build and buttress our profiles and bring new stimuli. These forces are changing industries and the nature of products, services, and experiences; they are changing what it is to be alive and human, and how we connect with each other personally and in the business world.

Connections, however, are twofold. First, the new digital world is connecting us in new ways to more people and more content as well as creating identity graphs that are a spiderweb of people, interests, and behaviors that we both spin and live within. We can connect to amazing hardware and software power by plugging into cloud-based computing and storage. All this is the digital, data-driven, and silicon side of connections.

But we are more than machine-stimulated people. We do not just compute using silicon chips or connect through Application Protocol Interfaces. We also feel, given our carbon realities. We feel and we dream and we are moved and we move others through storytelling. We connect through looks, glances, gestures, and unsaid words that are profoundly communicative but too nuanced for an algorithm or spreadsheet to compute.

When organizations forget this fact—and they forget it frequently—they roll out digital change that causes people to be anxious, fearful, cynical, angry, and rebellious. To avoid or counteract this response, here are two suggestions:

Face and create a conversation about the reality of the future.

Tomorrow is inevitable and cannot be stopped. We will live the rest of our lives there. We have entered what Klaus Schwab of the World Economic Forum calls the Fourth Industrial Revolution. At the Davos conference in 2016, he described it this way: "We stand on the brink of a technological revolution that will fundamentally alter the way we live, work, and relate to one another. In its scale, scope, and complexity, the transformation will be unlike anything humankind has experienced before."[6]

This means that leaders can't be in denial about AI, social media, and the like. It also means that employees can't give lip service to the new digital protocols and assume that "this too shall pass," resisting the changes openly or subtly.

We need honest, varied, and ongoing conversations about the reality of the future. This means companies have to do more than announce the changes. Leaders need to attend seminars and talk to industry consultants to understand the nuances of these changes and how to best implement them. Employees must talk to their managers and have access to online forums and other sources that explain the implications.

Ongoing dialogue will help leaders remove their heads from the sand; it will demonstrate that machine learning or blockchains aren't going to go away and that their realities must be faced and embraced. This dialogue will help employees grasp that this isn't like past change programs where management introduced something and then walked it back when it proved unsustainable. Once all the pros and cons of a given digital change are on the table, it's much easier for everyone to talk about them and, eventually, accept them.

Go slowly and deal with the complexities.

When you create digital change, it rarely happens quickly or without glitches. This is true whether you're installing a new software accounting system or if you're automating a plant. Recognize that this is not merely a cosmetic realignment but a twist of body, mind, and heart into a new shape. This is tricky stuff, so don't try to make it happen overnight or without dealing with all its permutations—from a lack of comprehension of how to use a new system to identifying and rectifying flaws in the tech design.

Taking Transformation Personally

Since the '80s, I've witnessed the effect that transformation has on organizations—not just as a consultant to clients but as an employee. This inside perspective is useful, in that the human dimension of change becomes much more visible when you're experiencing it directly as opposed to leading it or providing client advice.

In the mid '80s I was a young Leo Burnett employee working on a now-defunct toothpaste called Gleem for our Procter & Gamble client. It had once been America's biggest toothpaste brand, with nearly a quarter of the market, but had been reduced to a miniscule share by a new toothpaste called Crest launched by its parent company. The magic of Crest was one chemical and a badge. The chemical was sodium fluoride and the badge was from the American Dental Association, verifying that Crest was successful in preventing cavities. That chemical and that badge grew Crest to over a 40 percent share of all toothpaste.[7]

While our team worked to salvage Gleem's share by repositioning it as a cosmetic brand due to superior teeth-whitening properties, I spent the majority of my time helping prepare to launch what was expected to be another major new toothpaste with the therapeutic benefit of helping prevent tartar buildup. It was going to be called Professional Care Pace.

During this time, a soap-dispensing company from Minnesota called Minnetonka Inc.—the company that had given the world the pump-dispensed Softsoap—decided to launch a pump-dispensed toothpaste called Check Up.[8] We sneered as we worked on a real breakthrough versus some packaging trick. Check Up, though, was about convenience—even though it cost 20 percent more—and quickly made it to almost double digits in market share, much of it from Crest, which stood to lose its number one position.

At that time Procter & Gamble made a couple of bold decisions. First, they doubled down on the therapeutic positioning of Crest rather than packaging and second, they buttressed the brand by scuttling the launch of Pace and instead introducing the new antitartar breakthrough as an enhancement to Crest.

This was big business news, and Crest's decision helped return it to a strong leadership position, but I was looking at all these changes from a ground-level perspective. I was not a happy camper. The responsibility of launching the brand was taken away from our agency and given to another one—all my work on the account was shipped to them. I had hoped that my participation in the successful launch would result in my promotion to an account executive, and that hope was dashed with the change of agencies.

I learned three lessons about change that have held true, and the last one is particularly relevant from a story-and-spreadsheet vantage point:

1. **Technology can upend everything.** Sodium fluoride made Crest and took a category that was built on the cosmetic benefit of fresh breath and white teeth into one about therapeutic benefits—all within a thousand days.

2. **Change and competition often surprise by coming from outside the usual competitive set.** Check Up came not from Colgate but from a soap company, and instead of cosmetic or therapeutic benefits they promised convenience.

3. **Transformation has to be bold and is often painful.** Procter & Gamble made the hard call to cancel the launch of a new brand in which they had invested millions and instead buttress their flagship. The agency and I ended up on the short side, losing out despite doing everything right and following the rules. Anger and cynicism were reflexive reactions to the situation, and to continue to be productive and work effectively with our client, we needed to get past those negative feelings and recognize why their decisions would benefit their company and, ultimately, their advertising agency.

When the Publicis Groupe acquired Leo Burnett in 2002, I again felt the effects of transformation firsthand. While this transformative move was very positive—we became part of a major global, publicly traded company with the breadth and depth to compete with other global competitors in a time of change—two negative effects on the employees accompanied the change.

First, we had bosses in Paris and did not control our own destiny as we had before; we needed to adjust, and adjustment was challenging. Second, we had become part of a public company, subject to very different financial rules than we had followed as a private organization.

Many of the people at the Leo Burnett advertising agency never adjusted to the new reality. Some wondered why we had not been the buyer versus the seller. Others wanted to have their cake (the financial benefits that came with the acquisition) and eat it too (restoration of the status quo). I remember telling them that we were no longer the bosses and to stop pining for the past and adjust to the new reality. Even better, why not leverage the capabilities and opportunities of our new owner and combine them with our knowledge and expertise to better serve our clients and grow business? In time this attitude would have us influencing our new bosses and maybe even joining them in the boardroom.

Because of my other experiences—from Gleem to launching Burnett's first online marketing group to launching Starcom IP to helping clients with digital transformation—I was well aware that change has a diverse and multidimensional impact. Major alterations to workplaces can create self-doubt in some employees, set up a dysfunctional dynamic (new employees versus veterans or the employees of an acquiring company versus the acquired), and require climbing a steep learning curve and increasing workloads. As important as it is to address spreadsheet items—to make sure synergies exist between merging companies or a reorganization produces percentage gains in productivity—the people going through these changes all have their own stories.

We seem to forget that while computers are silicon-based, digital computing things, humans are carbon-based, analog feeling things. To change effectively, people need not only facts but also meaning, emotions, dialogues, and inspiration. True change leadership incorporates, understands, and leverages the human reality.

Change can be implemented artificially, or it can be nurtured organically. The latter doesn't mean redecorating the office or having touchy-feely bonding sessions or listening to the CEO give an inspirational speech about how change will be good for everyone. Instead, if you want to do one thing that will make change organic rather than artificial, I would prescribe *incentives*.

Incentives can address both the story and the spreadsheet. For spreadsheets, it helps measure what will be gained from the change. A range of incentives, for instance, can help people determine how much money they will make if they embrace the new systems. It can help organizations calculate the specific carrots they need to dangle to achieve goals (e.g., 95 percent adoption of a new work protocol).

From the story side, these incentives can have a huge, positive behavioral impact. A key learning from Steven Levitt's *Freakonomics* was that the best way to predict behavior was to understand incentives.[9] People will do what they are rewarded for, and if you want tomorrow but incentivize or measure yesterday, you'll create cognitive dissonance. Far better to align incentives with your change goals. This is a natural, caring way to get people to adjust their work behaviors. If you want to change the culture from one of individual contributors to teams, provide powerful motivation for this type of change. This involves not just financial incentives but communication on how a team structure will provide greater receptivity to big ideas and increase the odds of greater growth, innovation, and profit—meaning bigger bonuses, salary increases, etc.

Don't change your organization the heartless way—by getting rid of all the old employees who don't fit and bringing in a slew of new ones. I'm not saying don't bring in fresh talent. I am saying that you should heed this truth: the only way a company changes is by changing people's mindsets or changing the people, and companies find it is easier to change the people. Yes, it's easier, but it's ultimately self-destructive. You're bringing in the equivalent of mercenaries, and while they may be more in line with the change you're shooting for, many of them will have little loyalty toward the company.

Organizations should give veterans—especially individuals who have been loyal to the company and performed well—the chance to transition. With the right incentives, most will make the transition with flying colors and be grateful for the opportunity, motivated to perform well, and likely to remain productive for the long term.

KEY TAKEAWAYS

- Change is very difficult for most people, and companies must acknowledge this and realize that unless they make a savvy, strategic effort to bring their people along, it will be almost impossible to enact change.

- Successful companies ensure they communicate why the change is necessary and is good for employees, and how they will find a place for themselves in the company's future.
- Three tactics operationalize change: incentivizing the new behaviors; exiting people, regardless of level, who refuse to align and thus sabotage change; and staying the course with investment, despite the expected financial bumps in the road to change.

CHAPTER 6

UNLEASH CREATIVITY BY INSERTING POETRY INTO THE POWERPOINT

The skeptical among you may question this chapter's premise. It's all well and good to advocate straight talk and humanizing change, but poetry and creativity as a path to manage change and transform organizations?

Admittedly, the notion of bringing art into the workplace to counterbalance the data-heavy environment may seem like a stretch on the surface. Is gazing at a Picasso for an hour or reading poetry going to help an employee come up with a way to regain market share lost to low-cost foreign competitors?

Perhaps an hour of Picasso-gazing won't do it, but nurturing employees' artistic sensibilities will go a long way toward restoring the story-spreadsheet balance—a balance crucial for organizations that aspire to innovative approaches. Before providing some tips and techniques to foster an artistic sensibility, let's make the case for why it's necessary to do so.

Left-Brain Bias

This is nothing new. The spreadsheet-obsessed mentality has its roots in the start of the twenty-first century, and observers have noted the dangers of left-brain logic segregated from right-brain empathy and creativity. Naiman, who has written extensively about art in business, also asserted that "metrics are not enough. . . . The economic future . . . depends on its ability to create wealth by fostering innovation, creativity and entrepreneurship."[1] Naiman suggests that people with MFAs rather than MBAs are more likely to make this happen.

In Daniel Pink's *A Whole New Mind*, he made the point that left-brain, linear, analytical, computerlike thinking is being replaced by right-brain empathy, inventiveness, and understanding as the skills most needed by businesses.[2]

Interestingly, Pink and Naiman made these statements around 2005. Despite their beliefs and the similar ideas about this subject advocated by other thought leaders, the spreadsheet mentality still dominates most organizations. In fact, in uncertain, confusing times like today, decision makers often cling to logic and data for the seeming clarity they provide.

The spreadsheet, however, is not a clear window to view either the present or the future. Inherently, it's a backward-looking device that jails thinking within its cells. Some organizations recognize the limitations of spreadsheet thinking and hold off-sites, brainstorming, and other creativity-stimulating sessions to generate an alternative view to what data and logic deliver. The problem, though, is that breakthrough ideas emerge suddenly and organically rather than from these structured approaches.

Within many organizations, highly innovative, potentially game-changing ideas are born regularly. Unfortunately, the left-brain environment of these organizations often starves these ideas of oxygen and they don't survive.

If you doubt this last statement, consider all the times that one company incubated a great idea but the culture, leadership, or policies stopped the idea from seeing the light of day—and how the idea migrated to another company with a better left-brain/right-brain balance who turned the idea into gold.

The idea for new visual computing was built at Xerox but brought to the world by Apple.[3]

Nokia originated the concept of a great mobile phone, but management could not accept touch screens and the importance of software versus hardware.[4]

Two years ago at a Procter & Gamble Alumni conference, the ex-CEO of Procter & Gamble noted a mistake he had made: even though Gillette saw a market for a lower-priced subscription razor-blade delivery service long before the Dollar Shave Club, they didn't move quickly because doing so would cannibalize the profits of the existing product line.

Start-ups often use right-brain thinking to disrupt left-brain industries.

Even though incumbents often spot the outsiders' threat, they do little for the following reasons:

- The new idea challenges the logic of the industry and the old ways of doing business.
- The new idea makes no sense from a financial standpoint.
- The new idea requires a significant investment that will impact earnings.

At times, market leaders are able to fend off start-ups and other market challengers, but to do so they need to draw upon their right brain. Steve Jobs put an iPod in every iPhone, killing the iPod even though it was Apple's leading product. Netflix invested in streaming, which destroyed their DVD-by-mail business. Adobe transitioned from packaged software to a cloud-based system, reducing their revenues and hurting their stock price in exchange for long-term sustainability.[5]

A sure sign that a company is capable of right-brain as well as left-brain thinking is the ability to tell a story. The art of the story is something that great leaders understand and encourage in their people. They know that being able to construct a narrative draws people in and helps them relate to you and your message. Great narrative artists—fiction writers, playwrights, songwriters—know that they need more than great characters and a scintillating style. They need story.

Interestingly, the leader of a company that is known to be intensely data driven also gets the value of story.

Amazon's Jeff Bezos, speaking at his alma mater, Princeton, left graduates with five key words: "Build yourself a great story." Commenting on this, the website 234Finance noted:

Although everyone has a story to share, most people are shy about sharing stories about themselves, especially stories relating to our experiences of the good, bad and ugly. These are crucial stories that form the foundation of how to solve problems, critical reasoning and conducting business.

Storytelling transcends writing, and employing social media as the primary vehicle for sharing experiences is very effective to reach as many people as possible. Also, as humans, we learn best from our experiences and the experiences of other people. As a storyteller, it is your duty to create multiple opportunities to establish emotional connections to the key elements of the story, so the listener can learn and gain insightful information from you.[6]

Recently a colleague of mine—Linda Boff, CMO of GE—attended a session at Amazon with Bezos and noted that he paid particular attention to anecdotes. She told me that his belief in the power of stories is so strong that he often focuses on stories he picks up from customer complaints and letters rather than data, saying, "The thing I have noticed is when the anecdotes and the data disagree, the anecdotes are usually right. There's something wrong with the way you are measuring it."[7]

The ability to respond with right-brain, innovative strategies such as these requires an artistic sensibility. Here's why this is so.

Out-of-Sight Insights

I define innovation as "fresh, insightful connections." Let's break this definition down to its three parts. "Fresh" means new—every innovation has a sense of the new. "Insightful" involves perception—perceiving innovative possibilities that others have missed. In terms of "connections," Steve Jobs talked about connecting the dots in new ways, combining things in new ways to create something different.[8]

I came to my definition of innovation as fresh, insightful connections in watching our younger daughter, Rohini, who can get to the core of an issue and recognize patterns in frighteningly prescient ways.

She often connects things that shouldn't go together in various areas of her life: dressing a certain way, directing her sister and mother, figuring out how to get an advanced degree in marketing without doing too much finance or accounting, advising me on how to solve some issue I am lingering over, or becoming a social media expert by linking things that were not linked.

Her process is to identify three elements of a problem or possible solution (she gets this from her dad and has named her blog *The Power of Three*), then play around with them, stretching or combining or spicing them up, and then—lo and behold—an answer that connects the core elements in new ways.

Artists do all these things. They create something fresh on a blank piece of paper or canvas. They look at something familiar and then render it in a way that inspires or moves us with its ability to perceive the familiar differently. And they connect disparate elements—words, images, sounds, movements—so that the whole seems like nothing that has ever come before.[9]

The artistic sensibility that allows them to innovate is related to the way they question. As Pablo Picasso said, "Others have seen what is and asked why. I have seen what could be and asked why not."[10]

Great art helps us see differently. Walk into an art museum and look at a Picasso cubist painting or a late van Gogh work, and you'll see colors and angles that will cause you to reframe the way you perceive things. More specifically, here are four ways exposure to art facilitates business innovation.

1. **Reframing.** Art takes us out of our routines and out of ourselves, providing us with ideas that cause us to rethink our assumptions, giving us sounds or images that make us consider alternative ways of hearing and seeing the world. It shifts our viewpoint, and from this shift we can look at everything from business policies to strategies in a new light.

2. **Inspiring.** We read a great book or go to a terrific play and we're revved up, energized by the experience. Wonderful art motivates us in ways few things can. We return to work ready to grapple with a difficult project or take on a stretch assignment.

3. **Exploring options.** We see art that connects the dots in new ways, and we take the possibility of new connections back to our workplaces. We look at difficult or complex situations and are willing to try an unorthodox approach or test a new concept to meet the challenge.

4. **Overcoming failure.** The story of many artists is the story of one failed attempt after another—how a bestselling book was rejected by every publisher or how a great classical musician was ignored during his lifetime. These artists weren't deterred by their failures and pushed forward. Being aware of artistic failures helps businesspeople realize that failure isn't fatal and that trying again is not only a good idea but perhaps the best way to produce results.[11]

Art can also be a great teaching tool, telling us stories that help us look at issues differently. For instance, coaches and others have admonished command-and-control leaders about this leadership style, suggesting that it's no longer appropriate for the current work paradigm. These leaders hear what they're being told, acknowledge the value of the advice, but don't change their behaviors.

When this traditional leader "hears" the same message through an artistic form, however, he may be more motivated to change his behavior. For instance, one of my favorite films by François Truffaut is *The 400 Blows*. It is the story of a young boy navigating his way through a hostile world. There are many amazing scenes in the movie, including its classic ending freeze frame. One scene that is particularly relevant to the controlling leader, though, involves a gym teacher taking his students on a run along the streets of Paris. Furiously blowing a whistle, running ahead of all his students and oblivious to them, the teacher does not realize that all of his followers are peeling away from him.[12]

How many times do leaders bark out orders and run ahead to storm the hill without bringing their teams along? Either emotionally by "following but not really following" or physically by leaving and finding other jobs, some of the most talented folks leave the pack. I'm not saying that seeing this film will transform all order-barking leaders instantly and magically. I'm suggesting that this particular scene might have an impact, that the dramatic illustration of a leader's behavior can get past that defensive reflex and help see behavior in a fresh light.

Richard Thaler, the University of Chicago professor and Nobel Prize winner, notes that "nobody remembers some formula, but they remember stories."[13]

Round-the-Clock Innovation Capability

The spreadsheet approach to innovation is to designate a specific time and place for innovation to occur: offsites, brainstorming exercises, role-playing. The notion is that creativity can be planned for in a systematic manner; if you schedule X amount of time for innovation, you'll produce Y amount of creative ideas.

Yes, I'm overstating this position, but only by a bit. The belief that you can plan for and produce innovation on command underlies many of the so-called creativity exercises organizations use.

In truth, creativity is an everyday need in organizations, and innovation can and should happen all the time. Here are some tips and techniques to make it a more available competency for organizational employees:

ESTABLISH REVOLVING ARTIST SHOWCASES. It's not enough to place art on the office walls (and at a time of tight budgets, many organizations have backed off from this traditional practice). Why not bring a variety of artists to showcase their talent? Musicians, actors, performance artists, sculptors, writers, and dancers who are trying to get heard and seen would welcome the opportunity to display their talent to employees.

From poetry readings to glass-blowing demonstrations to dance recitals, these artistic endeavors could be scheduled for lunch breaks (or other times) and expose people to cutting-edge approaches and blazing creative talent. In addition, these showcases should include interactions with the artists and discussions about the art. None of this will produce instant innovation, but it will help people start thinking in more creative directions. Art inspires, provokes, challenges, and moves (emotionally). It stretches minds, allowing people to broaden their perspectives. With more cognitive and emotional space to roam, they are free to think about things in new ways—thus, innovation. Leo Burnett has brought in artists-in-residence to provoke and inspire creativity.

SET UP ART CLUBS. Within any sizable organization, you'll find employees who are opera buffs, closet novelists, poetry aficionados, painters, and theater lovers. Whether they're creating the art themselves or are simply fans, these employees would relish the opportunity to show their work to others or discuss what they're passionate about. Employee book clubs, movie clubs, and the like would be easy to set up and would help people think and talk about subjects from a creative perspective.

SPONSOR EMPLOYEE ART OUTINGS. Many cultural venues will work with organizations to provide discounts for large groups sales. Companies often subsidize employee health club memberships; why not do the same if employees want to become museum members or go to the symphony? These outings allow employees to experience great art, and by sponsoring them and defraying the costs, they incentivize people to do so in ways they might not otherwise. Again, this is a way to foster a creative consciousness.

CREATE AN $X-PER-EMPLOYEE ART BUDGET. This last suggestion will communicate to employees that an organization is putting its money where its mouth is. Allocating a dollar amount for artistic pursuits motivates employees to take advantage of them. For instance, an annual subscription to Criterion Collection, a selection of great movies accompanied by commentary from directors and actors in these movies, costs $100. It could also fund the books for an employee book club or help people purchase annual museum memberships.

How to Structure Your Artistic and Creative Endeavors

You can't impose artistic activities on people and expect the creative impulse to take root. Many employees have spent years being indoctrinated into the world of data; they've been told to follow the numbers, to take advantage of analytics and algorithms. Again, there's nothing wrong with this except that it has an unbalanced effect on the way they work. It's going to take some time and effort to restore the balance.

To that end, here are three ways to structure your "art strategy":

MAKE IT VOLUNTARY. You can't force art on people like you can a computer training session. Invariably, some people won't choose to participate or won't participate until they're ready to do so (perhaps after a colleague relates how much she enjoyed going to the company-sponsored movie night). This is an extracurricular activity, and no pressure should be put on anyone to attend any particular event. If you force people to attend a lecture by a guest artist or go to a concert, their reaction will be similar to when they were forced to read Shakespeare in school when they weren't ready for it—it will go in one ear and out the other.

KEEP IT DIVERSE. By diverse, I'm referring to the range of artistic activities and events. Within any organization, you'll find people who love going to the symphony and hate poetry and vice versa. If you focus all your energy on one particular art form, you'll attract only a small percentage of the workforce. Remember, the goal is to expose as many employees as possible to art. Obviously, you don't want to go too far in the opposite direction and offer zither lessons or other overly esoteric art forms. At the same time, it's a good idea to supplement the most popular forms—books, movies, museum outings, concerts—with experiences that challenge participants. Slam poetry readings, a concert of twelve-tone music, a provocative art exhibit—these are the types of experiences that prompt people to think outside the box, to push the envelope. Diversity, then, means combining traditional artistic forms with cutting-edge experiences.

COMMIT TO ONGOING EFFORTS. Singular events, no matter how spectacular (e.g., inviting Yo-Yo Ma to play a private concert at your organization), don't have much of a right-brain effect. It takes repeated exposures over time for people to broaden their thinking so that story is balanced with spreadsheet. Most organizations are limited in what they can do by budget and time, but committing to an art appreciation program doesn't have to be expensive or consume a lot of work hours. Scheduling four events a month—a book club, a movie showing, a trip to a museum, an in-house concert—may be enough if these events become regular events.

Art Is for Leaders Too

Leaders can benefit as much if not more than other employees from immersive art experiences. Too often, leaders exempt themselves from employee training and development programs. Sometimes this makes sense—they already possess the knowledge and skills being taught—or because they have to prioritize, and a particular type of training isn't as important as their main responsibilities.

But leaders, especially those who live and die by the data, need to broaden their perspectives, and art can help them achieve this objective. Think of it this way: leaders must develop their own points of view, their own styles of leadership. Today, authenticity is crucial, and people in senior positions must reject a one-size-fits-all definition of leadership and use their strengths and beliefs to develop a genuine personal style.

Art frees people to be creative in their approach to leadership, to adapt in response to changing environments. We constantly create our many selves. We have points of view. We select what we wear and how we appear. Events twist us into new shapes. Creativity is how we manage our own change. In a way, art gives people permission to take chances, to try new things. We see a mind-bending art exhibit and we're inspired to cross boundaries. We hear a hot new jazz trio and we get jazzed about a project or program—we want to improvise rather than play all the notes as written.

It's all too easy for leaders to fall into leadership ruts—to play their roles rather than transcend them, to lead by the numbers rather than incorporate their own story into the mix.

Art is liberating. Again, it's not an instant transformation. It's an incremental process, freeing your innovation capabilities by degrees. Accumulated exposure to art opens leaders to ideas that are untraditional and even risky. It exposes them to provocative ideas and imaginative leaps. Over time, it can't help but stimulate reflection and exploration.

Or consider two CEOs. John is a highly competent leader, great with financials. He started in accounting, received his MBA, and became great at operations. Outside of work, his interests are limited to family and exercise. He can't remember the last book he read, and he hasn't been to a concert or museum in years. Years ago he dabbled in painting still lifes, but he hasn't picked up a brush in years, convinced he lacks talent. John is considered a no-nonsense, by-the-book type of leader. He doesn't have much of a sense of humor and rarely spends much time on conversations that don't relate directly to the subject at hand.

Riya is also a CEO, and though her background is similar to John's, her interests and personality are quite different. She is a history-reading fanatic and knows almost as much about the Civil War strategy as she does about business strategy. A former violinist with her high school and college orchestras, she attends ten concerts annually at her local symphony. She also is a potter and has a wheel and kiln at her summer home. In the summer, she loves going to street art fairs and has taken a number of trips to Europe specifically to see works of art housed in museums. Unlike John, Riya is an open, transparent, and spontaneous leader. There's a steady stream of people coming into her office to talk to her about work and a variety of other subjects.

Which CEO would you want leading your company today? Which one will be better able to handle the major changes coming down the pike? Which one will respond more effectively when a smaller competitor disrupts the industry with a revolutionary product or service introduction?

I know this isn't a fair comparison—people aren't as black-and-white as Riya and John—but you get my point. CEOs like Riya can use their artistic sensibilities to respond to change in more agile and creative ways.

The Elements of Art Are the Elements of Change

Years ago, art was a much more integral element in people's lives than it is today. If you doubt this statement, ask a colleague when was the last time he attended the symphony; or went to a special exhibit at an art museum; or read a book that is considered a classic; or heard a poetry reading; or attended the ballet. Yes, people probably see as many movies as in the past, but many of these films don't really qualify as art—they're mass entertainment that are fun to watch but don't provoke or require much analysis.

Similarly, people lack the time to pursue artistic hobbies. In many cases, time is at a premium because of increasing work demands. In the past, people often had nine-to-five weekday jobs and saw painting or playing in a local symphony as a great escape from work. Now, many professionals work six or seven days a week for longer than normal hours; they also travel a lot for work. Even if they can maintain reasonable hours, the pressure of work is such that they're mentally exhausted after a hard day and prefer vegging out in front of a screen to practicing a violin sonata.

Consequently, they don't bring the same strong artistic sense to work as they might have years ago. This is a problem in a spreadsheet-dominant environment, especially given the times in which we live and work. Bear with me as I lay out one final and compelling reason for introducing art into the workplace.

Just about every organization communicates to its employees this truth: We are living in transformational times—times when people are empowered, things move fast, and the biggest opportunities and threats often arise from outside the category and traditional competition. It was not Schick or Gillette that hurt each other but Dollar Shave Club and Harry's. It wasn't GM versus Ford versus Mercedes but Tesla and Uber versus all the established automakers.

Given this environment, winning companies re-create themselves. They need to reimagine possibilities. They need to connect things in new ways to remain relevant. All of this requires innovation, and art fosters all the elements of innovation—re-creating, reimagining, connecting in new ways.

Recognize that spreadsheets, for all the value they contribute from a left-brain perspective, don't foster these qualities. As valuable as they are as tools that identify the need for change, they paradoxically stop change in its tracks by also identifying all the risks and costs associated with it.

Art can help leaven even the most diehard spreadsheet mentality. It's not going to change an archconservative accountant or a data-centric techie into an innovative leader overnight. It is capable, however, of providing the possibility of being more creative. It gives an option when facing a problem or opportunity—an option to try something different, to connect a different set of dots, to take a chance.

Listening to Beethoven, gazing at a Monet, reading Dickens, and watching an O'Neill play have many benefits, but one of the most surprising is helping organizations think and work in innovative ways.

CARLA MICHELOTTI

The Importance of Connecting Dots in New Ways

As a senior in-house lawyer for Leo Burnett, Carla Michelotti had few reasons to interact with a young account executive like me. For years, we only spoke a few times, when I was working on commercials that required Carla's senior expertise to address tricky legal issues.

Carla pioneered protections for advertising in multiple environments and especially advertiser rights on what then was referred to as the "information superhighway," better known today as the internet.

Carla's legal team and the little internet marketing group I had started for Leo Burnett were neighbors on the same floor. We bonded over our common passion for internet marketing.

Even though I was in a completely different function from Carla, she refused to "stay in her lane." Too often, spreadsheet-focused bosses define their responsibilities and relationships narrowly. Carla, on the other hand, was willing to cross boundaries to create synergistic connections. Carla had me accompany her to Washington, DC, for many summits on the role of advertising in internet marketing, including the first-ever meeting with the White House, at a time when the government didn't think there was going to be advertising on the internet. We became fast friends. Carla then introduced me to her boyfriend—now husband—Bob Colvin, who was a senior agent in LA at International Creative Management (ICM) and who was representing internet content companies and talent that wished to explore opportunities on the internet.

Through Bob Colvin and his introductions over the next year, the Leo Burnett Interactive Group, in conjunction with ICM, partnered with a small company with less than a million members, called America Online, to create an online celebrity-interview format using ICM talent. We helped General Motors by creating a promotional mapping CD-ROM—the first of its kind—which was used to induce buyers to drive a new model being introduced, and McDonald's ended up being the first nontechnology company to advertise on AOL. And we also created a deeply immersive, interactive experience, using a CD-ROM, for Dewar's Scotch.

These initial efforts in 1995 led to many positive changes in both my career and the work Leo Burnett would do. New frontiers opened because Carla refused to allow a rigid set of specs to define her job. She was willing to mentor me in ways that had nothing to do with the spreadsheet and everything to do with our intersecting stories.

KEY TAKEAWAYS

- People are analog and moved by stories and emotion, not just numbers and facts.
- Art allows people to see and feel differently, unleashing their creativity and fueling change; artistic experiences in various forms should be embraced, extended, and enjoyed at work.
- Successful organizations and people recognize that artists are entrepreneurs who start with a blank sheet of paper, frame problems in new ways, and see differently, which inspires innovation and creativity.

CHAPTER 7

RECOGNIZE THAT TALENT DOES NOT WORK FOR COMPANIES BUT RATHER COMPANIES WORK FOR TALENT

T alent used to work for companies. Today companies need to work for talent."[1] Emmanuel André, the chief talent officer of Publicis Groupe, is the author of this quote, one that reframes the relationship between employer and employee. In the past, it was a buyer's market. Organizations had an abundance of people to choose from and could dictate job terms.

While it's not fair to say that employees were treated like cogs in a machine, their preferences and dreams were often deferred or ignored in favor of the drive to meet group or organizational objectives. The most talented and senior people possessed leverage to achieve personal goals, but the majority of employees were at the mercy of organizational systems.

Today, organizations have enormous employee databases and numbers-based strategies they can use to match the right employee to the right job, to measure their performance, and to move them from team to team or from office to office where they're needed most.

The problem, of course, is that all this data tends to bias development in favor of the organization rather than the employee—or in this book's terms, the spreadsheet instead of the story. We need to rethink our development practices to align with André's philosophy. Before suggesting how to do so, let's make the case for why it's necessary.

The Evolving Talent Landscape

The talent landscape is rapidly bifurcating into two classes. One rapidly growing group is the contract or gig worker, with fewer benefits or job security in an "Uberized" and "TaskRabbit" world, who competes for the next assignment. A second group of workers, with rare or sought-after skills—from health care to databases to truck drivers—companies compete for.[2]

While legislation and worker demands for more benefits and rights for contract workers are always in motion, this chapter focuses on the segment of talent that companies compete for.

You may be aware that the power has shifted from organization to employee in recent years, but you may not be aware of how profound this shift actually is. Here are five factors that explain how deeply things have changed:

1. **The power laws of talent.** In today's networked world, a superior performer has a much greater impact than an average performer. Google pays its best people ten times as much as its average worker. People start specializing in what they are innately good at in order to maximize their skills and income.

2. **Information power has moved to talent.** Today, with resources such as Glassdoor and search and social networks, employees know what other people get paid, and they have built brands and LinkedIn profiles to attract recruiters; they know how to stand out in unique ways for their unique skills.

3. **Shorter half-lives of companies.** Industries are in flux; the time companies spend in the S&P 500 has declined from sixty years on average in the 1950s to twenty years today.[3] In many instances, people's careers will last much longer than the companies they work for. Thus, they need to focus on themselves more than on their companies.

4. **Networked age places a premium on mastery and diversity.** Today companies are often virtual, with a limited number of people and few assets, relying on specialists. We can get computing and storage power from Amazon, space from WeWork, and seamlessly access services online.

5. **Rise of knowledge-based and service industries.** More and more

companies are service oriented versus manufacturing. Today, services in the United States account for almost 80 percent of gross domestic product (GDP), while manufacturing is only 19 percent.[4]

All this behooves organizations that compete for talent to focus on employee needs. In *Drive*, Daniel Pink identified three key traits as employee motivators:

- *Autonomy:* freedom to work on whatever they like
- *Mastery:* the chance to develop something that they're experts in and truly care about
- *Purpose:* feeling connected to a high-visibility, exciting opportunity that matters to the company and is admired by their colleagues[5]

Today, even tech companies and investment banks that seemingly have their pick of the best and the brightest have become more accommodating of their people's requirements; they want to keep them for the long term, and to do that, they need to identify what their people seek and satisfy them.

Both organizations and individuals in a networked world face a common set of challenges and opportunities:

1. Talent and resources can be accessed from many places, and competitors come from many places both around the world but also outside the traditional competitive set.
2. There is a premium on speed of delivery. Today it is the lack of speed rather than speed that kills.
3. Downward pressure on prices exists, visible on Amazon and other sites or in goods from China and other sources.

As a result, organizations must transform themselves at speed in a changing world to remain relevant and gain competitive advantage—but do so in ways that minimize costs of doing business.

The challenge and opportunity for individuals is to ensure they grow their expertise in ways that maximize their current and future potential earnings—but do so in ways that reduce the uncertainty that comes with rapid change.

To maximize the opportunity and minimize the challenges, organizations and individuals need both sides to be flexible. The employer needs to be able to reaggregate and reallocate talent around specific projects in real time. This is very much like a Hollywood studio model, where talent comes together over a specific project and then disbands when the project is over.

Employees need to capitalize on opportunities quickly but also find ways to build skill sets and reputation to ensure they are building value for themselves as they move through their career, not just moving from gig to gig.

Companies are developing platforms that can enable and empower talent for this new world so they are linked in four ways:

1. To each other and experts in different skills around the world;
2. To knowledge across the firm and outside the company so they can grow;
3. To opportunities that allow one to be aware of and apply for projects and assignments; and
4. To productivity tools that make discovery and doing daily stuff easier.

Progressive companies realize that their people are more than numbers on a spreadsheet; they have their own stories that must be acknowledged or they won't be highly productive or may leave prematurely. It is essential that employees bring all of themselves to work.

Increasingly, companies are divided between ones that work for talent and ones that talent works for.

The company talent works for

- treats employees as production units whose output is constantly measured and monitored;
- provides training and performance reviews to maximize measurable outcomes that drive the company bottom line and agenda;
- believes there is a profile that successful people should fit into and there is a company "type" of person;
- prioritizes uniformity and scalability; and
- overlooks bad behavior as long as the numbers and goals are being met.

The company that works for talent

- gives employees opportunities, freedom, and the ability to participate and understand the end goals;
- offers access to training and resources aligned with what will make them successful;
- grasps that they need different skill sets, diverse talents, and multiple combinations of approaches in a fast-moving world;
- prioritizes flexibility and customization; and
- incentivizes behaviors that align with the company goal and calls out bad behavior.

Netflix represents the latter type of organization. They've been successful for many reasons (including their willingness to disrupt their DVD business by offering streaming options), but their talent philosophy has played a crucial role. They are a company whose story is not just that they distribute stories, but that they tell a story about what they value to their employees. They cut out the bull. They treat their employees like adults and trust their judgment. They give them freedom.

The culture document is a PowerPoint presentation that illustrates the company's belief in their people. Written in chapters shared with everyone inside and outside the company, the document evolves as customers and times change and employees provide input. The document focuses on outcomes that are expected rather than processes that must be followed. It is not about "how" but about "what." It is not about process but about people.

It expresses Netflix's key beliefs about what the company will do, including:

- encourage independent decision-making by employees;
- share information openly, broadly, and deliberately;
- be extraordinarily candid with employees;
- keep only highly effective people; and
- avoid rules.[6]

A Personal Brand

Working for talent translates into three developmental actions: helping people create their niche, voice, and story. Developing these three qualities not only satisfies a growing need among all types of employees but it benefits the organization—people with a niche, voice, and story work more productively. Companies must help their people create their own personal brands, combining expertise (which I call niche), a way of operating or a culture (a voice), and a reputation or credibility (called a story). More specifically, here is how I define these three assets:

NICHE. In a connected world, a premium on expertise exists. Experts tend to be more productive, and they tend to develop better solutions. Today they can promote themselves and often be available via the internet. Most successful companies tend to reformulate themselves into smaller organizations with particular skill sets; the huge, diversified conglomerate seems to be going the way of the dinosaur. Even well-regarded firms like GE proved to be too unwieldy. Similarly, companies look for specific expertise since experts tend to work more effectively and innovatively, as well as collaborate well with experts in other fields and attract and retain talent.

VOICE. Being good at something is not enough. It's equally important how the work is done, the character of the person doing the work, and the culture of the firm. These together make up the voice. It's what makes you special. Niche focuses on the product while voice focuses on the process. If niche is a fact, voice is a feeling, and both of these are critical to building a personal brand.

STORY. While a niche is what someone is good at and voice is what makes someone special, story provides someone's reason to believe. The story is about credibility. It's a combination of track record, which is fact-based, and reputation, which is feeling-based. It's the story you tell about yourself when you are in the room, and the story that people tell about you when you are not in the room.

It's All about Fit

A personal brand must dovetail with the organizational brand. Not everyone will thrive working for Google or a small start-up or General Motors or a high-powered consulting firm. A spreadsheet-dominant mentality, however, assumes that if an individual's experience and expertise jibes with the job specs—and that person is paid well—the employee will be productive at any employer.

I've found that people work best at places that are in sync with their personal brands. Obviously, they need to possess the right spreadsheet numbers—few people who lack the competencies for a job or who are being paid poorly will thrive. Still, people want to work where they believe who they are and what the organization represents are aligned. When this alignment exists, they often operate at peak capacity.

It makes no sense to invest the time and money in personal brand development if a given individual is a poor fit for the organizational brand. Therefore, we need to look at what that organizational brand entails from niche, voice, and story perspectives. Here are three types of questions that will help define each:

1. **What is its niche?** What does the company claim to specialize in and offer to their clients and customers better than the competitors?
2. **What is its voice?** What is the culture of the company? How does it want to "feel" as a place of work? What behaviors does it expect and reward?
3. **What is its story?** Where did it come from? Why are its promises or competitive claims believable?

Once you've defined all three elements, you can create alignment. You can use this knowledge both to develop your people and to attract the right type of people. If you're clear about what your company does, how you do it, and the different skills that you value, you can create a fit for people. More than that, you can give them the necessary knowledge to discern if they should join your organization or look elsewhere.

Our older daughter had the opportunity to work for Google after she graduated with a degree in economics. At that time, the company's reputation, training, quality of fellow employees, and compensation aligned with our daughter's need to learn about technology, burnish her résumé, and live in California.

Four years later, though, she had an itch to explore her options beyond a marketing career at Google.

Google is at its heart an engineering company, and engineers are their high priests and priestesses. Rightly so, given what the company does. People in other functions, despite being highly paid and treated well, are in service of the products that the engineers develop. In most firms "makers" are more key than "sellers."

For many who aren't engineers, the ability to work with Google's assets and resources is completely aligned with their own goals, and many of them have stayed for a long time and are among the best in their field.

For our daughter, it was not enough. As she told me, "Dad, in your company you are helping build and launch new things. I want to make things, and I want to be central to the core product of the company. I am not an engineer. I sell what the engineers make. I am a player. I want the ball."

A year later, with the strong support of her bosses at Google, she was admitted to one of the leading graduate schools of film to learn to be a filmmaker. She realized that though she was highly successful at Google and had received high ratings and raises, her personal brand did not fit with Google's.

My daughter's gain was *not* Google's loss; both of them benefited from her recognizing that her brand and Google's were no longer aligned.

Ironically, four years later, as YouTube increasingly invests in original content and studio productions, our daughter might end up working with or selling her work to the company she started with! Leaving with their full support will stand her well.

Raising organizational consciousness of alignment is essential for improved attraction and retention of employees. From an attraction perspective, aligned companies possess people who not only are productive but have a high degree of job satisfaction because personal and organizational brands fit. The word spreads that a given company is the perfect place for people whose personal preferences, requirements, and goals jibe with an organization's practices and culture. Like attracts like, and alignment becomes a recruiting tool.

Similarly, if employees are allowed to build their personal brands inside the company, they are more likely to stay than leave. They believe they've finally found a "home," and they relish working with other people who are flourishing in the organization (rather than complaining bitterly about its policies and practices). Talent leaves companies when they cannot build their own brands—when they feel like fish out of water.

To produce positive alignment outcomes, development is crucial. Here are some ways to foster the right type of development.

Aligned Development Techniques

To help people create personal brands that serve the individuals and their organizations, the starting point is identifying the niche, voice, and story of the organization. This may seem obvious, but it's not—people often have mistaken beliefs about their companies due to a theory-practice gap (the company is different from what it purports to be) and change over time (the company has evolved without widespread awareness of this evolution).

Therefore, ask the following questions of your organization:

- What are the critical areas of expertise? Have these skills changed over time? What is the highest-priority competency and is it in sufficient supply?
- How are things done? What approaches and styles of work are prized, and which ones are discouraged? What are the personality traits that are viewed positively, and which ones are viewed negatively? What specific qualities distinguish your company from others?
- What do people say about your company (at industry conferences, on social media, etc.)? How do your organization's history and current policies and culture provide a narrative for who your company is relative to other companies and the competition?

Once you know the answers to these questions, you can recruit and develop with much greater effectiveness. Bringing highly talented but misaligned people into organizations is a common mistake. Because they seem so smart and possess prized experience and expertise, they are attractive candidates. But even the best training and development programs won't help them achieve a good fit; sooner rather than later, they'll leave.

How does one ensure that employees fit companies, and vice versa? Here is a simple exercise that I've used with colleagues and clients over the years that has proven to be extraordinarily effective: identify three words that describe your niche, three words that describe your voice, and three words that describe your story.

Of course, you'll need to explain what you mean by niche, voice, and story, but that should be sufficient for them to create three words for each element.

Here is an example of my results (including explanations of why I chose these words):

- *Niche:* future, change, and innovation (what I specialize in)
- *Voice:* authentic (eat my own dog food and do what I say or advise), inspirational (supposedly!), and provocative ("I cannot believe he said that!")
- *Story:* global (have worked all over the world and am an immigrant), mongrel (worked in different skill sets), and reinventing (have morphed into new careers and opportunities)

Because I identified three words in each category, organizations can help me focus on and develop my abilities in areas in which I'm skilled (strategic, conceptual, longer-term thinking) and help me avoid positions I'm less skilled at (operational, executional). In this way, an organization helps me pursue the development path that will make me happy and avoid ones that will cause me to be unhappy and leave. It also helps the organization understand me as a person in the workplace—I'm likely to say and do things that are provocative, for instance, and I'm sufficiently agile that I've transitioned from and into a variety of areas. If they need a provocateur on a team, for instance, I'm their person.

In addition, organizations should set policies regarding niche, voice, and story that keep people prominent in policies and processes, such as the following:

NICHE. Encourage specialization as part of training versus only well-rounded generalists. Specialists should be promoted, paid, and celebrated as much as general management. In companies that are world-class—Goldman Sachs and Google, for example—particular experts are paid more than the CEO.

Put certain individuals on world-class expert development tracks; let them follow their passions rather than force them to follow the typical executive development path. Too often, the best and the brightest are singled out for general management when some of them prefer to remain in a specific function. All the data tells human resources (HR) that Francois or Kim is a high potential and should be groomed for an executive position. What the data may not be telling HR, however, is that Francois or Kim prefers to remain in engineering or sales and will make a reluctant and mediocre VP.

VOICE. Everybody is different, and a company that succeeds celebrates and integrates these differences. This is diversity not just of culture, geography, and ethnicity but of how people work, communicate, and speak. Some will be quiet and others loud. Some will inspire, and others will be supportive. As long as all these voices are linked together to achieve organizational goals, a multiplicity of voices adds value.

This means not only encouraging a range of personality styles within teams and cultures but using development to help people find their authentic voices. Too often, development encourages a singular style—polite, tolerant, straightforward, etc. All fine qualities, but they foster uniform behavior that doesn't serve diverse organizations well. People should be developed so that their authentic personalities emerge—idiosyncrasy should be seen as a positive. Obviously, you don't want people to violate cultural norms—you don't want to motivate people to become arrogant jerks. But some people communicate best through humor, others possess valuable skepticism, still others are dreamers. All should be developed to be their best selves.

STORY. Help employees build databases of their expertise and history that are available to all other employees. Development should be about enabling them to let their colleagues know who they are—what drives them, what their professional and personal interests are, what their goals are.

Provide them with opportunities to build out their social media profiles on LinkedIn and other relevant social media. People find it much easier to respect and form positive relationships with other people when they know their stories—when they have a deeper understanding of what motivates someone or what they love to do. As people learn and grow within organizations, they should share their stories of learning and growth with their colleagues, providing them insight about what they're currently excited about.

Individual Development Is Everyone's Job

This subhead should be the motto of every organization that wants to develop people with a good balance between story and spreadsheet. It suggests that it's not just HR that should be concerned with this issue; that the leaders of the company should be engaged in the process; and that the individuals being developed should be proactive in making sure their needs are met.

Before offering suggestions on how to make this motto a best practice, let me explain *why* it should be a best practice.

Differentiated and superior talent is usually the most—if not the only—important, competitive advantage companies today have in a networked world. All other resources and assets can either be accessed through third parties and "the cloud" or are often as much liabilities as advantages (scale, out-of-date factories or technologies, increasingly irrelevant brands). If talent is the key competitive advantage, it needs to be the responsibility of everyone, including CEOs. CEOs focus on two key areas: the strategy and business model of their company and the attraction, retention, and growth of talent.

Too often, however, the former receives the lion's share of CEOs' attention, and they cede much of the latter responsibility to HR. The big problem, though, is that managers get left out of the equation, and managers can and should play a key role in helping develop their people's niche, voice, and story.

Every manager is fielding a team, and each team needs to have different experts passionately aligned to achieve a common outcome. To obtain these skilled players, managers must ensure that each person excels at a particular niche; that these players are passionate about what they do; and that they are growing by building their story.

HR helps with this process, creating alignment with the law, implementing and overseeing the training and development process, creating measures to determine the progress people are making. But HR's historic role is to benefit the organization, not the talent.

That's why managers must facilitate the development of their people's niche, voice, and story. Here are three ways they can do so:

1. **Customization.** HR tends to think across the organization, since that is where they can best serve the company. An individual's immediate boss can structure opportunities specifically for them. The boss sees where their people thrive and where they struggle. They are aware of what they are good at and where they have weaknesses. By choosing work assignments with these issues in mind, they can provide people with opportunities to create their niche and build their story in ways they find gratifying.

2. **Continuous feedback.** HR tends to think in six-month or annual reviews. This is the spreadsheet approach to feedback, where you get locked into a formal cycle and offer feedback in specific ways relative to specific categories. Imagine a basketball coach who, instead of correcting a player's mistakes or building up his confidence in real time, confines his feedback to twice-a-year sessions after watching tape.

   Building a particular niche and voice requires continuous and iterative feedback. Only one's bosses and immediate colleagues can provide it. They can make suggestions and offer constructive criticism in real time—they can capitalize on windows of learning that open shortly after something is done or said. They can also help teach skills and impart knowledge that their people are motivated to acquire. Organizations need to encourage bosses to provide this type of continuous feedback consciously and consistently (versus unconsciously and inconsistently, which is more common). The rewards and recognition system should motivate managers to practice these behaviors.

3. **Integration.** Managers must put their people in positions where they can integrate what they're learning to create a powerful niche, voice, and story. Development of these elements doesn't take place in a vacuum—or a classroom. As they're being given the right assignments and continuous feedback, people must also be out in the field, testing their skills and assessing how those skills combine with others'. In this way, they can make adjustments on the fly. It may be that they learn they have to become more adept in the use of one particular skill or moderate the use of another one. They may discover that their team prizes their ability to cut through the clutter and articulate a consensus-building position, but that the team doesn't particularly like the way they try to lobby for their position. These can be skill nuances, but they're important, and only through in-the-field integration can people make these valuable adjustments.

As much as people can acquire these three elements on their own, they require the facilitation of bosses to accelerate the process and make it more effective. Ideally, this facilitation takes the form of mentorship. Managers who are mentors go beyond the traditional boss role, giving their people a safe space to develop their niche, voice, and story. Mentors are more tolerant of mistakes than bosses, more focused on providing learning and growth experiences. Not all managers can or want to be mentors, but the more that they are willing to take on this additional role, the better they will be at helping direct reports develop authentically and effectively.

Passion Projects

Earlier, when I mentioned that organizations should allow employees to follow their passions, some of you may have scoffed, thinking, *If we allowed our people to do whatever they were interested in, we'd never get any* real *work done*. I'm not advocating allowing people to do anything that interests them. It's necessary to be selective—there are some people who, if given the freedom to pursue their passion, would abuse that freedom.

Others, however, are responsible organizational citizens who burn to test a concept or to learn more about an emerging area. These are the people companies need to identify, determining if their passions are aligned with the company's strategy and goals. If not, these individuals may need coaching to help create alignment. But if their targeted development areas are within the general vicinity of the company's requirements, give them opportunities to pursue the knowledge and tasks that excite them. The company will benefit not only in employee retention and morale but because this can be a low-cost strategy to explore a potential new market.

In 1995, while working at Leo Burnett in direct marketing, I began to get interested in online services such as America Online and Prodigy. I went to our management and suggested that they let me pursue this passion full-time within the company, making the case that online might be the future of marketing.

The company allowed me to put together a business plan with two employees, myself and an assistant, to see if there was a way to gauge client interest and revenue. We called it the Interactive Marketing Group. This new assignment not only kept me working for the company but led to the launch of the first interactive agency, Giant Step, which grew to two hundred employees and tens of millions of dollars of revenue. More significantly, it also ensured that when Leo Burnett Media launched Starcom four years later, it did so with a focus on the future and digital, which was part of its incredible success. Today, more than half the $10 billion revenue of Publicis Groupe (which bought Leo Burnett) is digital!

Over the years, I have returned this favor and allowed selected people to pursue the endeavor that turned them on, from word-of-mouth marketing to gaming to music to product innovation. While many of them did not scale into large companies, in each case they provided three benefits to Publicis: (1) they retained some key talent for a few years more than if we had not let them pursue their passion; (2) they signaled to other talent that we were open to experimentation; and (3) they communicated to clients and prospects that we were willing to take risk and innovate.

Google is a good model for allowing people to pursue passion projects. For many years they've had a 70/20/10 guideline where top talent spends 70 percent of their time on their main job, 20 percent on some future corporate project, and 10 percent on their passions. This not only allows for innovation but fosters attraction and retention of talent.

If you study start-ups that disrupt industries, you'll often find that the big corporations being disrupted once employed the disruptor: an employee chafed against the limits of a job, left, started a company, and introduced a product or service that changed the entire category. If they had been given the opportunity to pursue their pet projects within their former employer, this large company could have disrupted the industry and reaped the many benefits.

Sachin Bansal and Binny Bansal were former employees of Amazon who left to start the e-commerce portal Flipkart in India. The two firms are competing today for market share in India, with Walmart having bought 77 percent of Flipkart for $16 billion in May 2018.

A decade ago, in 2008, I was on the board of a start-up called Revenue Science, whose strategy leader, Omar, was passionate about an idea to unbundle data signals from content and asked the board for permission to spend time and effort in this area. Our board decided we needed to focus on our core business, and Omar left to start a company called BlueKai in an emerging area called data management platforms.

In 2014 Omar sold BlueKai to Oracle for $400 million.

In 2017 Revenue Science (which became Audience Science) was liquidated and closed its doors.

Omar recognized that the correct strategy was to unbundle data from content rather than Revenue Science's strategy of bundling data with content. As in so many other companies, an existing employee had a disruptive idea that we did not embrace, and in time this inability to think differently and disrupt ourselves came back to hurt us.

The Personal Trend in Organizations

Many companies are starting to recognize that satisfied, challenged, and evolving employees are better employees. This is why there's been such an emphasis on helping people achieve a work-life balance; it's why organizations are adopting more liberal policies toward working-at-home parents and implementing other, more flexible work policies; and it's why training and development professionals are starting to take the whole person into consideration, not just the "worker."

For traditionalists, it may seem heretical to use development for anything other than meeting specific organizational needs. I would argue that whole-person development also meets these needs, but in a less direct (though arguably more effective) way. I would say that the separation between work and personal is difficult in a connected and networked age. In an era where a lot of people work from home and call, text, and email outside of the nine-to-five window (because of global time differences as well as other factors); where increasingly companies are global and conference calls occur very early or late; and when we are all connected via mobile phones, this separation is no longer a reality.

More than that, organizations are coming to understand that you don't leave your personal issues at home when you step into the office. If you're going through a divorce or just had a baby, you may struggle to focus on putting together a budget or running a meeting.

More subtly, but no less importantly, people want to do work that is challenging and meaningful. They don't want to repeat tasks ad infinitum, no matter how skilled they might be at doing them. They want to stretch themselves, to learn new things, to tackle issues that resonate with who they are as people and professionals.

Companies like Netflix, Google, and Home Depot get it. They have implemented policies and processes that go beyond organizational requirements and attempt to help people act and develop authentically. Indeed, a popular job search website conducted a survey to determine which companies were leaders in helping employees achieve a work-life balance, and their results were striking. Nike offers employees paid sabbaticals and discounts on fitness programs; Cisco's Human Network campaign helps people achieve more work-life balance and has formal and informal ways to adapt work schedules to people's needs; American Express has given employees who are new moms free 24/7 access to lactation consultants, while covering breast-milk shipping costs for mothers traveling on business.

Work-life balance, though, is the old frontier; the emerging one is development. In the coming years, we're going to see people demanding work that is meaningful. Development programs are crucial to helping employees evolve their jobs over time to become and remain fulfilling. Yes, they want jobs that satisfy the spreadsheet side of the ledger—well-paying positions that capitalize on their skills. But they want that story side, too, and growth needs to shift to accommodate this requirement.

———————————— KEY TAKEAWAYS ————————————

- The most successful companies are talent-obsessed because while firms are a collection of technologies, brands, and people, that last group is key, since they create the technologies and brands.
- Talent-focused organizations recognize that they can only grow if they unleash the potential of their people by aligning the company and its employees.
- The most successful people find their niche, their voice, and their stories, and this makes them credible; they maximize their talent for themselves and their organizations.

CHAPTER 8

DIVERSIFY AND DEEPEN TIME USAGE

If you've ever seen movies from the '50s depicting life in large corporate offices, you probably were horrified. Anyone who wasn't an executive sat in enormous bullpen-like areas at desks organized classroom-fashion. They were expected to arrive promptly at 9:00 a.m., were given one break for coffee before lunch, and were watched with hawklike vigilance by supervisors. They often had time cards, punching in and out so management could track their hours. The work was frequently monotonous—innovation, disruption, and agility were not on anyone's radar—and deadlines were sacrosanct.

We've made great strides since that era and have "loosened up" workplaces in many ways, including work-hour flexibility and flattened organizations. Despite these strides, we are still obsessed by time management, and in a spreadsheet-dominant era, we can use digital tools to track employee behavior by the minute. If you type "time management" into a Google search, you get almost 2.5 billion results.

Historically, time management has been an organizational obsession. Legendary management guru Peter Drucker said, "Time is the scarcest resource and unless it is managed nothing else can be managed."[1] From the early 1900s, when Fredrick Winslow Taylor pioneered time studies and Frank and Lillian Gilbreth conducted their time-motion studies, time management has been a business holy grail.[2]

Today, management of time has been taken to an entirely new level, from gathering input with sensors on delivery trucks that measure driver behaviors to analyzing output through state-of-the-art visual dashboards that compile and interpret data.

The heart of business beats to the inner metronome of time management with quarterly results, monthly management meetings, weekly status updates, daily outcomes, and hourly monitoring. This underlying beat of business often turns into a beast that oppresses our ability to be truly productive by replacing outcome with activity as we check in and check out, build our calendars around a rhythm of mundane meetings, and issue or read periodic reports that are cascaded up and down the organization.

In most spreadsheet-dominant organizations, time confines us to our routines rather than opening us up to new possibilities. More specifically, here is how time has a prisonlike effect on our work behaviors:

WE ARE CONTROLLED BY OUR INBOXES AND OUR OVERSTUFFED CALENDARS. Our calendars are packed to the gills with dull or routine meetings, and we let our inboxes or social media feeds colonize our minds and determine what we pay attention to and how and when we react.

WE CONFUSE ACTIVITY WITH ACHIEVEMENT, BUSYNESS WITH PRODUCTIVITY. We hustle and bustle. We boast of how packed our agendas are. We overschedule and we multitask. Part of this is due to increased workloads, reduced staffs, and constant incoming of signals, but a lot of it is our fear of the silence and the empty calendar. We might have time to think and maybe we are afraid of thinking. And if we do not have a packed calendar but instead swaths of unprogrammed time, we worry that maybe we are less relevant to our organizations and missing important things.

WE FOCUS ON WHAT HAS TO BE DONE VERSUS WHAT WE SHOULD DO. We narrowly define work as the tasks we are assigned and the expectations that must be met because we respond to how organizations define our jobs. As a result, we end up reliving every workday and they all blend into one. Work begins to resemble an assembly line of parts and pieces, even when we have white-collar and managerial positions.

Put another way, people who are obsessed with managing time can be narrowly focused individuals who dread certain job tasks, watch the clock, work at their desks, and rarely wander away—or into—anything that is not necessary. Organizations need to free their people from the tyranny of time and help them use time in a diversified manner. If they succeed, employees are more likely to look forward to work and find time flying by, spending less time at their desks and more time interacting with coworkers and in the digital world in search of new challenges and learning.

Playing with Time

Jeff Bezos of Amazon provides a good model for treating time with flexibility and creativity. Two *Wired* articles capture his time philosophy:

> "If everything you do needs to work on a three-year time horizon, then you're competing against a lot of people, but if you're willing to invest on a seven-year time horizon, you're now competing against a fraction of those people, because very few companies are willing to do that. Just by lengthening the time horizon, you can engage in endeavors that you could never otherwise pursue. At Amazon we like things to work in five to seven years. We're willing to plant seeds, let them grow—and we're very stubborn. We say we're stubborn on vision and flexible on details."[3]
>
> Bezos spends hours at a time thinking about the future: trawling for ideas, exploring his own site, sometimes just surfing the Web, particularly on Mondays and Thursdays, which he tries to keep unscheduled. "I catch up on email, I wander around and talk to people, or I set up my own meetings— ones that are not part of the regular calendar."[4]

Bezos thinks long term and refuses to be pinned down to the vagaries of quarterly and annual calendars. He also keeps looking for new stimuli to ensure that he is not falling into a rut or being "handled" by calendar keepers.

Organizations should take a cue from Bezos and help their people approach time in a similarly flexible and creative manner. To guide their efforts, they should keep the following four traits of time-savvy employees in mind:

1. **Be disciplined about being undisciplined.** They always find time to get off the grid and the programming. Just as some of the most memorable travel happens when tourists are not limited by the preplanned itinerary, the best learning happens unexpectedly. Bill Gates famously schedules a "think week," in which he goes off with books to ruminate and ponder.[5] This facilitates using time in diverse ways.
2. **Expose themselves to as many stimuli in a given time period as possible.** They seek out different people, surf the web as if they're free associating, and browse all sorts of online sites and books and articles.

They walk around. They seek out new experiences. Again, they use their time to pursue a variety of ideas and activities.

3. **Be intensely focused and present in the moment, and at the same time thinking very long term.** I call this "bifocal" time management. These individuals pay attention to details and stimuli in the short term while also thinking about how to process and understand the impact of these details and stimuli in the long term. They focus on the matters at hand, but they also consider future implications and tangential subjects.

4. **Understand the difference between the urgent and the important.** Dwight Eisenhower noted that "what is important is seldom urgent and what is urgent is seldom important."[6] These individuals aren't constantly in crisis deadline mode, grasping that if they treat everything like an immediate emergency, they'll miss out on ideas and activities that can help their organizations. They can differentiate between real deadlines and those that have been artificially created by machines and systems. These people create more diverse time for themselves because they don't become fixated on illusory due dates.

Time Is Not Our Own

If you were to survey people in your organization about whether they're using their time efficiently and effectively, most would probably admit they're not (assuming that they wouldn't be punished for their honesty). It's not that they're goofing off or don't know how to be efficient and effective in their work; it's that they are straitjacketed by policies, deadlines, paperwork, and monitoring. They possess so little flexibility relative to what they work on and how they work on it that they become robotic in their use of time—they know they must complete project A by Wednesday, that their boss expects a report on Friday, that their work is being monitored via their digital devices.

If you've ever had problems with your computer and given an online technician permission to view your screen, you're aware of how intrusive this technology can be. The Big Brother–like sense that your every move is being watched tends to make you acutely aware of how you're spending your time. More than that, it makes you reluctant to do things that may not seem relevant to the task at hand. You don't want to spend an hour exploring a seemingly tangential subject or creating a proposal for your boss that is unrelated to your primary assignment. You don't research an emerging market that is outside of your direct area of responsibility. Whether the fear is justified doesn't matter; you perceive that a "watcher" will think you're not doing your work, and this fear circumscribes how you spend your time.

One company that surveyed their people about how they use their time is consulting giant McKinsey. In November 2013, they surveyed 1,374 executives around the globe on how they spent their time and found that only 9 percent of the respondents were "very satisfied" with their use of time, while fewer than half were "somewhat satisfied," and about one-third were "actively dissatisfied." Only 52 percent of those surveyed said that the way they spent their time was aligned with their organization's strategic priorities. Nearly half admitted that they were not concentrating sufficiently on guiding the strategic direction of the business.[7]

While McKinsey's survey didn't address the impact of a spreadsheet mentality on time use, it makes you wonder why some of the world's best and brightest with high-paying positions are not "very satisfied" with how they're using their time. They're smart enough to figure out what they should be doing at work, but perhaps they lack the freedom or resources to use their daily hours as productively as they might.

The McKinsey study concluded that those who were satisfied spent their time in three areas: (1) meeting with key reports one-on-one or at clients' offices; (2) working on solving operational issues or on long-term strategic initiatives; and (3) spending time alone, thinking and producing work.

In short, these were the areas that mattered most to satisfied employees. I would also argue that these are the areas that *should* matter the most to the company. Too often, however, there's a gap between how people want to spend their time and how organizations require them to spend their time.

Meaningful Time Management Methods

Author Annie Dillard wrote, "How we spend our days is, of course, how we spend our lives."[8] Work environments that fill days with routine; unmanageable workloads; constant, meaningless, or mundane meetings; and regular, oppressive monitoring signal a less-than-pleasant life in and for the company.

I have distilled six meaningful time management methods from observation, experience, and research that counteract the often meaningless ways many employees spend part of their workdays. If organizations want their people to be more productive, they should encourage the following behaviors:

ELIMINATE. The first of these methods is simplest to state and hardest to execute. For people to start using their time in a more varied and meaningful manner, they need to stop doing a lot of similar, meaningless things. Many people recognize the limitations of time and try to do as much as possible. They multitask and run around in a frenzy. Usually all they achieve is more multitasking and more frenzy. Doing more stuff is not the same as achievement.

ACTIVITY IS NOT PRODUCTIVITY. Showing how busy you are does not show how important you are. Give people permission to get rid of unessential tasks, whether it's paperwork-related or jobs that could be done better via outsourcing, part-timers, or in other ways. Encourage people to prioritize based on what's meaningful to them and what's meaningful to the organization—when a task is meaningful to one or the other but not both, it's a candidate for elimination.

FOCUS. Here is what organizations should communicate to their employees: once they have additional time, focus it on a few things versus many. Diversifying time does not mean skipping from one thing to the next like a dilettante. The more things people do, the less opportunity they have to become expert at any one of them. They should focus only on things that they can do particularly well (comparative advantage) or that have great impact or meaning for them and their organization (positive outcome). The first, comparative advantage, means prioritizing activities that they can do better than most people. To create this focus, though, people need organizational permission to delegate tasks that they don't do as well—either internally or through outsourcing. The second, positive outcome, means concentrating time based on likely, advantageous results such as creating revenue, learning something new, helping someone else or the team get better, or having a meaningful experience.

SCALE. While your people cannot make more time, they can make their efforts more impactful through the use of scale. This is a great way not only to save time but to help people feel they are using their time in ways that possess power and significance. There are three ways to execute this strategy: leverage, coached delegation, and momentum.

- **Leverage.** Today technology and scheduling allow people to leverage. They can use social media with good writing and speaking skills to reach many people with whom they need to communicate and to whom they want to sell their thinking. They are not limited to small meetings and groups, especially if they're a senior manager. Instead, they should gather folks at the right conference or meeting versus repeating themselves ad infinitum.
- **Coached delegation.** One of the best ways to scale is to delegate tasks to others with direction and coaching. If others become good at this task, it's like you've cloned yourself; you imbue others with the input and direction necessary for them to do as you would do.
- **Momentum.** The trend is your friend. To avoid wasting time, understand the underlying trend that is driving the firm or the business and, in most cases, align with it. The world is going global. The world is going digital. Every company has a built-in DNA. If they are going to go against the flow, they need to prepare for loss of time as well as resistance. I am not suggesting to go along with every trend, especially leaders and managers—if you believe strongly in an alternative, fight for it. Just be aware that you'll need to prepare a great argument and enlist others to win the battle, and that it's not going to be easy.

DO NEW THINGS; TATTOO THE MOMENT. Day-to-day repetition of tasks and calendar scheduling creates boredom and robs people of their creativity; they try to get through the day rather than make the most of it. New experiences deepen time and create more diverse work tasks—people who take on stretch assignments or volunteer for new training make their work time memorable because they're engaged in something fresh and different. New experiences stretch your people, helping them learn and grow as employees, managers, and leaders. These experiences can be as simple as attending a conference they've never attended or volunteering for work on a new, diverse team. It may be taking on a big challenge or creating a new project for themselves or their teams. The new experience, if it's sufficiently successful (or even if it's a spectacular failure) will tattoo itself in people's memory. They can draw on it and learn from it; it is time well spent.

GIVE TIME TO OTHERS. Donating time to direct reports, bosses, customers, suppliers, or trade associations is another method to increase the meaning and diversity of workdays. When people mentor others, for instance, they feel their time is purposeful, that they're appreciated. They can tolerate the time they may have to spend on a necessary-but-boring task because they are infusing their time with an activity about which they care that varies from the routine. Developing people, providing assistance to a client, helping a trade organization, doing pro bono work—all this is a generous use of time that benefits the individual as well as the larger entity.

Facilitating Better Ways to Use Time

An employee's time is not their own. Work has to be done, and not just at work. We have to juggle responsibilities at home and everyday living. Deadlines have to be met. No one can just do what they want when they want.

While companies can't allow employees to eliminate whatever they want to focus on whatever they choose, they can be far more sensitive to time pressures by finding ways to change organizational philosophies toward time management:

ASSESS ALL MEETINGS TO ELIMINATE ONES THAT WASTE TIME OR WHOSE TASKS COULD BE HANDLED MORE EFFICIENTLY IN ANOTHER SETTING. In the next chapter, I'm going to advocate for more meetings of significance and substance. Unfortunately, the majority of meetings are inefficient and boring. Here's a radical amendment to this policy: Cancel all meetings and start with a blank sheet of paper. Then assess which meetings are the best ones in the organization—the ones that feature lively discussions, diverse viewpoints, disruptive ideas, and productive outcomes. Of these premium meetings, assess the minimum number of times they should be held in a year with the minimal number of attendees and the maximum acceptable gaps. "Bad meeting creep" is a problem for most organizations, and this approach may be the best way to stop meetings from being a time suck.

CONSIDER TIME A FINITE RESOURCE AND BUDGET FOR IT LIKE YOU WOULD BUDGET MONEY. Every time an organization funds a new initiative from a fixed budget, they eliminate the budget of some other program. Why not do the same with the allocation of time? Whenever a new meeting or initiative is added to the calendar, identify what gets canceled or reduced. Resources aren't infinite, even intangible ones like time. Organizations cannot keep launching new initiatives and projects without paying a price—people will be overwhelmed and overbooked and won't have enough time to focus on what matters most.

ESTABLISH ELECTRONIC-FREE TIME PERIODS. This isn't just my idea; some companies already designate time during the day—or an entire day—when electronic media use is forbidden or discouraged. Yes, people can look at their emails and texts for critical messages, but a general understanding exists that during certain time periods, digital messages won't be answered or sent. This policy frees up people's time to try new things, to focus on key tasks, and so on.

Diversify Time Based on Goals

In the 1990s, a new productivity tool called the Pomodoro Technique became popular. It called for twenty-five minutes of intense work toward a goal, followed by a five-minute break. After the break, people had the option of returning to the existing task or moving on to a different project. After five Pomodoro repetitions, the technique mandated an hour break.[9]

The Pomodoro seems designed more for individual than team work and also doesn't take into account modern business realities. But if the technique isn't directly applicable, its principles are even more relevant today than years ago. Specifically, this technique suggests the following principles: (1) a single-task focus is more productive than multitasking, (2) humans work best in short spurts with breaks to recover, and (3) we should strive for a diversity of tasks *over time* versus at *the same time*, breaking up a job routine and considering various tasks comparatively.[10]

These principles, though, work only if they are tied to well-designed goals. Here is how to create time-sensitive goals:

ORGANIZE A LIMITED NUMBER OF GOALS INTO TWO SETS. Determine short (daily and weekly) or mid-term (monthly or quarterly) goals for up to six tasks or objectives. Having a list of more than a dozen (six short and six mid-term) goals means either too many goals have been listed and they become unachievable or they will produce a lot of switching between tasks and making lists or monitoring goals. Diversifying time is good; overdiversifying is bad. An overabundance of goals overwhelms people. Some goals will need more time (usually the important ones or ones that facilitate growth) and some less time (usually the urgent ones and the ones that must be done but rarely promote growth).

FIND THE SWEET SPOT BETWEEN SHORT-TERM AND LONG-TERM GOALS. A list of goals should not be just about getting work done. While these are important to include, they are insufficient by themselves. People should spend some of their time getting better, not just getting work done. Allocating 20 percent of one's month to enhancing and expanding skills is manageable. This may include attending training sessions, going to conferences, helping colleagues so you can learn what they are working on, and reading or visiting websites that help grow skills. Employees can best give to their companies by giving to themselves. By growing their skills, they not only become more valuable to the company but are more likely to stay longer because their growing skills are relevant and rewarded.

This is how I have learned to manage my time over the years. I allocate time into four buckets:

1. **Client work.** Projects specific to clients, including meetings and presentations. This tends to take up about a third of my time.
2. **Corporate work.** Since I was part of management and often worked on our strategies and broader overall objectives, this takes another third of my time.
3. **Learning.** I try to set aside 20 percent of my time over a week (the equivalent of one day a week or an hour or two daily) to learning, ensuring my skills continue to be relevant. It would be hard for me to be useful to clients or inform our corporate strategy without keeping abreast of key advancements in technology, strategy, competitors, and clients. This learning time is not limited to just work-related topics and includes things that will help me become more innovative or be

stimulated to think differently—going to museums, seeing new films, attending university lectures, and so on.

4. **Giving back, mentoring, teaching.** One of the ways I can be of help to our company is to teach others, either one-on-one or in groups. I communicate what I have learned about my field and managing a career. Teaching and guiding people is often the best way to scale since you are now teaching people to fish rather than fishing yourself.

Finally, be aware that this is not a static process. Once I diversify my time based on my goals, I often have to recalibrate and rebalance the activities to which I've allocated my hours, based on emerging realities.

Situations change. A sudden customer crisis, the realization that a new skill will soon be crucial, the restructuring of a team or department—all of this can affect people's goals and priorities. Therefore, organizations need to make sure that people reassess their goals and time allotments monthly or even weekly. Diversifying time is similar to diversifying investments; rebalancing the portfolio is essential.

Quality Versus Quantity

As I wrote this chapter, I thought about how productivity-obsessed leaders might respond. In an era where organizations are trying to do more with less, some companies are attempting to wring every single second of work from every employee.

A company's productivity is defined as output divided by input, and one of the key inputs is time. Therefore, one way of increasing productivity is to increase output per unit of time. It is a key variable monitored by many manufacturing and certain service businesses (e.g., call centers that measure the number of phone calls a service agent completes in an hour). Less formally, other organizations focus on incentivizing their people to work longer hours for rewards and recognition.

This measure frequently fails to capture the quality of the product or service, as opposed to the quantity of the product and service. Particularly in the service sector, which is now more than half the economy of advanced countries, the degree of variability of output is particularly extreme and more is not necessarily better.

Many experts have believed productivity came through focus and repetition. Just as increased practice and monomaniacal focus make for an improved athlete, it makes for a more productive employee—or so the thinking goes. While this may be true for some manufacturing companies and service providers, focusing on repetition has a negative effect on productivity for the following reasons:

- *Customization* is often a key to quality of product. Imagine a hairdresser who cut everyone's hair the same.
- *Constant repetition* of a task leads to burnt-out or bored employees, increasing turnover and its negative impact on productivity.
- *Collaboration* makes superior service possible in a connected world; varying and adjusting collaborations to fit customer needs and markets helps boost productivity, while a single-minded focus and universal repetition does not.
- *Competition* usually comes from outside one's industry, where new ways of doing things can change the game. This was true even in manufacturing, where Toyota's new "just in time" inventory approach plus close collaboration—with suppliers and between employees—upended the traditional, focused assembly-line approach of US car manufacturers.
- *Computerization and robotics* allow machines to handle repetitive tasks, giving humans the time to deal with sensitive issues, handle emotion-related concerns, or customize responses.

For both organizations and employees, increasing the depth, quality, and variability of work ensures increased productivity and job security. This won't happen, however, if organizations don't actively invest in programs and policies that encourage quality as well as quantity.

--------- KEY TAKEAWAYS ---------

- It is a mistake to allocate and measure time only in economic or numeric ways. The quality of how people spend their time is as important as the quantity of what they produce during that time.

- Successful people do not allow the vagaries of calendars or incoming emails to determine their days but rather have technologies or practices that allow them to allocate their time to things that are important to them.
- To get the most out of time, organizations need to sanction doing less and open spaces to do nothing.

CHAPTER 9

SCHEDULE MORE MEETINGS

As long as there have been people, there have been meetings. One-on-one meetings; team meetings; organization-wide, all-hands-on-deck meetings; check-in meetings; weekly update meetings; and many more. There have been meetings about meetings. Meetings on how to conduct meetings. Meetings to eliminate meetings.

In the nearly four decades I have been working, all types of meetings continue to proliferate, but many more of them today have a spreadsheet focus that minimizes or eliminates the story aspect.

This needs to change. In an era when interactions in the workplace are increasingly digital and transaction oriented, we need to inject more life into our meetings. Instead of being part of the boring routine, they need to become meaningful and memorable. In this way, they can help people become more valued as employees and more excited about the tasks they perform.

Let's start by looking at the nature of meetings and how they've evolved so that we tolerate them at best and dread them at worst.

All about the Data

If you've been working in organizations for a sustained period of time, you've noticed that your meetings have changed. In the old days, let's say ten or twenty years ago, meetings were looser and their content more varied. While they may have been run by bosses and organized through agendas, they often could veer off topic. Participants might become involved in heated exchanges. Meetings could start out organized and logical and devolve into free-for-alls. At times, they were chaotic. At times, they produced great ideas through free-form discussions.

I'm not suggesting meetings were better years ago—they were often boring, dragged on endlessly, and were used to further someone's agenda or scapegoat someone. They certainly weren't always efficient. They were, however, more human.

Today, new technologies have greatly impacted meetings. Given almost universal access to screens and improved conferencing and connection apps (Skype, Hangouts, Chat, Slack, etc.), being in the room for a meeting is no longer as common or necessary as it once was. As a result, some or all participants are communicating from different locations. Just as significant, when people are in the same room, they are often staring at screens rather than at each other.

Add to the mix an increasingly global workplace, accelerated work pace, and a growing number of remote workers, and you have a recipe for meeting metamorphosis:

MORE VOLUME; LESS IMPORTANCE. As the work pace has quickened, meetings have proliferated because people need to check in more often to ensure coordination of effort. In a more connected, more collaborative world, the invitee list to meetings has expanded, since more people have ownership of a given issue. Plus, meeting software makes it easy to convene people, especially because invitees don't have to be there physically. Invariably, these frequent, "crowded" meetings are often focused on issues of secondary or tertiary importance; in the past, they would have been handled by Miguel walking down the hallway to Sheila's office.

MORE PROCESS DRIVEN; LESS PURPOSEFUL. Meetings tend to be about getting work done rather than how to get better at doing the work. They are increasingly about informing and aligning rather than improving and inspiring. They focus on meeting numerical criteria (deadlines, percentage increases, etc.), and they pay scant attention to quality of work or long-term goals.

MORE TIME; LESS ATTENTION. Most people tolerate meetings rather than look forward to them as opportunities to develop ideas and relationships. They are similar to boring classes in school—we're constantly looking at the clock.

As a result, we denigrate meetings. We complain about how they're destroying productivity, taking over calendars, and need to be eliminated. There is a veritable cottage industry of books, seminars, and consultants that proffer advice on solving the plague and pestilence of participatory gatherings. They suggest reducing the number of meetings, limiting the participants, using technology as an information-sharing substitute for meetings, and so on. All good suggestions that focus on increasing productivity via meeting alternatives and alterations, but they miss a key point.

Too often, most meetings are about data. Sharing it. Interrogating it. Aligning around it. They are about the spreadsheet side of business.

These meetings miss the opportunity to integrate story into the mix. They fail to provide a forum to communicate the story of the business—the story of how people are growing in the business. They don't create unusual combinations of employees, giving someone in finance the chance to interact and form a relationship with someone in marketing. They don't allow for chance interactions and unplanned collaborations.

In many ways we are the accumulation of the places we have been and the people we have met. Meetings both planned and ad hoc, large and one-on-one, help determine who we are as professionals.

Organizations need to be proactive in creating policies that promote meaningful meetings, that help people develop their abilities rather than bide their time. Instead of letting meetings plan employee days, we should plan meetings that let our days be as meaningful as possible.

Five Types of Meaningful Meetings

When you think about it, meetings vary considerably. They range from spontaneous, involving only a few people, to regularly scheduled, large, formal gatherings. Some last for hours and others for just minutes; some are highly focused with clear goals and others are wide-ranging and open-ended.

And some are primarily about story, while others are about spreadsheet.

All this is fine. What's not fine is when one type dominates, and in recent years, spreadsheet meetings have been dominant. Too often the large, regularly scheduled, agenda-driven meetings have become the norm, and their emphasis on data-based outcomes has created a spreadsheet-story imbalance. How many meetings have you attended that were about detailing and debating data points? About discussing numerical objectives? About fine-tuning budgets?

These are necessary and can be valuable, but organizations need to do a better job of integrating story. To facilitate that, consider the following five types of meetings that are meaningful and relationship-focused:

Unknown Meetings

These are meetings with individuals who are unknown or little-known to employees. For instance, people who are looking for advice, sharing new ideas, or interested in meeting someone for other reasons (e.g., a friend or colleague recommended they should meet). This meeting could be with one person or a small group. It should not be with someone who is trying to sell something. That's because the value of these meetings is that they stimulate fresh and creative thinking. Their goal is often learning, and a side benefit is forging a relationship that may prove valuable to the organization. In a sales situation, learning is not the goal, and relationships are often predicated upon a purchase.

Unknown meetings help people voyage outside of their bubbles. Over the years, these meetings have led me to people I have wanted to hire, who taught me about things I had no idea existed—or that they insisted would be a "big deal" in the future (I first heard about Bitcoin and cryptocurrencies in this type of meeting). Some didn't yield anything substantive in terms of practical learning or relationships, but they opened my mind to ideas and possibilities that I would never have considered otherwise.

"Can You Help?" Meetings

Here the purpose is to provide assistance without receiving anything in return—at least anything tangible and immediate. In reality, you receive other people's gratitude and willingness to go the extra mile for you in the future. I'd argue that you get more than you give from these types of meetings.

As I have grown more senior and well-known, I spend a lot of time helping people who are between jobs, students, and colleagues grappling with particular challenges. They are surprised that I am accessible and willing to give them my time. I remind them that I am getting as much out of the meeting as they are—the satisfaction of passing on whatever learning and wisdom I've acquired over the years.

"Can you help?" meetings are opportunities for people to give back to their organizational communities, whether one-on-one or to larger groups. They help people feel good about what they've accomplished, the expertise they've developed. Givers emerge from these meetings with a renewed sense of purpose, and receivers emerge with knowledge that can help them do their jobs better.

Woodshed Meetings

As the name implies, these are instances where you have to reprimand, warn, or punish people. Yes, this may seem like an odd meeting type to include in the story category. Most of us hate disciplining others even more than we hate being disciplined. Emotion-filled, pressure-laden, and unpleasant in other ways, these meetings are challenging.

But it's much better to have these meetings than avoid them. In spreadsheet-dominant companies, the culture often gives tacit permission to avoid woodsheds. These meetings are messy emotionally, and numbers-focused people don't like mess. As a result, people are often allowed to continue down the wrong path—no one confronts them about their mistakes or attitudes or lays out a meaningful plan of improvement. Meetings often lack the straight talk and emotion necessary to catalyze behavioral change. Employees are allowed to function at a marginal (or worse) level for a sustained period of time. Perhaps they receive warnings or reprimands, but they don't improve and are eventually let go. The organization, however, tolerates mediocrity for months—or longer.

Woodshed meetings determine our success or failure. They provide the opportunity to help people change, learn, and grow rather than retire in place or exist for months or years as marginal contributors. Whether it's conferring one-on-one with a problematic employee or speaking with a team that isn't delivering results, these meetings represent opportunities to get people back on track.

Jerry McGuire–Inspired Meetings

In the movie of the same name, the protagonist storms out of his workplace spewing harsh, angry truths. While it was entertaining (for movie viewers) to see Tom Cruise vent, organizations should not encourage similar practices. If a Jerry McGuire–like employee did the same thing in your office, it would be disruptive in a negative sense—it would hurt morale and probably cause other employees to start sending out their résumés.

Instead of public venting, Jerry should have discussed his issues in a frank, one-on-one meeting with his boss or with senior leaders, where he could speak truth to power.

We often are scared of going to management and telling them harsh truths. It's tough to inform leaders that they've missed something or that they are putting profits before their people. As someone who mustered the courage to have these meetings with senior people earlier in my career, and who has been on the receiving end later, I know they can be uncomfortable experiences.

Generally, however, people emerge from these meetings with greater respect for their bosses, and bosses usually emerge with greater respect for the honesty and courage of their people. Just as important, critical issues surface that may otherwise have simmered for months before boiling over. These meetings allow people to tell their stories—to express what they've experienced and the perspectives they've formed. Their opinions may not always be right, but the meeting itself gets their story heard, which is an excellent goal in and of itself.

"Let's Get a Beer" Meetings

These have no agenda; they are designed to allow people to catch up with each other. Informal and spontaneous, they build morale and camaraderie. Whether it's going out for beers or lunch or coffee or other social activities, these types of get-togethers build relationships, allow employees to see one another as individuals rather than as colleagues, direct reports, supervisors, specialists, etc. Even if nothing related to work is discussed in these agenda-free meetings, the organization benefits. People work best when they know, like, and trust their colleagues, and beer meetings help achieve this objective.

I have also found that when gathering a group for a beer meeting, having fun activities can enhance the proceedings. At Starcom IP, whenever we had a beer meeting, everybody who had just joined the team had to "justify their existence" as to why they were special enough to join our group, and a senior employee had to "justify" what they had done recently to be good enough to stay. This way we learned about each other and our work with minimal formality.

Foster a Spirit of Generosity

In many organizations, the meeting leader is selfish—not in personality but in outcomes. The people who run meetings are usually focused on what they can get out of the people in attendance—how to help them achieve data-driven goals.

This is the main reason people resent and sometimes avoid meetings. Instead of looking only at what we can get out of meetings, we need to also think of what we can give. When we value a meeting by how much we can help others, no meeting is wasted. Too often, leaders and managers spend the majority of their meeting time imparting information. As necessary as this may be, this implied transaction ("I'll give you the data; you give me the results") is a poor basis for a meaningful meeting. Much of this information distribution could be done digitally.

Instead, focus on the following generous meeting goals:

KNOWLEDGE. Information is data and facts; knowledge is distilled wisdom and meaning. The first can be contained in a spreadsheet. The latter's vessel is a story. Storytelling—through personal examples, historical reference, and relevance to the listener—should be the operating principle for how team leaders communicate to meeting participants. Helping them have "aha!" moments of understanding is all about knowledge; perfunctory head nods are all about inputting data.

GUIDANCE. Most people leave meetings with marching orders—tasks to complete in a certain way by a certain date. I'm not saying you can ignore to-dos. But the concept of giving people a compass for guidance, rather than a list of exact directions, means you provide participants with both tools and a certain amount of freedom to use them. This is empowering; people are grateful that their bosses trust them to achieve outcomes using their own initiative. A compass ensures that they don't get lost when exploring solutions on their own. I usually try to leave people with a tool kit of sorts to take away with them. This may be some combination of reference materials (books, websites, etc.), techniques (recall my earlier "three words to build your brand"), and other people to meet.

APPRECIATION. Give people the gift of appreciation. You discern their point of view. You know where they are coming from. This requires listening carefully and watching for emotion and body language, not just words. When people leave meetings feeling like you "get them"—their fears, hopes, and ideas—they move forward with confidence and enthusiasm.

RELEVANCE. The meeting should be about them, not you. Even if you share your own knowledge and experience, it should be relevant to their needs and situation. Self-love in storytelling does not help the other person. Think in advance about what will be most significant to meeting participants—the stories, tools, and ideas to which they are most likely to resonate.

To put these generous principles into action, meeting leaders should adopt what I refer to as a LIFT mindset: Listen, Interact, Feel, Transform:

LISTEN. Open a meeting by listening to the person or people with whom you are meeting. Resist the urge to lecture or criticize or drown participants in information. Where are they coming from and what do they want from this meeting? Find that out before you focus on your agenda.

INTERACT. Allot time for questions when you're done speaking. Too often, people leave meetings frustrated because they never had a chance to respond to the information or the assignments made by meeting leaders. A question period allows people to provide you with feedback about what you're telling them as well as focus the conversation on issues that concern them and will help them accomplish meeting goals more effectively.

FEEL. Are you responding emotionally to the meeting discussion or more like a spreadsheet-focused robot? If you're talking about the need to downsize, are you allowing people to see that you're upset or sad? Meetings shouldn't only be about matters of the mind but about heart and spirit. Showing feeling and conveying that you understand their feelings creates resonance that has more value than subject-matter relevance.

TRANSFORM. Perhaps the most generous thing you can do in a meeting is help other people think, feel, and do things differently. You are giving attendees a fresh perspective, a better sense of what customers want, a new approach for a challenging problem. This isn't the easiest goal, but it's one worth striving for. By helping others see and act differently, you may also be giving yourself the gift of transformation. By pushing others to explore alternatives and shift perspectives, you confront your own ways of seeing and may open your mind to fresh possibilities.

Establish Empathy

Do people leave meetings feeling like you and other participants have walked in their shoes? Do they believe that you "get it" and "get them"? If you're just acknowledging their data (the dates they've targeted, the percentage increase they've achieved, the budget they required) but failing to communicate that you grasp what their concerns and hopes are, then they will leave meetings feeling dissatisfied at best, disgusted at worst.

Creating empathy in a meeting means not just getting what other people are feeling but communicating that you get it. You can do this with a group as well as an individual, and you can do it through both words and gestures. Sometimes, a knowing nod or locking eyes with another person can help them see you understand what they're feeling. In group settings, however, words are crucial.

Here are ways leaders can establish empathy:

UNDERSTANDING. Listen carefully and ask follow-up questions to ensure that you truly understand the issue. Three questions I ask are (1) What else is bothering or troubling you? (2) Why do you think this is an issue? and (3) If you could solve this, what would you do? Probing the causes and possible solutions of a problem ensure that everyone understands the real problem.

In some meetings team leaders say they understand, but participants know this is a surface understanding at best. "I understand your complaints that the customer is being belligerent, but you have to figure out how to deal with his attitude and please him to the point that he stops being so belligerent," a leader might say. Participants, though, feel this customer has crossed the line, that he's been abusive, that he is impossible to work with, and that only an intervention from the team leader and the customer's boss will remedy the problem.

REFRAMING. Put what you hear in an illuminating context. Share examples or analogies that help participants know that you grasp what they're facing and that this situation isn't unique. Ask yourself where you have seen or heard about this situation before. This may provide a way to reframe the problem or opportunity in a way that shines a spotlight on a given issue.

PERSONALIZING. Empathy is not about a general situation but a particular person. Make what you say personal: "A few years ago, I was dealing with a similar problem at Company XYZ. It was making me crazy, and I thought I was going to be fired until I did some research and . . ."

People relish stories that go beyond dry case histories. They love meeting leaders who are willing to be vulnerable and transparent about their own past situations that relate to the matter at hand. Sometimes it's appropriate to share a story where you overcame obstacles and achieved a goal. But it's just as effective (maybe more effective) to communicate a mistake you made or a failure you endured and what you learned.

As I suggested earlier, empathy is not just what you say but what you show. It is about tone of voice. It is about silences. It's as much about what is *not* said as what is verbalized. It is about not looking at your watch. It is about body language and gestures. It is not about what you say but how you say things. It is not about whether you listen but how you listen. It is not about what you react to but how you react.

In meetings, leaders can be abrupt, impatient, dismissive, and myopically focused on ticking off items on their agenda. They may think they're being empathic because they ask questions of others and solicit their ideas, but they negate what they say by what they show. Empathy is about feelings more than anything else, and feelings are often signaled in nonverbal ways.

Therefore, be open and patient during meetings, conscious of your tone of voice and body language and whether they're projecting openness and patience. Don't fidget or stare daggers or keep checking your watch. Don't let your body say one thing and your voice another.

As Maya Angelou wrote, "I've learned that people will forget what you said, people will forget what you did, but people will never forget how you made them feel."[1]

Generating Energy

For every meeting I lead, I have a consistent goal: ensuring that the participants leave the meeting more energized than when they entered.

We all have experienced meetings that drag on interminably, and sometimes even an hour-long meeting can feel like an eternity. When people exit the room, they are enervated. More than that, they may be dispirited, confused, and scared. For a number of reasons, the meeting sapped their initiative and energy, and they struggle to execute their meeting-assigned tasks well or with much enthusiasm and creativity.

If *generosity* ensures that attendees will depart the meeting believing that their requirements have been addressed, and if *empathy* helps them feel that they've been heard and understood, *energy* provides them with the drive to accomplish tasks at a high level.

By energy, I do not mean that you or the participants have to emerge with high fives and gung-ho, charge-the-hill attitudes. Instead, you turn the meeting into an energy source by offering clarity, belief, and a plan.

Clarity

The worst thing about a meeting is coming away more confused than when you went in. People hedge, obfuscate, fill meetings with buzzword bingo (e.g., *disrupt, transformation, platform*), and generally circle around an issue like a jetliner circling a busy airport but never landing. They cite statistics ad nauseum, and the combination of too much data (some of it redundant, some of it contradictory, a lot of it confusing) and too much nonsense causes participants to feel like they don't understand whatever was being conveyed.

To avoid this, I try to restate the problem or issue in three or fewer points. Ideally, a simple sentence suffices. I work hard to distill, to find the core versus the fluff. When people can grab on to a clear, concise articulation of an issue, they feel good. More than that, they can derive energy from clarity. It's galvanizing for them to feel like they get it.

One recommended technique: listen carefully for both words and emotion. At some point during the meeting someone will express a thought that is emotionally deep, but the words will be vague or convoluted or hard to grasp. *Emotional depth combined with inarticulate expression is often a sign of a critical issue.* Pay attention and use that information to help clarify the real takeaway from the meeting.

Belief

Do people believe they are capable of tackling the issue, of solving the problem, of capitalizing on the opportunity? Many times leaders assign tasks to individuals or teams, and they secretly believe they're in over their heads.

While this may be true in some instances, it's often just reflexive anxiety about a challenging assignment.

To counteract this eminently human response, communicate that you believe in them and their abilities. It is as simple as letting them know you are in their corner and see in them strength and capabilities they may not see.

You can also bolster belief by sharing stories of how others tackled this issue successfully or how you faced a similar situation while wondering whether you could handle it. Stories dramatize as well as humanize situations, allowing people who doubt their abilities to recognize that they're not the only ones who didn't believe in themselves—and others handled a task effectively despite initial anxiety.

When people believe, they are emboldened. They have confidence. They can draw on their belief to move forward and power through obstacles that would otherwise stop them in their tracks.

A Plan

People have the energy to move forward when they have a clear and viable map to get them where they want to go. When participants exit a meeting, leave them with steps to take to create forward momentum. It may not be the ultimate plan to solving the problem, but it's an interim plan for taking action. This is sometimes referred to as "chunking" work into doable blocks.

Help people leave with the answers to: What now? What next? What to do? It may be as simple as suggesting the first step, whether that is to research a topic, or interview an expert, or go online and find a supplier who can help. You can also schedule a follow-up meeting to assess progress. Making sure team participants understand the immediate steps to take following the meeting (and making sure those steps are doable) will leave them eager to get started.

A Small but Significant Meeting

Perhaps the most common type of meeting is the one between a boss and a direct report. Many times these meetings are short and task oriented, but others can delve into deeper issues. Some bosses use these meetings negatively, exhibiting bullying behavior, and other bosses are so spreadsheet oriented that they avoid any transparency, vulnerability, and empathy. Today these meetings are especially sensitive given cases of harassment and bullying by senior management.

I'd like to share an example of a boss who focused such a meeting on the story side of things. I'll warn you that this was not a politically correct interaction by today's standards, but back then people were less sensitive to these types of issues, so don't focus on what may seem like ethnic profiling.

In 1983, after a year in my job as a media buyer for the Leo Burnett Company, I had just received a stellar work review from my media supervisor and had been invited by her boss, Don, the media director, to stop by his office for a chat.

Don began our meeting by noting that I was doing a terrific job as a media buyer and that I brought a new level of analytical rigor, discipline, and drive to every task. He also said that I got along with everyone, actively sought new assignments, and took initiative.

As I was basking in this praise, Don asked me to close the door. I did so, and then I heard him say, "I am sorry to say that you are unlikely to be as successful as your skills and drive should ideally make you, because you are too different and people will not be comfortable with you."

The implication, of course, was that my dark skin and Indian ancestry would work against me as I attempted to move up the career ladder. Don outlined a number of obstacles that I would face:

- I failed to indulge in small talk with clients or with any of my colleagues. I focused my conversation on work or world events. I came off as always serious. My personality would tend to limit hanging out, going for beers, etc.
- I didn't understand the culture of the United States, and it showed. I knew US history but did not understand baseball, football, or a host of other things. All my colleagues had gone to US colleges, and I had attended school in India. It was hard for them to relate to me on any topic besides work. People liked me but had me pegged as a serious, monotrack worker bee.
- I needed to take more risks, speak up more even if I was not sure of the answer. Don noted that "bullshitting" is part of the American business style.

As you might imagine, I was stunned and mortified by Don's articulation of these obstacles. At the same time, I recognized that he was not telling me these things because he was mean-spirited. Despite their political incorrectness by today's standards, his words and his body language reflected his essential kindness; Don was known throughout the agency as being a soft-spoken gentleman.

Don moved on from the obstacles I faced to how I might overcome them. "I believe all of these issues are fixable," he said. "And I personally will help you overcome these obstacles if you accept what I have said is true and if you are willing to commit to addressing them."

I croaked out, "Yes, of course," still reeling but seeing light at the end of the tunnel.

Don laid out the plan he had created for me. It was, as you'll see, highly personal and unusual. It involved me committing to going to two sports events monthly (since we were in the media business, we got free tickets), accompanying his kids and some of my colleagues to college campuses in the Midwest and watching movies about college life, becoming a member of certain clubs (my boss facilitated my memberships), and a list of to-dos that had no relation to media planning, handling clients, or marketing.

I may have been initially upset during the meeting, but I left energized. Why?

First, Don provided *clarity* by speaking directly and specifically about my problems.

Second, he expressed his *belief* that I could be successful, and he was willing to take the time to help me fix my problems.

Third, he created a *plan* of action, even though it seemed strange to me to be required to see movies, attend ball games, and join clubs.

Fourth, Don exhibited *generosity* through taking the time to display his concern about my career in the company.

There was no reason for a very senior director to take a meeting with a junior employee. There was no reason for him to address issues that would impact my career in the future but had no impact on my productivity in the present. And there was no reason to spend the time and expend the effort to help me address obstacles.

But Don turned what is often a spreadsheet-type meeting into one that was also about story. He treated me as a person, not just as an employee. He taught me two things I always remember: (1) tell people where they stand, and (2) suggest and show them ways to improve.

It was a meeting that I am convinced provided the catalyst for what became a highly successful career.

———————————— KEY TAKEAWAYS ————————————

- The received wisdom of minimizing meetings and only going to ones that create value for you is wrong. More meetings create more opportunities for productive relationships.
- Meetings aren't just about numbers but also about people. To capitalize on the collective capacity of meeting attendees, managers should use the full range of LIFT tools at their disposal: Listen, Interact, Feel, and Transform.
- To make the most out of meetings, understand what type of meeting you are in, so you know how to listen empathetically, give generously, and leave people inspired and energized.

CHAPTER 10

UPGRADE YOUR MENTAL
OPERATING SYSTEM

In a digital age, employees can easily think like the algorithms to which they're exposed. Because they use social media and search engines so often, they are subjected to what mathematician Cathy O'Neil refers to in her book *Weapons of Math Destruction* as "opinion embedded in code."[1]

An algorithm is a step-by-step set of instructions written into code. While algorithms are code and enable much of life today, they have not been immaculately born and often contain built-in bias, having been created by people to achieve certain goals.[2]

As a Pew Research Center study concluded, "Algorithms have the capability to shape individuals' decisions without them even knowing it, giving those who have control of the algorithms an unfair position of power."[3]

My point isn't to beat up on algorithms—they obviously are crucial in a digital age—but to suggest that if we leave organizational employees to their own devices (pun intended), they will be reactive and biased in their thinking. They won't consider options beyond their own narrow beliefs; they will see the trends they're exposed to rather than explore ones on the periphery; and they will fail to consider that their ideas might be wrong or outdated since their screens are confirming their biases.[4] Or, in this book's terms, they'll fail to create their own story and instead follow the spreadsheet.

Organizations need their people to be the architects of their own minds. Let's describe what architecting means and why it's beneficial.

A Science and an Art

Architecture is about building things. It's the art of designing something creatively and the science of structure. It's about connecting dots into a unified whole. It's about integration. It's about the physical object being built based on the data and the aesthetics and the emotion it conveys.[5]

Goethe described architecture as "frozen music,"[6] and that term captures the solidity of a well-designed building as well as the art it represents.

Organizations need employees capable of thinking from both story and spreadsheet perspectives. They need people who are proactive and independent in shaping their ideas, who can rely on the data when necessary but can also depart from it and form their own ideas and opinions.

We must create work environments where this type of independent, self-directed thinking can thrive. When companies speak about growth, they need to move beyond the growth of financial numbers that can be captured in a spreadsheet and toward the growth of the people who work for them. They need to think about the story of growth. As much as personal and professional growth is an individual responsibility, leadership can do a lot to stimulate this development.

Obsessed with productivity and measurement, some companies fail to give the freedom people need to develop their own ideas and innovations relative to work. When organizations overstructure their work environments, they are like parents who sign up their kids for so many playgroups, lessons, and other activities that no time exists for reflection and exploration. The parenting analogy gets the point across, and who better to make it than Jack Ma, founder of Alibaba, who said this about work-life balance: "I told my son: you don't need to be in the top three in your class, being in the middle is fine, so long as your grades aren't too bad. Only this kind of person has enough free time to learn other skills."[7]

People are also more likely to architect where they feel free to take risks and speak their minds as opposed to in a workplace filled with bully-bosses, where they are taught to do as they're told *or else*. Similarly, environments that stimulate thought—that encourage creativity through exposure to diverse people and ideas—also facilitate architecting.

If you're a leader, at this point you're likely to say, "Our company has created this type of environment." No doubt most leaders are sincere when they make these statements. Too often, however, what they say and what their companies do are two different things. Even in an age when agility, innovation, and risk-taking are esteemed, many organizations remain focused on the spreadsheet—on order, control, repeated processes, numerical outcomes, and the lack of surprises.

CEOs especially hate surprises. A company's stock price crashes or soars whenever there is a surprise. No boss likes to be surprised. Jennifer Mueller noted in *Quartz* magazine that "IBM recently asked 1,500 executives which leadership characteristics they most desired in employees. The number one trait: You guessed it, creativity. But the same study noted that more than 50 percent of executives said they struggled with, and felt unprepared to recognize and embrace, creative solutions. Study after study shows that new ideas are chronically rejected at many companies, even businesses that say they want more innovation."[8]

To counteract this cognitive dissonance, organizations should create environments in which the following three traits are present:

A SENSE OF BALANCE. People are most likely to form their own opinions and think independent thoughts when balance exists. The most obvious balance—at least to readers of this book—is between story and spreadsheet. This translates into more specific balances in different areas.

First, there is a need to balance ends and means. If the goal is to achieve a numerical goal at all costs, balance is missing; people will ignore rules and even laws to achieve goals. For instance, Wells Fargo's focused efforts on rewarding and promoting people based on accounts opened and cross-sales made, regardless of whether customers needed these services. A second form of balance is recognizing that people have different skills and the company should not force consistency and conformity. Give people the freedom to follow their passions and do tasks their own way as much as possible; they will respond by developing their own ideas and styles for getting work done.

A MINIMUM OF FEAR. Certain types of fear serve a purpose and help people grow: fear of not doing a good job, fear of letting people down, or fear of not being able to support oneself. However, if fear becomes pervasive in an organization, it can limit thought and action. It not only shuts people up, since speaking up can lead to negative consequences, but it also shuts their minds down, since they know that thinking disruptive thoughts may also lead to disruptive actions. When people are constantly afraid, they don't think clearly or well. Instead of architecting, they hide in existing edifices.[9]

A GROWTH MINDSET. Psychology professor Carol Dweck writes about growth and fixed mindsets. A growth mindset embraces challenges, learns and grows from mistakes and criticism, and is persistent and resilient. A fixed mindset avoids challenges, ignores feedback, and gives up easily. Dweck's research shows that people are capable of changing their mindsets, and this is partially impacted by the environment in which they work and the feedback they receive.[10] A workplace that punishes mistakes and celebrates only success feeds a fixed mindset, while one that acknowledges effort and learning from failure and mistakes allows for building minds and skills.

Make Iteration and Improvement an Organizational Constant

Organizations transform when people transform their minds. It's not about redesigning work spaces or buying companies or creating new social media strategies. Part of mind architecture is a desire to learn, to grow, to acquire new knowledge and skills, to improve.

As a leader, you can implement the most sweeping, well-funded transformation plan in history, but if it's all external, it won't work. People must be able and willing to embrace iterative change and improvement for it to succeed.

Companies need to get people in the habit of setting and working toward small goals, of visualizing something that they might do differently and how they might put that into practice.

Transformation sounds like a huge leap, but it is only possible when lots of people take lots of tiny steps in the right direction. "A journey of a thousand miles begins with a single step," Lao Tze wrote in the *Tao Te Ching*.[11]

This concept of small steps applies to modern software writing and agile approaches through the idea of releases. Companies release software in an alpha or beta form and then continuously improve upon it.[12] Eric Ries talks about Minimum Viable Product—launching products into the marketplace and then continuously improving based on feedback.[13]

Encourage people to practice this same method of improvement: a goal, a plan to get to the goal, executing the plan frequently or daily, and then evaluating progress, which then feeds back into modifying the goal, plan, and execution. By thinking this way, people can build their minds and skills in a changing world.[14]

ADAM AND ERIC HENEGHAN

A Giant Step

Companies with soul are open to new people, ideas, and businesses. They are not rigid when it comes to culture or strategy. Instead, they invite people in whose perspectives may be different from their norms. They know the value of having a diverse group of stories under one roof.

In 1994, while leading Leo Burnett's fledgling Internet Marketing Group and looking for individuals with creative and production skills, I was introduced to the Heneghan brothers.

They had learned at an early age that the computer could be a creative tool. In college they started a digital marketing firm called Giant Step Productions that went on to count several Fortune 500 and Silicon Valley companies as clients. They then moved their company to Chicago and began working with agencies and their brands.

Around this time, Ed Artzt, Procter & Gamble CEO, gave a groundbreaking speech to the advertising community. In his address to agency CEOs and brand CMOs at the annual 4As gathering, he predicted the impact that technology would have on our lives and marketing. He believed that advertisers would divert much of their spending to interactive delivery, even before the internet was a platform for advertising.

The speech was a milestone for the ad community. The brothers' proven work created interest in a formal arrangement among the agencies that they had been working with.

We initially agreed to a deal where they remained independent and would co-reside with the Leo Burnett Interactive Group, bringing us both their creative expertise and their credibility.

In less than a year's time it became clear that the real value in interactive marketing was not necessarily the marketing and strategic plans but the ability to create, design, and deploy programs. What made us, and the small handful of similar agencies, different was having strategy informed by the people creating and pioneering the work. It functioned in tandem, as the marketing insight pushed their boundaries as well. This is what clients wanted and were willing to pay for: an early insight that is the current reality.

After working together successfully for a few years, they agreed to sell a majority to Leo Burnett and simply be called Giant Step. As part of the discussion, it was agreed that anybody joining the new group would be a Giant Step employee (I was the single exception), and we would in time move out of the Leo Burnett building at 35 West Wacker.

It was a giant step for Leo Burnett: this was the first time they had ever allowed an "outsider's" name to be on the door, as they replaced the Leo Burnett Interactive Group with Giant Step. Until then, taking the name off the door was tantamount to heresy.

But it allowed me and others in the agency to take a step forward. Adam and Eric brought something to Burnett that was previously missing—not just their expertise but their entrepreneurial zeal. They were a generation younger than me and lacked formal business or organizational training, but they gave me a master class in what it was to be an entrepreneur. I and others learned from them how to take good risks and also how to push back and walk away from clients who failed to provide the necessary revenue. Nothing clarifies the mind on the importance of cash flow like trying to make payroll. These were things I never had to bother about when I was at big Leo.

Ultimately, I moved away from Giant Step and back to Leo and other challenges, but Adam and Eric were instrumental to my and Leo's growth, bringing skills and experiences—their stories—that were absent from the company until their arrival.

In my thirty-seven-year career at Publicis Groupe, I have continuously reinvented what I have done by focusing on areas that I determined would be important in the future for my company, my industry, and my clients. I have moved from managing client accounts, to becoming an expert in direct marketing, to launching a start-up focusing on interactive marketing, to helping launch a spin-off media company, to becoming a digital expert, to becoming a strategist and innovation leader.

I've learned how to learn. It is the most important skill employees can possess. *Autodidact* means "self-taught." It suggests people who don't need formal training to learn; they have the impetus and ability to learn on their own. You want a company of autodidacts.

Here are three lessons every manager and leader should convey about how to learn and improve continuously:

1. **Be attentive to your discomfort.** Sometimes in a meeting or a conversation I hear people discussing things that either I was not previously aware of or do not understand. I write a note to myself about those topics or terms. To improve, we need to be aware of where we fall short. Addressing and listing knowledge gaps is a first step. Ignoring your lack of knowledge, or hoping that it won't be noticed or affect your job performance, is a bad idea. View this knowledge discomfort as a challenge.

2. **Invest time.** Learning requires time-consuming effort and practice. Convey to people that they can and should devote time each day to learning and not just completing tasks. Encourage digital exploration of a range of work topics, trying out new software, engaging on social media. Suggest they target areas of ignorance and seek sites, books, articles, and the like that can provide knowledge they lack.

3. **Practice or do.** When people architect minds, they don't confine this activity to their own minds. Two decades ago I began to hear about a company called America Online (AOL). So I bought a modem and went online and talked to other people about AOL. By doing and talking—and by thinking about what I heard and said—I began to understand the possibilities of this medium and its implications on the marketing business. If I had not gone online, I would not have understood. Similarly, when social media took off, I spent hours using Twitter, LinkedIn, and Facebook while reading books and articles about them. More recently I have played around with Bitcoin, AI, and other topics that seemed foreign to me.

Be aware that your people each have their own style of learning. Accommodate their different styles, but establish that everyone must have a goal (what they are learning about), a time to learn, and an opportunity to practice. It costs companies very little in out-of-pocket expenses to give people a few hours a month to pursue learning or offer people the opportunity to develop new skills by working in new areas. In fact, these actions telegraph that the company is serious about transformation and improvement. It communicates that they want their people to architect minds.

Recognize the Opposite Is Also True

To create the type of organization where people move beyond what algorithms tell them and allow their minds to expand and explore, encourage them to think in opposites. Here's a story that explains what I'm suggesting.

In 1982, when I applied for a job at Leo Burnett, I had to include an essay as part of the interviewing process. After I got the job, a couple of the interviewers noted that my essay had been a significant factor in their decision; thirty-four years later, one of those interviewers still remembered it. The essay's theme stated that the only way to be sure of your position on an issue is to build the strongest possible case for why the opposite belief is true.

To this day, whenever I make a recommendation, I build a strong case against it. Three compelling reasons exist for this practice:

1. **It helps sell your recommendation.** Whenever you build a strong case against your position, you can answer questions or address opposing viewpoints much easier since you have thought about the other side. It also communicates that you've considered the opposing position seriously—you're not making your recommendation lightly, which increases the power of your argument.
2. **It allows you to delineate areas of compromise.** A key to making a sale (to an external customer or an internal boss) is the willingness to compromise. By building an opposing case, you have a better understanding of what is (and what is not) essential. In this way you are more astute about what you can sacrifice to close a deal.
3. **It allows you to monitor and change your mind.** Considering the opposing point of view is a valuable cognitive exercise. It creates agility,

producing insights about all aspects of an issue that you might not otherwise consider. In a volatile world, understanding a range of positions is crucial, since you may need to adapt your position as circumstances dictate.

To a leader of an organization, oppositional thinking confers two advantages in an intensely digital age.

First, *it helps overcome the danger of filter bubbles.* We live and work in a world where opposing points of view are filtered by search engines, social media, and recommendation engines aligned with our interests. As a result, we find it increasingly easy to see only validating evidence and facts or to find a friend circle of only like-minded people.

No less of a digital authority than Bill Gates agrees, saying that technology "lets you go off with like-minded people, so you're not mixing and sharing and understanding other points of view. . . . It's super important. It's turned out to be more of a problem than I, or many others, would have expected."[15]

Second, *the speed of change means that the best position today might not be the best position tomorrow.* The metabolism of society works at a faster frequency. A single device like the mobile phone has upended everything from photography to taxi services to mapping to music. New breakthrough technologies from AI to biotech are moving so quickly that even IBM's Watson is finding it difficult to keep up-to-date.

In an age of disruption, disrupters challenge the status quo by questioning many of the assumptions of current models. To prevent being disrupted, you have to disrupt yourself, which means looking at ideas and decisions from an opposite point of view.

Consider using Red Team/Blue Team exercises, in which two teams build opposing points of views or solutions to a problem. This formal way of stimulating double-sided thinking creates the reflex to consider opposing concepts.

Upgrade Employees' Minds

In times of transformation, two ways exist for companies to remain relevant: transform existing employee mindsets or hire people with new mindsets.

Companies usually do both. Bringing in talent from outside has significant advantages in that it makes a company less insular and ensures that a constant stream of new skills are added to the company DNA. However, relying too much on external talent has significant disadvantages in the cost of hiring, the time it takes a new person to learn the ropes, and the signal this sends to talent inside the company whose growth opportunities may be capped.

Enter the architecture solution: upgrade the minds of as many employees as possible. Provide them with the means and the encouragement to learn continuously—or rather, to learn and unlearn. People need to forget old methods and processes while acquiring new skills and approaches. And learning needs to be ongoing both because change is continuous and because learning requires constant practice and upgrades.

Organizations can help people architect their minds relative to learning by providing three things:

1. **Knowledge.** This can be in the form of training or underwriting training, bringing in external speakers, sharing case studies, etc.
2. **Incentives.** Provide time to learn or rewards for new skills with increased compensation and promotions.
3. **Culture.** People need to feel comfortable practicing new skills, being learners, and making mistakes.

To help people take advantage of the learning environment, offer internal sharing and learning platforms, from Slack to AI-based bespoke platforms like Marcel, which we are creating at the Publicis Groupe.

Look for sharing platforms that are available and comprehensively connected. Being always available is key because people will have the need to learn and the time to learn at different times of their week or day; platforms should be optimized for mobile devices.

Besides availability, these platforms should have four types of connectivity:

1. **Knowledge.** From case studies to outside resources and document links.
2. **Tools.** Such as enhanced ways of dealing with time sheets and scheduling meetings.

3. **Experts.** A person who is the veritable fount of wisdom on a given topic and is willing to talk with interested parties.
4. **Opportunities.** Learning without doing is not very effective, so the link here is to opportunities to test new abilities in new situations.

I have used a combination of different online resources over the years to enhance my skills and learn at my own pace. Here a few that everyone can capitalize on:

KNOWLEDGE. In addition to Google or Baidu (if in China), here are two incredible free sources of deep knowledge: (1) podcasts available on Apple or Google Play and (2) free online resources such as Coursera and Khan Academy, which have amazingly helpful lectures and practice applications.

TOOLS. The two tools that I use for learning are: (1) Feedly, a reader application that fetches information from a variety of resources that the user selects. I have Feedly streams on a number of topics, enabling me to keep updated. (2) Evernote, a digital, always-available, easily searchable filing cabinet. I can copy and organize ideas and information that I discover online, adding pictures and attachments and much more.

EXPERTS. Three great resources for connecting and learning with experts are: (1) Quora, which is an Q&A site, (2) Twitter, where you can create lists of experts and follow and learn from them, and, of course, (3) LinkedIn.

OPPORTUNITIES. Companies can create proprietary tools that link people to teams seeking assistance in given areas, and others provide simulations that allow users to practice new skills in situations that mirror typical business scenarios. Invariably, however, most people receive opportunities daily in their emails and through other company digital forums—opportunities to take a course, to go on a retreat, to participate in a team-building exercise, and so on. Opportunities for learning are just a click away.

Best Practices for Digitally Saturated Minds

Some companies grasp the value of helping their people grow and develop their minds in a boundaryless manner. They understand the importance of counterbalancing the groupthink that can dominate in a digital age, and they go the extra mile to implement cognitive best practices. In some instances they create formal training programs that help employees architect their minds, such as GE's legendary program at Croton or the mind-opening programs at organizations like Amazon and SAS.[16] In other instances they create less-formal ways of encouraging people to think for themselves and figure out what methods and models make sense in their areas of the business.

Through my observations of these organizations, I've identified four best practices:

A WIDE VARIETY OF LEARNING OPPORTUNITIES. From training programs to workshops to guest speakers, forums exist for conveying all sorts of knowledge and ideas. In some ways, these companies mirror universities and have a rich array of learning experiences available for their people. The cultural norm is that learning is good, that people are expected to educate themselves continuously and broadly.

PRIORITIZING CUSTOMER COMMUNICATION. Jeff Bezos of Amazon and John Legere of T-Mobile encourage this practice among all employees, and Procter & Gamble's board and management also emphasize the need to listen to the customer voice. Most companies talk about the importance of listening to customers, but in some organizations, it's more than talk. They insist that people regularly spend time interacting at customer offices. They offer digital tools so that every employee has access to customer complaints, praise, and questions. In architecting their minds, employees need stimulation from the most important stakeholders in their universe. By accessing a steady stream of information from this source, people can formulate their own ideas about how best to meet customer requirements.

ROTATIONS. Organizations move people physically and cognitively, and they do so regularly and with as many people as possible. This can mean having people work on teams outside of their function or cross-functionally. It can mean opportunities to work in different divisions and offices. It can mean working in offices outside of their native country. The goal is to provide fresh perspectives by placing people in situations that are figuratively, and sometimes literally, foreign.

OPPORTUNITIES FOR BREAKS. Universities recognize the value in offering their professors the opportunity to take sabbaticals—it provides time away from the routine to reflect, to research, to theorize, and to see things in a new light. Similarly, companies are offering certain employees sabbaticals as well as insisting people take their allotted vacation time. Sometimes, workplaces can be all-consuming mentally. Enmeshed in stress-filled and task-filled environments, there isn't sufficient mental room to view initiatives and projects with a fresh eye. Breaks are critical for this purpose, offering the chance to step back and then return with renewed energy and ideas.

I've been fortunate to work for a company that has also embraced these best practices, but ultimately it's up to employees to take advantage of them in their own ways. For instance, the cultural norm that encouraged learning prompted me to pursue self-education in a manner that might not suit everyone. I wake up at 4:30 a.m. every morning and study for an hour or an hour and a half by reading books, visiting websites and exploring apps, and learning skills or tools. Even today, when I am invited to speak at a conference, I stay to listen to other speakers.

I take between 120 and 150 flights annually to interact with clients around the globe, and I have a goal of meeting and getting to know three or four new people weekly.

I have rotated through jobs in every area of my company in both operational and staff roles, both small and large, in emerging and established units.

And I take breaks, thanks in part to my wife, who calls my assistant and blocks out vacation weeks, and in part to my own practice of adding a day or two of vacation time to explore every new city I visit for work.

But these are just my own responses to my company's best practices. As long as companies make sure these practices are in place, employees with the initiative will find ways to adapt their own work behaviors to take advantage of them and, in so doing, view their jobs with increasingly creative, agile minds.

KEY TAKEAWAYS

- Regardless of how senior or established employees are, they all possess the capacity for growth and relevancy in changing times.
- Organizations need to set aside time for their people's mental self-improvement. They can encourage employees to escape digital routines and engage in tasks and conversations that stretch their minds.
- Today there are many amazing new ways of self-learning and improving, of which every person can take advantage of.

SECTION III

FUSING THE STORY AND THE SPREADSHEET:

Soul for the Machine Age

CHAPTER 11

ROBOTS COMPUTE. PEOPLE DREAM.

Imagine a world where driverless cars are the dominant mode of transportation and how this will change everything. Think about how the driving experience will be transformed into a sleeping, reading, movie-viewing, or working experience. Consider the spillover effect on the economy and how it will change the entire automobile industry. Think of the implications of a world without traffic jams, accidents, or parking lots.

As you reflected on this transformed universe, perhaps you thought about the implications of an employee-free workplace. No, I don't believe that employees will disappear, but I absolutely believe that what we're seeing today is only the start of a trend. As increasingly digitally dominant workplaces proliferate, we're in danger of losing crucial elements of organizations. The losses are insidious, doing their damage incrementally. They are eating away at the values, intrinsic satisfaction, and fun of work.

To understand what we're in danger of losing, we have to lift our eyes above the daily grind and see the big picture. We need to ask ourselves tough questions: What's wrong with everyone working from home in their pajamas? What do we lose if too many of us become figuratively or literally remote workers? The best companies will reflect deeply and continuously on these and other issues. And then they'll create policies and programs that prevent these losses.[1]

Go back to the opening analogy of driverless cars and consider not what is gained in this new digitally dominant world but what is lost: the feeling of joy and control when driving on a country road on a beautiful summer day with the windows down and the radio blasting a great song. This is the story side of driving, and it may be impossible to maintain this in the future.

But we can maintain story in a digitally transformed workplace if we're conscious of the issues. To foster this consciousness, let's look at one type of loss that's occurring.

The Loss of Deep Engagement

Companies used to talk about their people as family. In the wake of downsizing and in the midst of workplaces where people work remotely, travel constantly, and change jobs frequently, *family* no longer seems an appropriate term. But should workplaces be the opposite of family—impersonal environments where people measure their satisfaction by the size of their paycheck and bonus?

To address this question, let's start with the highly influential paper "Measuring Meaningful Work," which examines a number of studies and concludes that this type of work is aligned with passion and seen as a higher calling; growth in a job and making a difference in the world represents a greater purpose than income.[2]

Similarly, CEO Tony Schwartz identifies twelve attributes of a great workplace and notes that a key to these attributes is standing "for something beyond simply increasing profits. Create products or provide services or serve causes that clearly add value in the world, making it possible for employees to derive a sense of meaning from their work, and to feel good about the companies for which they work."[3]

Most organizational leaders probably agree with these notions of meaningful work, at least in the abstract. Yet in reality, many don't create the necessary conditions. Willis Towers Watson, a global advisory firm, found that two out of three workers were not fully engaged at work, with almost one-fifth completely disengaged.

"The most significant factors relate to how their supervisors support them on the job, their levels of stress and the severity of their workloads. For the detached, by contrast, company leadership stood as the focal point. Detached workers lack an emotional connection to the organization, stemming from feelings that they do not work for a company *with strong values, clear vision, and a leadership team that takes employees' interests and needs into account"* [emphasis added].[4]

Organizations possess a lot of physically and emotionally detached workers these days. Think of it from a landscape perspective. There's the physical landscape of offices, common areas, off-site meeting spaces, and so on. There's also the emotional landscape of relationships with bosses and fellow employees. People *feel* spaces and connections both emotionally and physically, and therefore work environments are key for establishing meaning and purpose. This is where the culture of a company is created and sustained.

In these spaces, stories are told: stories about values as related to customers, employees, communities, and shareholders. Stories about the company's founders, how it was founded, and why it exists beyond creating products and services. Stories that employees create as they find purpose and growth and meaning.[5]

These stories are lost, or at least diminished, when people fail to occupy physical and emotional spaces. When they're enmeshed in data, working remotely, transfixed by screens and not fully present for other reasons, people don't tell or hear the stories that imbue the workplace with meaning.

Companies such as Apple are brilliant at merging stories and spaces. In their offices, spaces become art, expressions of its stories and related values. As dependent as they are on digital, they keep the stories flowing.

This is the challenge in spreadsheet-dominant companies across the world. We need to make sure that we don't lose our stories as we become increasingly dependent on data. We need to make an extra effort to facilitate conversations and relationships in the spaces we occupy.

If George Orwell Could See Us Now

In Orwell's *1984*, he introduces the notion of Big Brother. If he were alive today, he might write about Big Employer. For years, blue-collar workers have complained about feeling like their every move is being monitored, first through punch-in time clocks and supervisors and more recently through video and digital techniques. Now this sense of being watched also applies to white-collar professionals. We know that our organizations are aware of when we're on our computers and phones, when we've stepped out of the office (via scanning technology), and when we're at our desks. They are especially aware of the apps and sites we're visiting on our devices and the messages we're sending via text and email.

This feeling is not paranoia if you're actually being watched. Workplaces are diminished when people feel as if they're being spied on. The loss of privacy is the initial problem, but it leads to a loss of free will—it feels like your choices are limited to what Big Brother wants you to do.

In this environment, we are less likely to share stories that we think might be interpreted negatively. Yes, digital vigilance can be warranted if shrinkage is occurring or productivity levels are low. Organizations also believe that by monitoring screen activities, they may be able to make suggestions to employees about how to improve their performance (i.e., "Mary, we noticed that you're overly blunt in your emails to your customers"). But what is lost because of this digital monitoring?[6]

It's not just the monitoring that affects corporate cultures and employee attitudes but also the overemphasis on translating everything into measurable terms. The eminent management theorist Peter Drucker is often misquoted by having the following attributed to him: "If you can't measure it, you can't manage it." He never said nor wrote this. Instead, Paul Zuk notes that Drucker's take on this subject was more qualitatively than quantitatively focused:

> [He] certainly did believe that measuring results and performance is crucial to an organization's effectiveness. . . . Drucker also knew that not everything could be held to this standard. "Your first role . . . is the personal one," Drucker told Bob Buford, a consulting client then running a cable TV business, in 1990. "It is the relationship with people, the development of mutual confidence, the identification of people, the creation of a community. This is something only you can do." Drucker went on: "It cannot be measured or easily defined. But it is not only a key function. It is one only you can perform."[7]

Another quote about this issue has been attributed erroneously to a famous individual known for his emphasis on measurement. Albert Einstein supposedly said, "Not everything that can be counted counts, and not everything that counts can be counted."[8] It was actually sociologist William Bruce Cameron who made this statement in his 1963 text *Informal Sociology: A Casual*

Introduction to Sociological Thinking. Cameron's quote is over five decades old and is from a time when computing machines were on the rise: "It would be nice if all of the data which sociologists require could be enumerated because then we could run them through IBM machines and draw charts as the economists do. However, *not everything that can be counted counts, and not everything that counts can be counted*" [emphasis added].[9]

Over the years I have watched presentations go from being about perspectives, words, and nuances that were supported by numbers to spreadsheets, displays, and mathematical probabilities with little insight or discussion. We are confusing numbers with facts, data with insights, and computation with decisions.

Think back to the Willis Towers Watson study that found two out of three workers weren't fully engaged. How can we expect to engage our people when data is so dominant? People feel constrained by all the data flowing across their screens, by their hyperconsciousness of being measured, by their knowledge that too soon their jobs may be replaced by AI.

On top of that, their jobs have become boring and unchallenging. So much of what people do at work these days is dictated by studies, reports, and trends. They aren't asked to use their experience, their gut, their creativity. Instead, they're asked to follow the numerical analysis.

Data is critical, but too much of it too much of the time sucks the meaning and joy out of work tasks. When our jobs lose excitement and challenge, we're never going to perform at as high a level as we should.

A Win-Win Scenario

Leaders don't want to lose the essence of their cultures, the values and practices and traditions that make their companies good places to work. They don't choose to sacrifice any of these assets. But the speed of the business, the need to be "always on everywhere," the ability and impulse to measure everything—all of this can overwhelm best intentions.

Walk through a large corporation today and observe what people are doing. What you're likely to find is that they're checking in, leveraging Slack, managing and monitoring social media feeds, creating "agile" routines and "scrum" meetings, and receiving alerts from mobiles at the slightest irregular data heartbeat. In this environment, people often aren't motivated to tell their stories, to go to the adjacent office or cubicle and shoot the shit. Leaders can preach the importance of this behavior, but their words often bounce off the data-buzzed brainpans of their people.

It takes more than talk to preserve cultures, and Starbucks is a company that has done a good job in this regard. Starbucks is at the leading edge of data and technology. With ninety million transactions a week in twenty-five thousand stores worldwide, the coffee giant uses big data and AI to help direct marketing, sales, and business decisions. Its mobile app is consistently one of the most downloaded apps. Starbucks leverages data to decide where to open stores and what flavors of coffee to promote at retail, and they are leveraging AI to create virtual baristas.[10]

At the same time, however, the company strives to be values-driven, inclusive, and cognizant of the individual requirements and development of employees. This starts at the top with founder Howard Schultz and flows down through the organization. The emphasis on story is consistent and wide-ranging. You can see it even in data-centric operations—the company has more than thirteen million rewards members, and the data derived from this usage helps the company personalize services and build relationships.[11]

For years, Starbucks has been recognized as a leader in providing extremely generous benefits for employees; they even offered health insurance for part-time employees. They also provide excellent education stipends for their people who want to go back to school. The company is environmentally conscious and supports good causes. And even though they've received their share of criticism in some areas (e.g., an incident in a Philadelphia Starbucks when the manager called police because two black men refused to leave the store[12]), they have a remarkably positive record when it comes to diversity policies and environmental issues.

Howard Schultz recently said, "Everyone one [*sic*] of us here, regardless of product or service, we are all in the people business. It's the humanity of a company that is going to create the long-term value. Without humanity and without values, you end up with a company that makes money but doesn't stand for anything and really has nothing to be proud of. So, lead with your heart."[13]

Companies like Starbucks have strong humanistic streaks. They do a lot of good in the world, donating money to worthy causes as well as being active philanthropists in a variety of ways. For them, doing and being good go hand in hand with making money and other performance measures. Making life better for others and making money are not mutually exclusive.

Schultz recognizes that people—both customers and employees—need to believe in stories that are more than data stringed together. From a barista's innovative solution, to a customer's problem, to the company's commitment to recycling and reducing waste, Starbucks attempts to do far more than pile up the numbers.

Contrasts: You Can Choose Not to Lose

Organizations need to ask themselves: Do we want to be like Southwest or United Airlines?

When I give talks about spreadsheet and story, an audience member often protests that at his or her company, tech is advancing so fast that people are devoting all their time and energy to just trying to keep up; that new software, social media initiatives, and technologies are being introduced daily, and leadership has to focus myopically on the tech side of things or they'll fall behind competitors; and that their workplace represents a new world of work where people are clicking, coding, and measuring constantly.

I don't know about you, but I don't want to work in such a place. More to the point, I don't believe people can work effectively when they've lost the ability to hang out, brainstorm, reflect, and feel free of the pressure to constantly measure what they're doing. Even more to the point, people don't want to do business with organizations where the spreadsheet-story balance is out of whack.

Look at Southwest and United. Both companies are absolutely dependent on data and technology, and they're measuring their performance consistently. Employees at both companies must have an almost religious adherence to processes and procedures, given how crucial safety and timeliness are in their industry.

At Southwest, though, they prioritize customers over process (though certain processes must be followed), view employees as family, avoid layoffs, and encourage people to express themselves creatively. At United, individual expression is discouraged. That's why a captain flying a Southwest plane might get on the intercom and provide passengers with the score of a pivotal game being played in the city they're flying to or from. On United, they act like this game doesn't exist.[14]

It's not surprising that United has been grappling with a series of ugly PR incidents recently, while Southwest boasts the following results:

- 2.4 percent voluntary turnover
- 44 consecutive years of profitability
- Lowest number of customer complaints
- 85 percent employees proud to work for Southwest
- No layoffs and no furloughs ever[15]

United is not alone in their focus on the spreadsheet. In fact, it's alarming how many companies have fallen into this trap. Wells Fargo continues to struggle with a culture built on driving results at all costs, even if it meant selling completely irrelevant and costly services to their customers. The University of Phoenix has been the subject of a series of state and federal investigations that allege the company used aggressive and deceptive recruiting, advertising, and financial aid practices. Negative perceptions of the University of Phoenix may be one factor contributing to the decline in the school's enrollment. In 2012 the university announced it would be closing 115 locations and laying off 800 employees—5 percent of its workforce. Between 2010 and 2017, student enrollment fell by 70 percent.[16]

I'm not suggesting that all companies obsessed with profit and measurement are guilty of unethical or illegal practices. I do, however, think that every company in every field is feeling the competitive heat, and the response can be to cross a line in order to make more money. As a former math major, I know how seductive the numbers can be. It's easy to become enmeshed in numerical calculations and manipulations and fail to see the larger picture.

But even if companies don't commit ethical breaches, an obsession with digital and data can diminish their cultures. In the coming years, more companies are going to be introducing sophisticated blockchain and AI systems, and these systems can dominate the workplace. Do we want to entrust decision-making to machines? And if we do, how will this affect the morale and creativity of the people who remain?

In her book *Retirement and Its Discontents*, Michelle Pannor Silver's research reveals that for millions of people work is much more than the output or income they generate. It is a source of meaning and social identity. It is where they feel intellectually stimulated and can express their creative selves. It is where they feel a sense of community and connection.[17]

If organizations lose these attributes, they will struggle to attract and retain the best talent. Admittedly, this is a challenge when they feel in a mad competitive scramble and think that only by devoting all their time and money to data, measurement, and the like can they survive. At the same time, they need to find a middle ground, a place where they make room for story, for meaning and identify. If they lose these crucial elements, what does it matter that they can measure stuff in nanos?

Why We Can't Lose Community

When workplaces become as bland and impersonal as a room at a discount hotel, organizations are in a lot of trouble. Though we're not there yet, we're heading in that direction. In companies with high turnover rates, where people do a lot of traveling and often work remotely and on screens, it's difficult to develop relationships and an esprit de corps.

People are looking for work to provide a sense of community as never before. In a *Harvard Business Review* article, Lori Goler and her colleagues identified three factors as necessary for job satisfaction: career, community, and cause: "Community is about people; feeling respected, cared about and recognized by others. It drives our sense of connection and belongingness."[18]

You might think that community is only important to certain types of people holding certain types of jobs in certain countries. Goler, however, found that community (as well as the two other factors) transcend types. In fact, on a 5.0 scale, engineers rated the importance of community at 4.18—a surprisingly high rating from a group that is often thought of as idiosyncratic loners.

Think about community as a forum for storytelling in the broadest definition of that term. In any organization where people have a strong sense of community, they also are constantly telling and listening to stories—stories about the behavior of bosses, about the machinations of teams, about the heroic efforts of one leader and the villainous actions of another. More than that, stories about the organization reside in all employees' heads. A major merger with a competitor a few years ago is analogous to a historical treaty signing between formerly warring nations—this event and everything that led up to it is embedded in people's consciousness.

The multiple stories of an organizational community provide people with common language, ideas, and personalities, offering a narrative of which they are a part. As Goler asserts, community fosters a sense of "connection and belongingness," and these positive attributes emanate from the ongoing organizational story.[19]

At a time when people change jobs with almost the same regularity with which they change their passwords, community keeps people loyal to their organizations. More than that, in a volatile, uncertain world of work, it provides certainty and satisfaction. We need to be aware that in our rush toward all things digital, we're endangering this sense of community.

In author Don DeLillo's landmark novel *Underworld*, he writes:

I was driving a Lexus through a rustling wind. This is a car assembled in a work area that's completely free of human presence. Not a spot of mortal sweat, except, okay, for the guys who drive the product out of the plant—allow a little moisture when they grip the wheel. The system flows forever onward, automated to priestly nuance, every gliding movement back-referenced for prime performance. Hollow bodies coming in endless sequence. There's nobody on the line with caffeine nerves or a history of clinical depression. Just the eerie weave of chromium alloys carried in interlocking arcs, block iron and asphalt sheeting, soaring ornaments of coachwork fitted and merged. Robots tightening bolts, programmed drudges that do not dream of family dead.[20]

This paragraph has stayed with me for a long time, particularly these three lines:

Hollow bodies coming in endless sequence.

There's nobody on the line with caffeine nerves or a history of clinical depression. . . .

Robots tightening bolts, programmed drudges that do not dream of family dead.

All industries are becoming increasingly automated. While DeLillo's book described robots in an auto plant, we now see robots of some type nearly everywhere. With the dawning of AI, the rise of intelligent objects with the IoT, and new interfaces such as voice, we will see our workplaces augmented, encrusted, and infested with machines of every type.

In today's distributed workplace, where we interact across screens with machines that spew data that is collated and compiled by computers, how do we maintain a sense of community? If people don't gather regularly around the water cooler or in the coffee room, if they don't each lunch together, if they don't gather after meetings to dissect and discuss what took place, if they are 50 percent less physically present in the office than ten years ago, then how can we create work communities?

Yes, they can be created virtually, but I guarantee you that online gatherings do not provide the same meaning and satisfaction as getting together after work for drinks or exchanging stories about the brilliant speech a company leader just made.

To understand the value of community, consider that one of the fastest-growing and most valuable private companies in America is WeWork. Their selling proposition includes creating a sense of community and connectedness among professionals, particularly today's growing cohort of freelancers, remote, and gig-economy workers, who are willing to pay for connection versus working in isolation.[21]

This hunger for community and connection can be seen everywhere, from Starbucks to SoulCycle. The more we glower at screens and the screens glow back, the more we need to feel connected with others even if all of us are sitting side by side, glowering and basked in glow. If organizations do a good job of creating a community within an increasingly digital space, they increase the odds that we will strike up a conversation, share a smile and a story, and build a resonant bond, which is hard to do with machines—even if they now speak back to us.

How Tech Companies Fight Against Loss of Meaning

You would think that Silicon Valley companies would be the most unbalanced of them all, that because they're all about digital and data, they would be spreadsheet-focused to the extreme.

Yet that's not the case. Jeff Bezos spoke to the Economics Club of Washington and said, "All of my best decisions in business and in life have been made with heart, intuition, guts . . . not analysis. . . . If you can make a decision with analysis, you should do so. But it turns out in life that your most important decisions are always made with instinct and intuition, taste, heart."[22]

Not coincidentally, Amazon is one of the few companies that has banned people from using PowerPoint presentations and insists on written narratives.[23]

Similarly, when Marissa Mayer became the CEO of Yahoo a few years ago, she insisted that remote workers return to work so they could reignite teams and connections that she believed were keys to innovation.[24]

Surprisingly the most technology-oriented and left brain–oriented companies are often the most driven to create community at work and encourage their people to take risks, to express their feelings, and to work in teams. They value play more than many traditional corporations, and they recognize that innovation often starts in the heart or the gut rather than the head. Perhaps it's because they're more aware than most of the effect that a digitally intense environment can have on policies and practices. Perhaps because tech is in their blood, they're more sensitized to what happens when people spend most of their day staring at screens.

This sensitivity may explain why so many tech companies have integrated the university campus model into their organizations. Campuses represent places to study, places to play, places to congregate, but most important, communities of students. The ultimate value of the experience is as much learning from other students, forming relationships, and making connections as it is the classroom experience. University campuses prevent the loss of creativity, cognition, collaboration, and communication.

Apple, Facebook, Google, and others have modeled their office headquarters after university campuses. We see this same model used by tech companies around the world, including Tencent in China and Infosys in India.[25] A cynic might say that these companies like the campus model because it enables people to spend their entire waking hours at work and therefore become more productive. With food and laundry facilities and break rooms with video games and exercise equipment, there's all the comforts of home—and all the more time to spend writing code or selling product.

No doubt, there's some validity to the cynic's perspective. Still, the bigger issue is the type of culture and work environment these campuses foster. The leading tech companies know that providing work spaces that are warm, comfortable, and offer all types of resources and activities are preferable to cost-efficient, relatively spartan, traditional office spaces. In fact, it would not surprise me if a growing number of employees are provided "bed and board," encouraging an integration of the personal and professional.

A Cautionary Note: The Loss of Ethics

In recent years some spreadsheet-dominant companies, feeling the pressure from Wall Street as well as motivated by their own personal gain, have done everything possible to make their companies look great on paper—downsizing, insisting on across-the-board cost reductions, pursuing short-term profits at the expense of long-term sustainability, and even fudging the balance sheet. This mercenary, short-term numbers approach can create a loss of a different sort—the loss of morality.

One of the world's premier cancer institutions is Sloan Kettering in New York City. By mid-2018 the institution was facing turbulent times as it became increasingly clear that top executives and doctors there were leveraging clinical data to help start-ups that they were investing in on their own. This was after the chief medical officer resigned when it became apparent he had failed to disclose some of his financial ties to the health and drug industries in dozens of his research articles.[26]

Today the institution is facing a breakdown in trust across various stakeholders as its lack of transparency and increasing focus on personal and financial gain versus medical service is impacting its reputation and its ability to attract government and charitable funding and pioneering research.

If a well-regarded brand like Sloan Kettering that is not even focused on making money begins to get greedy, we can only imagine what happens to institutions where intense pressure exists for profit. When companies focus on financial as well as other numerical metrics and leadership creates a culture of short-term urgency and importance on making the numbers at all costs, the companies begin to rot; their leadership has stopped managing the firm and is being managed by numbers.[27]

In turn, employees quickly understand this focus and work at optimizing their own numbers at all costs since they see all decisions are short term and that helping others or thinking long term will put them at risk.

Fortunately, most organizations have not lost their ethics completely. Most are fighting to retain their values. But my warning about this loss is not hyperbolic. The more we become obsessed with measurement and the need to produce better numbers, the easier it is to rationalize behaviors that value performance to the exclusion of all else.

KEY TAKEAWAYS

- People need more than their screens and social media. They need purpose, meaning, and community. They do things that do not compute and are moved by things that do not fit in algorithms.
- The best businesses find ways to marry the math and the magic, the silicon, digital, data-driven landscape with the analog, carbon-based, feeling souls that fill the landscape.
- Focus on goals beyond the immediate and measurable, if sustained success is the goal. Weigh the balance sheet of numbers and assets against the balance sheet of reputation and goodwill, and accommodate both.

CHAPTER 12

HOW TO LEAD WITH SOUL

B eing a manager today requires a different mindset as well as a different skill set than even ten years ago. In a digitally transforming world, bosses need to know their spreadsheets—they have to be adept at managing people using all the data at their fingertips. At the same time, they need to lean away from the numbers so they don't lose the story side, the qualities that build human connection. If they fail to empathize and inspire, for instance, they might as well be managing robots.

If you're a boss, you might think that combining spreadsheet and story is relatively easy. It's not. As you'll discover, numerous factors favor managing by the numbers, discouraging the types of interactions that cause people to be engaged, energized, and creative.

It's not that bosses had it easy in the old days. Being a good boss has always been a challenge. It's just that today the degree of difficulty is higher because many managers have become overreliant on data and it colors their relationships—especially with their direct reports.[1]

To find the right balance between spreadsheet and story, bosses need to be aware of the factors that have had a profound influence on their management style and substance.

Seismic and Interconnected Forces

If you think of boss types on a continuum, on the extreme left are the touchy-feely managers. They manage by instinct and experience, and they encourage their people to come in and talk to them—their door is always open. On the far right are command-and-control bosses, and they follow orders and expect their people to follow them in turn—they believe strongly in being authoritative and decisive.

Both types have positive attributes, but being only one type is no longer feasible in our changing world. Let's look at some of the major, interconnected changes that are affecting how people manage in organizations.

Mindset Diversity

Generation Z turned twenty-one in 2018. Forty-six percent are not Caucasian, and none of them recall a world without mobile phones, search engines, and social media. Members of this generation are joining companies whose most senior leadership is still primarily white men that used to work with typewriters rather than computers and who had to search for information in libraries rather than online.

It's not just technology that divides older and younger employees, but also mindset. And it's not just the difference between baby boomers and younger generations. Generation Z is showing startling differences in mindset from millennials in that they are far more risk averse, having borne the brunt of a serious economic downturn, student debt, and other generation-specific issues.[2]

On top of all this are the more obvious differences created by a more diverse and global workforce. As a result, bosses can't manage all their people the same way. They need to adapt their style to meet the needs of a range of mindsets and preferences.

Globally Interconnected, Flexibly Structured

The combination of a global workforce and flexible work environments (e.g., working from home) demands a new style of management. How do you motivate people you rarely see? How do you connect and communicate with people in different countries, on the road, and in open work areas?

Data Intensity

I've discussed the availability of and dependence on data in previous chapters, but think about it from a "noise" standpoint. How do bosses get their people to listen when they're constantly receiving messages from mobile devices and social media apps? How do leaders convince them to follow a path that isn't dictated by the data, that flies in the face of information they're receiving?

Velocity

The global workforce is always working somewhere day or night, is equipped with social and mobile tools, and possesses computational abilities to monitor and measure every heartbeat of the business. All these factors allow us to accelerate work on projects. Should bosses feel free to engage with their people at 2:00 a.m.? Should they expect them to work far harder and faster than in the past? Should they impose deadlines that require breakneck work speed?

Here's the result of all these workplace changes: the best bosses have learned to change their own behaviors. Specifically, these changes have had the following effects on managers:

- **Negated the command-and-control style.** When the workforce is diverse, spread out, and moving fast, it is difficult to shout out orders. People no longer respond well to bosses who tell them what to do, who act like they know everything. They are much more responsive to bosses who know how to influence—who suggest ideas and steer people gently.
- **Mandated fast decision-making.** As the metabolic rate of business picks up, so does the need to make decisions quickly. Slow decisions are often decisions in themselves since it means you decided not to decide.
- **Motivated big-picture thinking.** We live in a connected age, and if you can't step back when you manage and see the links between dots, you're not going to succeed. Bosses need the vision to see far and wide and then help their people make connections between disparate ideas and information.

Given these effects, you need both spreadsheet and story abilities to be effective. Let's look at a story-side capability that many traditional bosses underuse.

The Notion of Emotion

In diverse, data-centric, fast-moving cultures, bosses must balance their natural cognitive reflexes with less familiar affective responses. Or, put another way, in a world of machines, people long for the human touch. The last thing they need is a robotic boss who provides them with all the information they need to do their jobs but none of the honesty, empathy, humility, inspiration, and vulnerability that help them do their jobs better. These five emotional qualities will help bosses communicate with and motivate their people more effectively.

Honesty

The basis of any relationship is trust. If you cannot trust your boss, nothing else matters. Trust is about honesty. Will your boss tell you the truth to facilitate your improvement even if it hurts? Will your boss level with you about your chances for a promotion?

In today's fast-moving and highly competitive environment, the less time people spend worrying about what a boss "really means," the more likely they are to succeed. Rock-solid trust between leaders and their followers not only saves valuable time but provides insights about how to improve and achieve goals. I often say that "trust is speed."

The honesty of bosses also has a cumulative benefit to the organization. In a world where a breakdown of trust has occurred, people yearn for transparency and authenticity. The more honest bosses an organization has, the better its reputation. Remember, it's not companies that are inherently dishonest or immoral; it's the people who work at these companies. When the majority of leaders and managers possess integrity, the odds are that their institutions reflect these qualities. Today, when trust is a key factor around the world, bosses with integrity are crucial.

Empathy

Most often people quit bosses, not jobs. While they might not like their assignments, they can tolerate boring or routine tasks for a period of time as long as they have a boss who empathizes with them. In stressful, challenging environments, people need bosses who get what they're going through. The unempathetic boss who, when a direct report complains about a difficult customer, says, "I don't care that he's difficult; figure out how to deal with him," crushes the spirit of the direct report.

People want to feel that their bosses "get them," that when they're having problems at work or with family, health, and other challenges, their bosses demonstrate understanding of them both as a person and a professional.

Humility

To understand an employee's needs, bosses must be both approachable and willing to look beyond their own self-interest. Humility makes these two essential actions possible. Humble bosses recognize that success is a team effort often driven by the people whom they coach and delegate work to. This ability to share the spotlight and promote others attracts talented people who want to make sure that their achievements are recognized.

Humility also fosters learning and growth. When bosses recognize that the company is bigger than just them, they are more willing to manage people in ways that help the company rather than build their own egos.

Inspiration

This is a powerful driver to unleash employees' potential as well as provide the energy to overcome challenges. Inspiration is about being a motivating role model, but it's also about reminding people of their potential and ability to thrive regardless of circumstances. It's not just a bright, glowing star to steer by but also the ability to stoke passions and ensure that the spark of potential produces achievement and action.

Vulnerability

Bosses are people too, and like all people, even the best of them feel unsure and confused and feel out of their depths at times. Brené Brown has written about how vulnerability is a sign of leadership.[3]

These five emotional qualities are soft skills in an increasingly hard world; more than ever before, they drive great organizational performance. For more than fifteen years I worked closely with two of the most successful people in the advertising and communication business: Maurice Levy and Jack Klues. Both were honest, empathetic, humble, inspiring, and vulnerable, but they were also intensely competitive people who hated to lose. They understood and drove financial results and made one hard decision after the other. They held people to impossibly high standards and drove themselves and their teams hard.

What differentiated them from other hard-driving leaders, though, was their willingness to sit and listen, their straightforwardness, their ability to motivate. Working for them, I always appreciated their emotional openness and intelligence, even though they were focused on quantitative results. They didn't shy away from difficult client conversations, nor did they put themselves above the company—they loved being flag bearers for the company's traditions and practices.

As busy as they both were, they always made time for me when I needed their help. Yes, they were capable of kicking me in the butt if I messed up, but they also gave me the flexibility I needed to explore what I was passionate about and reduced my workload if I had personal issues that needed addressing. And I never worried that they would undercut me or fail to deliver on promises. All of this made me intensely loyal to Maurice and Jack and work harder to achieve our goals.

In a world where everything is measured and compared—especially salaries—companies should understand that money and other financial incentives are only short-term tactics to keep people in place and working hard. To create sustainable employees, companies need lots of bosses who are like Maurice and Jack.

While they had been my bosses for nearly twenty years, they had been preceded by many other great bosses, including my first full-time boss, Kathryn Milano.

KATHRYN MILANO

Let Your Direct Reports Shine

Some managers boss by numbers. I'm not just referring to managing by using data but to being a stereotypical boss: issuing orders, failing to offer much support, taking all the credit. These bosses get stuck in a box that narrowly defines how they should act instead of managing authentically.

In 1984 I was a media buyer and planner on the Allstate Insurance account reporting to Kathryn Milano, who in addition to being an amazing media thinker was besotted with all things Jane Austen. Initially I believe the only redeeming quality I had in her eyes was that I had read Jane Austen and so was seen as civilized compared to many of my Western-trained colleagues who were not familiar with the author. Kate always wanted to ensure we used language well, even if we were describing and making math cases.

From day one Kate would take me with her to bosses' and clients' offices and note that I had worked on the project that she was presenting. Once she had socialized me to them, she began having me present the work that I had done under her guidance. After a while, she would review my presentations before the meetings and often have me go by myself.

My counterparts on other accounts were flabbergasted and wondered whether Kate was planning to leave; they couldn't believe that she had moved so far from the boss norm and was allowing me to present on my own.

Kate had explained that once she was comfortable that I could handle these tasks, she wanted me to present for clients because it would make my work more rewarding, and I would grow and learn faster. Her motivation, though, wasn't completely altruistic; freeing up her time in this way, she could tackle bigger and more difficult assignments that would prepare her for being a director. She became known as a great trainer, which attracted more talent and let her offload more work and take on more of her bosses' work.

Kate taught me how to shine a light on people who work for you. Many other supervisors have their buyers do a lot of the work and then present it to their bosses and clients themselves. Kate didn't care that her managerial approach wasn't like that of most other bosses. Instead, she saw the value of sharing the limelight and the credit. She didn't boss by the numbers, and through her actions, she allowed me to avoid working by the numbers.

Over the course of my career, I've learned that the best bosses let others shine. As someone once told me, if you see a lot of bright, shiny planets all around, there must be a star in their midst.

The Problem with Bad Bosses Today

While bad bosses have always been problematic, they are of special concern in today's business environment. As we'll see, their behaviors drive employees into full-spreadsheet mode; they create fear, and fear leads their people to seek refuge in data to cover their butts and justify their actions.

But I'm getting ahead of myself. To grasp the impact of bad bosses today, we need to identify their distinct types and how they affect their people. Leo Tolstoy wrote, "Happy families are all alike; every unhappy family is unhappy in its own way."[4] Similarly, each bad boss is terrible in his or her own way. Nonetheless, I've managed to group all these "unique" terrible traits into the following four categories:

THE NARCISSISTIC GOD. These bosses believe that only they know the answer, only they are capable of handling the major meeting, and only they should get the credit for their teams' success. They often believe they transcend the company. In many instances, they create a godlike cult that worships their every move, using public relations and social media to spread the word.

Their people worship them by following their commandments. Direct reports lose their own individuality when they're working for Narcissistic Gods; they also lose their ability to draw upon their own experiences and skills to solve problems or capitalize on opportunities. Their story gets lost, and they become mindless followers.

THE MICROMANAGING FIDDLER. These folks are terrific operators—they know how to get things done—but as managers, they retain their obsessive detail orientation. They tell their people what to do and insist they check in with them at every stage. They are insecure and can't let go of anything. They often manage via spreadsheets or the need for slavish following of systematic procedures. Micromanaging Fiddlers fail to understand the outside world since they are constrained by the cell of the spreadsheet or slaves to historical procedures.

Obviously, direct reports are driven to spreadsheet thinking by these managers. If they deviate—if they suggest risky ideas or do things their own way—they face censure or worse.

THE OSCAR ASPIRANT. These types emote, loudly and dramatically. Erratic and unpredictable, they are a roller coaster of emotions. They greet bad news with histrionics and good news with hyperbole. These drama kings and queens are tolerated by management because they can be effective in certain roles—they can present well and even inspire others with their visions and speeches.

At the same time, they make their people crazy. People are expected to praise the boss's performance or to raise their spirits. More to the point, these managers only want one story told, and it's theirs. As a result, direct reports aren't allowed to bring their own ideas, experiences, and views to the group. The story of the boss overwhelms everything and everyone else.

THE DOUBLE AGENT ASSASSIN. While the previous three types are expressive in their terribleness, Assassins are soft-spoken, well-behaved, and self-controlled. Behind closed doors, however, they take credit for other people's work, create animosity by speaking ill of people to others, and find ways to trip up others and make them fail. They are like Reese Witherspoon in the movie *Election*: smiling and ruthless. They win people's trust and then undermine them.

People working for Assassins become guarded and monitor everything they say and do for fear that it will be used against them. They carry out tasks with little creativity and take little risk, knowing that even a minor slipup will give the Assassin an opportunity to target them. They are driven to spreadsheet thinking because they fear for their work lives—keeping a low profile and cleaving to their tasks is the only way they can escape the Assassin's bullets.

All four bad boss types know that if they deliver their numbers and meet their objectives, they can continue to exist in most organizations. This is especially true if these organizations have spreadsheet-dominant cultures where measurement is constant and meeting quarterly numbers is the highest priority.[5]

Bad bosses are the enemies of balance; they provoke extreme reactions from their people. If the employees don't leave the company, they work in fear or expend all their energy on managing their managers. No doubt you've witnessed employees go into survival mode to deal with a bad boss. They become obsequious, robotic, and myopically focused on their boss's every action and reaction. As a result, they may be able to carry out assigned tasks effectively and help their bosses meet their numbers and objectives, but they are loath to take risks or deviate from norms. At a time when innovation is crucial, they fall short because innovation requires behaviors that bad bosses hate. The balance is tipped heavily in favor of playing it safe.

Bad bosses unbalance companies in another way: they force people to face inward instead of outward. Whenever I hear people speak more about what their bosses have done or how to manage their idiosyncrasies, I remind them that they were hired to listen to the marketplace and customers.

In the advertising and marketing world to which I belong, clients need people to bring them outside perspectives and to keep the customers in mind. Our real bosses are the people we wish to develop relationships with and sell to—not someone in our organization or even our clients' organizations. The best thing we can do for our internal bosses is to make sure our external bosses do not fire us. Which is why looking outside and seeing tomorrow versus looking inside and being nostalgic for yesterday helps provide balance. Bad bosses keep us staring at our shoes. Good bosses encourage us to lift our heads and look around.

The Best Bosses Apply the Story to the Spreadsheet

Great bosses think about how to maximize not only the outcome of the job but the impact of the employee. By growing the skills and confidence of the employee, they double and triple the results of the short-term, self-aggrandizing boss. They seek balance—between the internal and external, between the short term and the long term, between team outcomes and internal employee growth. And between the spreadsheet and the story.

Great bosses impact the spreadsheet through stories:

- stories that inspire;
- stories that teach;
- stories that resonate; and
- stories that motivate.

They share their own stories of failures as well as successes. These bosses encourage their people to talk about their own experiences and offer their perspectives. They believe in ongoing dialogues, whether in person or through various devices. As long as they get their people engaged and thinking widely and deeply, they've done their jobs.

And it's not that they fail to hold their teams accountable to deliver results and meet goals. They set and deliver deadlines. They leverage facts and data to feed decision-making. In these ways they are left-brained and spreadsheet-driven.

But these bosses also realize that the spreadsheet is the scoreboard and not the ball or the player. They keep an eye on the ball, which is the market and their customers, and on the players, who are their employees. Like great coaches they goad and inspire, push and commiserate, and speak to the unique strengths and vulnerabilities of each player. They empathize, and they keep things in perspective.

I referred earlier to Jack Klues, my boss between 1999 and 2013, who connected the story and spreadsheet better than anyone else with whom I've worked. Jack was driven, understood numbers and spreadsheets, and held people accountable to high standards of performance and behavior. This helped him go from running $100 million of revenue in 1999 to nearly $4 billion of revenue in 2013, relying on the combination of double-digit organic growth and skillfully integrating a series of mergers and acquisitions.

But for all his business acumen and delivery of the numbers, he understood that success would be driven through motivated and inspired teams of people with diverse mindsets. Jack surrounded himself with different types of people from different cultures and backgrounds who shared his drive to excel. He supported these people even when they disagreed, listening intently to people with fresh thinking as well as ideas that opposed the current plans. In fact, he often put me in the role of chief provocateur, encouraging me to question his thinking and decision-making.

Despite his seniority and sterling track record, Jack never forgot that he was one person in a company, and the company and its long-term success mattered more than any individual. He was always approachable and willing to fight for what was right—even if it meant angering a client.

While I have described what good bosses and bad bosses are, the reality is that all of us have within us the ingredients of being a good or bad boss, and we must be aware and resist the bad tendencies while feeding the good tendencies.

In addition, we need to be aware and fight against two additional forces that detract from being a leader with soul.

Resisting Screen-and-Process Management

First, the legal department and human resources are driving the documentation trend. Not only do they want to minimize the emotional messiness of dealing with people (e.g., the anger and tears when people are passed over for a promotion, terminated, etc.), but they are scared of lawsuits and regulatory bodies. By documenting a process to make a decision and by reducing the numerical ranges and variables to make qualitative calls, they can more easily justify their decision . . . and if it comes to it, make their case in court.

In our litigious society, bosses need to be aware of the possibility of legal action, and they need to follow processes that ensure fairness as well as protect the organization. At a certain point, however, following process and procedure hamstrings managers. It prevents them from responding to employees as individuals. It stops them from using their knowledge of and relationship with an employee to provide direction and explanation. They become the equivalent of telemarketers, forced to follow a script.

If a boss can't personalize conversations, what's the point of developing manager–direct report relationships?

Again, balance is the solution—a balance between story and spreadsheet and, more specifically, between personalization and process. Document rules, procedures, and expected behaviors. Be transparent on what is and is not acceptable. Create clear performance metrics and spell out criteria. Identify and report issues. Involve HR up front and when necessary in meetings where things may turn unwieldy. This is the scaffolding that not only protects the company but telegraphs fairness.

At the same time, give bosses room to empathize, customize, and personalize by recognizing that each employee is unique. They have different skills, dreams, concerns, and constraints. They and their careers are stories, and at any given time they are in different chapters of their growth. Accept that some interactions can and should deviate from the norm. The best bosses are insightful about their people and empathetic about their issues. Organizations should encourage all bosses to use these insights and empathy to help their people learn and grow—and give difficult feedback when necessary.

Second, technology that makes "remote" management possible is also a force that can become an obstacle. By remote, I'm referring both to the geographical distance between manager and direct report and the emotional distance. It's now possible to work with people with whom you have little or no daily, weekly, or even monthly contact. You can monitor their performance via the data they enter into the system and communicate with them through text, email, and video conferencing. Even when a boss meets in person with a direct report, they can both be staring at screens, the conversation centering on charts, reports, and other digitally displayed data.

Jeff Bezos of Amazon has at his beck and call more data than probably any other businessperson on the planet, and if he wanted to, he could run his global company from his office, relying on technology that allows him to give direction to his people through various devices. But Bezos flies to his many markets and walks around the offices he visits. He continuously learns and spends a week every year at TED.

Diversity of thinking is encouraged, but then Bezos gets people to move forward once a decision is made. He calls this "disagree-but-commit."[6] Voice your point of view, build a case, but once a decision is made, commit to delivering.

He also resists the pull of technology management consistently and effectively, unlike Eddie Lampert, chairman of Sears. Having watched Eddie in action, I know that he is a highly intelligent, passionate, and committed leader. At the same time, he seems to revert to remote mode frequently. As an article in the *Wall Street Journal* observed, "He visited the Hoffman Estates, Ill., headquarters a few times a year, preferring to beam in via conference calls from ESL's Florida offices, they said. While most retail executives visit stores weekly, Mr. Lampert urged Sears executives to hold video chats with store managers, arguing that they could collect more data, more quickly."[7]

Eddie tried to take on Amazon from a distance, depending on numerical spreadsheets and video conference calls with a continuously churning staff. He saw the data but rarely recognized what it signaled. When he saw the signals, he did not know how to go where they were pointing and failed to hire people who could get him where he wanted to go. And if he went in the wrong direction, apparently no one told him to come back since they either were no good or too afraid or reconciled to being always overruled.[8]

Eddie gave long talks about technology and marketing via screens, and while he spoke with certainty, his on-screen persona was intimidating and unapproachable. Sears has had (and still has) a lot of problems, and it seemed like Eddie had an opportunity to rally the troops. But it's tough to rally anyone if you're overly dependent on devices to do so. While screens are great tools to convey data, they aren't so great when you need to motivate and inspire.

Yet I understand the temptation of managing through screens. It is faster and more efficient. It filters out the messy emotions of face-to-face interactions. It fosters a sense of control and power. But if you're tempted to make screens your primary managerial tool, consider these negatives:

- **You won't get the whole story.** Data is always massaged or flows from the questions being asked. Through firsthand observation and dialogue, you are stimulated to ask additional questions, to engage in spontaneous conversation that often uncovers ideas or information that is missed in pure digital management.
- **You won't motivate your people to go beyond what's required.** You won't be able to communicate powerfully and personally, causing them to stretch their abilities and think innovatively about an issue.
- **You may put yourself out of a job.** If your managerial method is to compute and respond to what is on a screen, you can be replaced with an AI bot or tool that can process much faster without any of your biases.

Of course, we're never going back to a time when screens were a minor part of our management. They provide all sorts of benefits that no manager can do without. So I'm not saying to put your screens and data in mothballs. I am suggesting that you integrate the following behavior into your management tool chest:

Make yourself move and see beyond the screen and the spreadsheet. Running a company by managing teams remotely via a spreadsheet on a computer screen is often like trying to influence the world from a prison. There is a reason that the components of a spreadsheet are called cells! The data captured filters out things that do not fit and filters out the human emotion behind the numbers.

Since data is available to you anywhere, you're free to be mobile. Get out of the office, walk the floor, travel to different offices and conferences. Discuss their data and their work rather than use their data to determine what to discuss with them. They have stories about themselves and their business that don't fit in the predetermined cells of spreadsheets. You want a boots-on-the-ground presence combined with all the data that flows across your screen. This combination will broaden your perspective and make you a much more effective boss.

KEY TAKEAWAYS

- Each of us has worked for good and bad bosses, and each of us has in us the traits of being a good or bad leader. Bosses may be tempted to manage their people via devices, but if they fail to mix in a sufficient amount of personal interaction, they will be leading with too much algorithm and too little heart.
- To ensure leaders accentuate the positive while minimizing the negative, they need to understand whom they work for and how both of them behave in different circumstances.
- Becoming a good leader is a continuous journey, with some detours and dead ends and no finish line. Leaders require continuous learning, from both story and spreadsheet. No matter how successful leaders are and the goals they achieve, they still need to dedicate themselves to learning from screens and from people.

CONCLUSION:

Thriving in the Third Connected Age

In 1989 Tim Berners-Lee invented the World Wide Web and launched the modern era of the internet. Between 1989 and 2007—for eighteen years—we lived in the First Connected Age, where the key connection was a link on a web page. The company that best monetized how to organize and search through the links was Google, and the company that best monetized e-commerce on the other side of the link was Amazon. Search and e-commerce were the big benefits of the First Connected Age, and they reordered everything from newspapers to magazines to retail. Amazon and Google are two of the most valuable companies in the world.

In 2007 we entered the Second Connected Age, where the modern mobile device and social networks came to be. We were now connected all the time and connected everywhere. The company that best monetized mobile was Apple, and the one that best monetized social was Facebook; both joined the ranks of the most valuable companies.

Today we are entering the Third Connected Age, where there will be four additional connection points building on search, e-commerce, social, and mobile. These are data connecting to data via deep learning that drives AI, things connecting to things via the IoT, new ways of connecting such as voice and augmented and virtual reality (VR), and much more powerful ways of being connected via 5G.[1]

The coming years are going to bring all types of digital breakthroughs—some foreseeable, some not. I don't think anyone would argue against the premise that the world of work is going to change in the next five or ten years, that everything from robotics to AI will transform workplaces again and again. No doubt we'll be staring at screens even more intently in the future than we are now.

Despite this, I'm convinced that the majority of organizations will not become soulless machines, cranking out products and services with great efficiency and little empathy or creativity. Instead, they'll find ways to integrate story and spreadsheet and by doing so will restore the soul of business. They'll recognize that, ultimately, organizations are most effective when they're places in which relationships, ideas, and risk-taking are allowed to flourish; that as important as measurement is, meaning is equally important; that people who think blockchain is the holy grail are blockheads.

The story and the spreadsheet isn't a contradiction but a paradox; you don't have to choose between the two but find the right balance. To see how to move forward in a balanced direction, let's look at emerging trends and how they might play out in the future.

The Implications of Intense Connections

According to a November 2017 McKinsey study, while only 5 percent of jobs can be fully automated, 60 percent of all jobs have some parts that will be automated to a great degree. By 2030 this will result in the displacement of 400–800 million people around the world from their jobs, requiring them to be retrained. Physical jobs that are repetitive, office support, and basic customer support and retail will be the most impacted.[2]

This is not just a US phenomenon but a global one. For instance, according to CNBC, between 2012 and 2016 massive iPhone producer Foxconn's operating revenues increased slightly, but its head count declined by almost one-third. More than four hundred thousand jobs were eliminated as tens of thousands of "Foxbots," factory robots, were deployed. Foxconn is targeting 30 percent automation by 2020.[3]

Amazon, which today employs more than six hundred thousand people, is increasingly automating its warehouses, where it has more than one hundred thousand robots. Its algorithms for pricing and recommendations are getting so good that its machine learning is replacing humans.[4]

These and many other studies and projections suggest we're on the cusp of the Third Connected Age, where a combination of AI, the IoT, and new communication technologies of voice, augmented, and virtual reality will change everything; they will take work and play to a new level, building on changes wrought by the First Connected Age of search and e-commerce and the Second Connected age of social and mobile.

We will be surrounded by devices that sense and anticipate what we need, that will embed and extend themselves everywhere as everything accelerates because of faster chips and 5G speeds.

In this world, what will our roles be as humans generally and as leaders and managers specifically? Where can and will we add value to ensure a productive and meaningful life? Will we use advanced machines to extend ourselves or will advanced machines extend so much into our worlds that there will be little place for us?

Again, I'm an optimist about science and people as well as a mathematician with an abiding interest in technology. I believe we can and will be better off as humans and organizations in the future, but the path forward will require courage, political leadership, and patience.

Here are the challenges we must meet to realize this optimistic future:

THE SPEED OF CHANGE. While things have been changing relatively fast in the past decade, the rate of change will increase exponentially in the next decade as we enter the Third Connected Age. In fact, it may outstrip human capability to adapt and the ability of political and legal institutions to keep pace.

Part of the problem is that some of us react to change without questions or conscience; we aren't concerned that we've ceded decision-making to machines. Some of us, though, have the opposite reaction to change. We long for a slower, more easily understood past and distrust all the changes speeding by us. We become insecure and tuck our heads in the sand; if we ignore it, maybe it will go away.

It won't. We need to learn how to work when everything is moving a lot faster than previous speed limits.

THE GLUT OF DATA AND COLONIZATION OF TECHNOLOGY. According to a recent *New Yorker* article, the average doctor in the United States spent two hours in front of a computer for every hour they spent with a patient.[5] Scientists are overwhelmed with the reality that 2.5 million new scientific papers are published every year and this number is increasing. The constraints of a twenty-four-hour day and the limits of the human mind are no match for the infinite speed and abilities of machines.

Accept that data is everywhere and that you can't process as fast as machines, but don't think for a second that human instinct, experience, and creativity are "less than" data. That doctor's hour with a patient is far more valuable than the two hours in front of a screen.

THE HYPERCONNECTED WORLD. The world is with us too much. Between updates, notifications, breaking news, FaceTime calls, instant messaging, social media, and more, we feel ourselves enmeshed in a web of impulses, stimuli, and expectations. Much of this stimulus is algorithmically optimized to get us addicted and engaged. As technology improves the stimuli of computing—through virtual reality and other means—we will be increasingly drawn to digital connections and increasingly more likely to be isolated from others. Again, we must strive to resist the pull to digital so we live and work in a balanced manner.

If these challenges seem daunting to businesses seeking balance, never fear: opportunities exist in equal measure. Technology has given organizations the opportunity to help their people:

LIVE AND WORK MORE MEANINGFULLY. As machines take over mundane or boring jobs, they will free up people's time and minds to do more fulfilling things—to come up with better products and processes or create innovative tactics and visionary strategies.

While technology eliminates some jobs, it gives birth to others. Because of advances in transportation and the wealth created due to globalization, more jobs exist today in tourism than years ago, despite many travel agents having lost their jobs. In the Western world, one million more people work in tourism than in agriculture. In organizations, we have more opportunities to pursue impactful, fulfilling assignments rather than repeat rote tasks.

EXPLORE AND SEIZE OPTIONS. Modern technology allows us to work from home, the road, anywhere we choose. While Uber has negatively impacted the price of medallions and the livelihood of taxi drivers, it has made us a more mobile society and created alternate revenue streams. Modern technology offers more choices even when it eliminates some options and industries. Yes, many great movie theaters and record stores are gone, but surely a world with Netflix and Spotify is a much better one than if these services didn't exist. More to the point, technology offers us all sorts of fresh ways to work, from incorporating social media into the mix to offering tools for instant research.

MAKE CONNECTIONS. Our minds and our sophisticated language separate humanity from other living beings. Companies like Google, Apple, and Facebook are so valuable because they amplify our minds and our ability to communicate. These and other technologies help us connect with each other more than ever before. Even since we've made a connection leap—from the first seafaring lanes to internet cables—the world has been better off. The more we find ways to capitalize on enhanced connectivity, the better off our businesses will be.

Capitalizing on these opportunities, however, can be a challenge when you're swept away in a daily data avalanche. It's all too easy to tip the balance toward the spreadsheet, and it's just as problematic to tip it too far in the story direction. We need to face the following realities, and in so doing, find a viable midpoint:

IN WHATEVER JOBS OR PARTS OF JOBS TECHNOLOGY CAN DO BETTER THAN PEOPLE, THEY WILL REPLACE PEOPLE IN THOSE PARTS OR JOBS. This is inevitable because of the Darwinian reality of capitalism. Productivity drives wealth and growth, and if one can get more output for less input, the economy or company that optimizes this will win.

LEADERS AND INSTITUTIONS SHOULD INVEST IN PREPARING THEMSELVES FOR THIS REALITY. You can't fight the future. Leaders of countries and companies need to recognize that a significant percentage of their respective populations will possess skills and knowledge that are no longer as valuable as they once were. This means we need programs for retraining people so they can acquire valuable skills and knowledge and find good jobs.

People who are too far on the story side of the continuum may resist this reality with good intentions and bad results. And there are reality-deniers who blame immigration and globalization for people losing their jobs, while the truth is that we in the West are never going back to the "good old days" of big factories everywhere that depended on lots and lots of workers.

INDIVIDUALS SHOULD INVEST IN THEMSELVES AND IN UNDERSTANDING HOW TO ADD VALUE IN THIS NEW WORLD. To paraphrase John F. Kennedy, ask not what your company can do for you, but what you can do for your company. Individual responsibility for relevant skill development is a key to future success—for both the individual and the organization. Perhaps more to the point, we need to maximize our value by melding our uniquely human traits to technology.

Creativity and empathy are hugely important overlays for maximizing tech value. Creatively, we can find new ways to use social media to benefit the organization. Empathically, we can recognize the pain points employees have when working with a given system and find ways to eliminate the pain. We must leverage our human abilities to maximize machine capabilities.

Tech Is Nothing without Talent

This last point has been the subject of some debate. At this point, I hope I've waved the yellow flag with sufficient vigor. The worst-case scenario is that our embrace of technology may leave people in the dust: as we become ever more reliant on data and measurement and robotics, organizations will lose the ability to rely on instinct, to draw on experience, to take risks, to be innovative and agile.

It doesn't have to be this way. As much as I've warned about the dangers of too much digital without enough analog, I believe that organizations will recognize the value of people even as they're becoming increasingly dependent on machines. Most organizational leaders aren't *technomaniacs*; they realize that historically, people have been responsible for their companies' success and that people will be responsible for it in the future.

Leaders do need a nudge toward this realization. They must think about the implications of the rise of data: how every company is becoming a software and data company to survive, and the rules of cold, calculating math and algorithms could drive out the people and ideas that lack a spreadsheet-only focus.

Fortunately, a number of highly tech-oriented company leaders have thought through this issue and pursued a balanced strategy.

Among the most valuable companies in the world is Apple. It has harnessed technology and logistics to an unprecedented extent by building an incredible supply chain in China and offshore financial engineering, among other financial and data-driven decisions. But what makes Apple valuable is its creativity and design. Most people forget that when Apple first launched the Apple Store, Dell was a market leader in the category, having built the ultimate low-cost manufacturing and distribution machine through direct sales. Dell machines were cheaper and often better powered than Macs but a combination of design, ease of use, and the Apple brand and stores helped them dominate Dell and made Apple the leader. Today Apple is investing deeply in all things community and creative with its stores, in content and in its advocacy for privacy.

It's not just Apple; many other companies from Rolex and Patek in Swiss watches to Domino's Pizza combine technology and humanity to win in their categories.

Rolex today sells 70 percent of all watches that cost more than $5,000, and they have used the most modern of technologies to run their factories. The premium they or Patek receive for their products has nothing to do with the machines but everything to do with the art. Both companies have used technology for what machines can do better, and both—particularly Patek— have hundreds of artisans whose work, as well as the design and legacy of their brand (all of which is emotion and not rational), creates the value for them.

Domino's Pizza went from a low-cost, low-quality pizza with fast home delivery to a much higher-quality pizza with technology that customizes delivery and customer monitoring (of the pizza's progress from ovens to the customer's door). Domino's uses technology as an ingredient to separate itself from competitors, and if you had invested in them ten years ago you would have a better return than if you'd invested in Apple, Google, or Amazon. Domino's realized that when it comes to fast food, people wanted greater control over where their food was delivered and wanted more transparency about when it was delivered. They used technology to meet this human requirement.

The best companies leverage technology and data to be successful today, but they do more than this to ensure their success tomorrow. To sustain success, they do more than find a brilliant way to use blockchain or to capitalize on an algorithm. Technology has only limited value without the human component for two reasons:

Technology is a commodity.

First, with a few exceptions, almost all technology can be outsourced and rarely is a long-term form of competitive advantage; even the most innovative technologies are knocked off quickly. Combining technology with other ingredients, however, creates sustainable edges. The other ingredients are almost always noncomputational and irrational. These include provenance (the history of a brand or its people), design, experience, innovation, branding, and storytelling.

Talent is a differentiator.

If a company is run purely by data and machines, it will quickly fail because the most talented people in such companies will have no meaningful role. In these organizations, math is the decision maker. Just as important, while technology is good at detecting patterns and projecting the predictable, it's poor at anticipating anomalies and surprises. People do a much better job at reacting on the fly to sudden twists and turns; they're the ones who have to recalibrate and re-engineer the machine.

The path forward seems obvious when we're looking at it from the removed perspective of a book, but it's tougher to see when you're in the thick of things. Think back to a time when new modes of transportation or electricity were being introduced. Companies that failed to leverage these developments fell by the wayside. At the same, relying exclusively on electricity or transportation for a competitive edge was not an effective long-term strategy (because every successful company possessed these resources).

Now and especially in the future, organizations must find the sweet spot between the two. Focusing on organizational design and the mindset of its talent is a way to find it.

As you've read, I love the phrase, "the future does not fit in the containers of the past." It is no use leveraging data and technology if you're trying to stuff tomorrow into today. Think about how Uber is organized; or rather, think about how it is not organized—like a taxi company with taxi company skills. It has no medallions, full-time employees or drivers, and no depots. Instead it has mapping, computational technology, and recommendation engines. Uber leadership designed a company and its talent to what the customer needs and how they buy or use the product.

In addition, the talent in the company must be trained and incented to optimize the future while defending the past. In his book *Freakonomics*, Steven Levitt shows time after time that if you want to understand someone's behavior, you must study their incentives.[6] Too many leaders talk about tomorrow but organize for today and incentivize to protect yesterday.

Why? Because cannibalizing your own business feels suicidal and demolishing your legacy structure is expensive. Leaders may also know that their people lack the skills necessary to thrive in the future or may be scared by the expense of hiring people who possess these skills.

So it's scary. But it's also necessary. Companies can't map future strategies and expect to succeed unless they hire the right people, give them the right incentives, and develop them in ways that help them leverage new technologies.

That's a tall order, admittedly, but it's one that can be filled if companies seek balance. The problem, of course, is *exponential* change.

Runaway Machines

When technology advances exponentially, society and organizations benefit while some people suffer. Yuval Harari, author of *Sapiens* and *Homo Deus*, worries that a combination of AI and advanced biotechnology will so alter society that more and more people will be replaced by machines, creating a group of individuals who belong to the "useless class." Harari rails against a quasi-religious order that embraces "data-ism," concentrating power and wealth within a "super class."[7]

It's not only Harari who warns of the danger of exponential change. Luminaries such as Elon Musk and Bill Gates worry that the capabilities of AI have become so advanced that managing their use is too important to be left to technologists alone; government and societal groups must be involved.

I'd offer similar advice to organizational leaders: don't turn over all the power for tech decisions to your tech people. Leaders and managers in nontech disciplines need to be involved in the decision-making process. They're the ones who have to raise yellow or red flags when the harm a new tech innovation causes outweighs the good. They're the ones who always have to ask: What is the people downside of this innovative _____? (Fill in your company's digital blank.) Are our employees, customers, and other stakeholders going to be frustrated, confused, dispirited? How many people will lose their jobs because of this?

With technology adoption comes responsibility. It doesn't matter whether you're a parent, a technocrat, or an organizational leader. You're responsible for the technology you've brought into the world.

Part of this responsibility is legal. Governments are paying attention since the algorithmic power of digital media impacts elections and outbreaks of violence and civil strife. The monopolistic tendencies of Google, Amazon, and Facebook may lead to antitrust action.

As technology spreads, parents worry about the impact of screens on children. Harari believes in disconnecting and silence to such an extent that he does not speak for two hours daily and two months yearly.[8] (I've already shared my own less radical disconnecting routine.)

Ultimately, humankind will master machine and restore the balance between technological advances and human concerns. Doing so, however, will require a heightened consciousness about these issues and corresponding actions—an investment in education and retraining to minimize social impact. We will also require leaders who can find ways to align people with technology (versus those leaders who turn a blind eye to technology's effects or who have a Luddite-like opposition to technology).

Here is just a sampling of emerging technologies or technology-related trends that will have a huge, lasting impact:

1. AI, from machine learning to natural language processing
2. Biotechnology, particularly gene-editing technology such as Crispr and CAR T-cell therapy
3. Computing advances such as Quantum computing
4. Data transference at high speeds everywhere to all devices as we move to 5G
5. Environmental changes driven by global warming and new frontiers of ocean agriculture and mining
6. Full-scale changes in big industries: automobiles with electric, self-driving, and on-demand cars; finance with computer-driven portfolios and trading; retail with omnichannel juggernauts such as

Amazon and Walmart; and new direct-to-consumer brands such as Dollar Shave Club and Casper; and health care and education, which are still stuck in the past even though both medicine and knowledge have soared into the future

We need leaders who not only adopt and promote exponential technologies but who speak out about the negative effects of these technologies. From Tim Berners-Lee, who created the World Wide Web and is calling for a less commercial and snooping web, to Salesforce CEO Marc Benioff, who is speaking out on the societal evils of inequality, we need leaders with a conscience, leaders with empathy, leaders who recognize the value of finding the middle ground.

Making the Connection

I've touched on this point earlier, but I want to expand it based on three future developments. Digital connectivity leads to analog empathy. The more ways we have to connect with other people, the more opportunities we have to develop empathy and meaningful work relationships.

Your organization may be filled with tech geeks, but behind their external obsessions with cryptocurrency, blockchain, and coding reside beating hearts. Human beings crave connection and are communal animals. More than two billion people check into Facebook every single day, and many of them want nothing more than to reach out to someone who is their friend. Historically, people used to do this all the time at religious and community gatherings, but today they're connecting online.

Many people criticize online connecting as superficial or tribal. In the former instance, we're sharing trivial information, the type of exchange that fails to build relationships. In the latter, we connect only with people who share our points of view, denying ourselves the chance to debate and reflect, learn and grow.

Real empathy and meaningful relationships develop only when we connect on a deeper level. I believe three existing and spreading technologies will facilitate empathy and meaningful work relationships:

1. **Voice.** More than a billion people already have phones with the equivalent of translation machines, which allow people speaking different languages to converse with each other. In 2018, during the World Cup, one of the most popular apps in Moscow was Google Translate, which connected people from all over the world. Siri, Alexa, and Google Assistant represent another form of voice technology.

   In global organizations, translation apps make it far easier to communicate with people in offices around the world—it's a lot easier to empathize with others when we can understand them. Siri, Alexa, and Google Assistant facilitate our search for information and ideas, providing easy access to knowledge that we might never have encountered before. This knowledge can range from a provocative business theory to case histories of innovative companies. Whatever it is, it can be a catalyst for conversations—new and stimulating ideas prompt us to share them with others.

2. **5G.** It's one hundred times more powerful than today's technology. Imagine a world where everybody can access applications, services, and utilities instantaneously. 5G will make today's connection feel as slow and dilapidated as dial-up modems. The faster and more pervasively we can connect, the more ideas we can access and the more people we can touch and be touched by.

3. **Visual, augmented, and mixed reality.** Talk about empathy: virtual reality will allow us to be educated about and to literally walk in the shoes of others. Or imagine visiting an office in another city for the first time and flowing across a device connected to our eyes are facts and figures about every person and object encountered—this is augmented reality. It will help us find kindred spirits in other companies as well as people who possess opposing but credible viewpoints. Augmented reality can make us aware of people we need to talk to and get to know—we might not even be aware of these individuals' existence without this technological tool.

These technologies are as much about connection as computation and provide organizations with the chance to implement an organic balance of spreadsheet and story. Savvy businesses will leverage these opportunities, recognizing how valuable these inherently balanced technologies are.

In fact, we're already seeing this happening in the hospitality sector. Major hotels are embedding voice technologies into their rooms, allowing guests to run room functions or learn about the property and city they are in. Soon their destination guides will embed AR and interactive voice response and translation to make individuals feel more at home and informed wherever they are.

Business will use these not only to decrease costs but to increase the experience of customers. Beyond the customer experience improvements resulting directly from the new technologies, employees will gain valuable minutes—or even hours—daily to focus on tasks that use their experience and expertise, their creativity and relationship-building abilities. As information retrieval and dissemination become automated and delivered through easy interfaces, people will no longer be spending the bulk of their time doing mindless or repetitive tasks.

Service reps, for instance, will be able to listen carefully to the requests that cannot be handled by machines. This could be people who—due to age, training, or disability—are not able to get the information they need or because new information systems give rise to new, unexpected questions. It also will give reps the additional time they need to engage in two-way, deeper conversations— the kind of conversations that are most helpful to customers and that provides reps with the most satisfaction. This is what leads to connection and empathy.

Of course, spreadsheet-minded organizations will only concentrate on the efficiencies of these new technologies. Spreadsheet-story organizations, on the other hand, will look at the benefits beyond cost savings and maximize the empathy and relationship-building aspects inherent in these technologies. Training in empathy and relationship-building will become even more common in the future.

Technology Opens the Door for New Stories

Again, I'm defining story in the broadest business sense possible. People have ideas they want to test. They have improvements to processes, new product concepts, and more effective ways of managing customer relationships. Customers and suppliers have their own stories too—stories about bad service as well as ones designed to put their own spin on the supply chain.

As I've discussed, screens, social media, algorithms, and other products of our digital age can suppress these stories; the emphasis on data and measurement, the lack of face-to-face time and other factors can discourage people from articulating their ideas and convincing others of their value.

But technology is also capable of communicating stories. Let me tell you about my older daughter, an aspiring filmmaker. In October 2018, I assisted her on the set of her second movie, *Shadows*, which she directed and wrote. My job was that of the "best boy" grip: picking up equipment from rental houses, moving lighting and rigging equipment from location to location, and filling in wherever the crew needed help.

Over my five days on set, I marveled at how modern technology was allowing her to tell her story. Here are seven ways technology facilitated the process:

1. **Access to studio-level equipment.** The superior capabilities of digital camera and sound equipment, which are increasingly portable, allowed her to rent for a few thousand dollars what would have cost millions of dollars ten years ago.
2. **Fund-raising.** Our daughter raised the funds for her movie via a crowdfunding site called Seed and Spark, to which she uploaded videos, distributed updates, and set out a menu of benefits for different levels of investment.
3. **Locations.** All of her locations were rented via Airbnb, and we moved from locations in Queens to Brooklyn in a rented U-Haul truck, finding our way with Google Maps to neighborhoods with which none of us were familiar.
4. **Casting.** A combination of mobile video and online sites allowed her the ability to cast a wide net and find unique characters for her movie. By sharing her script via a former colleague, she even had a leading cast member of the Netflix show *Orange Is the New Black* available for a day to play a key role.
5. **Logistics.** The script called for shooting primarily at night, and most days the shoot ended at 3:00 a.m. But being in distant parts of Queens and Brooklyn was no hurdle, as a cavalcade of "limos" provided by Uber and Lyft arrived to take the crew home. They conference-called with each other on their mobile phones, plotting the next day as they

were driven home. And, of course, online restaurant menus and Uber Eats made food services easy.

6. **Dailies.** At the end of every day's shoot, the film was captured on hard drives, uploaded to the cloud, and could be accessed and viewed and listened to in real time.

7. **Distribution.** While filming her second movie, our daughter was negotiating distribution of her first movie with a couple of streaming sites.

Modern technology reduced the film's cost from around $1 million (the estimated cost a few years ago) to less than $15,000 today, but the real breakthrough was the opportunity for my daughter and others to tell a story. Her movie touches on religion, family, and fear of the "other," and it was made despite not being as commercially viable as, say, a superhero movie. It was also a film whose director, cinematographer, writer, producers, assistant director, production designer, and sound mixer were all women.

And it was a movie whose primary cast members were Hispanic (one of the reasons a lead character from *Orange Is the New Black* agreed to be in the movie was the rarity of featured roles for Hispanic women).

My daughter's experience is just a microcosm of a larger trend. The Time's Up movement is leveraging social media to enable fairness in hiring practices. And streaming options, from Netflix to Amazon to niche platforms, are creating a renaissance in storytelling that is more inclusive and offers a broader spectrum of film that resonates with diverse cultures.

Organizations should endeavor to use social media, new software programs, digital communication tools, and other technologies to help tell people's stories—from employees to customers to vendors to partners. When doing so, they need to keep the following two pieces of advice in mind (one of which I've shared, one of which is new):

1. The future does not fit the containers of the past.
2. The future does not come from the heavens but the slime.

The future does not fit in the containers of the past.

Giving people a voice means more than allowing them to blog on the company website or setting up a digital forum for customers to air their complaints.

That is nothing more than the old suggestion box approach. Every aspect of business is being rewired, and embedding the new technology into the old ways of working will not be enough. Uber did not just become a competitor to taxis but an alternative to car ownership. No garages. No vehicles. No drivers.

Mary Meeker of Silicon Valley venture capital firm Kleiner Perkins speaks about how every business must learn to reimagine themselves for the future.[9] What will GM be when fewer people own cars or the cars are increasingly electric and shared? Will internal combustion and dealership knowledge matter? Will driving experience matter if most of the time the car is driven by someone else or is self-driven?

A company that has reinvented itself with great success after being written off by Wall Street is Best Buy. Here is a company that married cutting-edge technology and speed by being willing to match any competitor's price immediately in the store, leveraged their store locations to arrange even faster deliveries than Amazon, and most important, used knowledgeable people—whether it be blue shirts in the stores or the Geek Squad—who would help install and wire homes for the modern age.

New stories need to be told in new ways. I would bet that people exist within GM that have fresh, vital visions for the industry and the company, who have tremendous ideas that need not only to be articulated but discussed and tested and measured. The suggestion box approach won't work with such powerful, potentially revolutionary ideas. Admittedly, it's difficult for organizations to break with their pasts to reimagine their futures. Unlearning what you've been taught is even more difficult than learning new ways of doing things. Perhaps that's why few companies have reinvented themselves, especially when the leadership that built the legacy business remains in place, even as that business is being disrupted.

The future comes from the slime.

A less slimy way to make this point is that future innovations and breakthroughs will emerge from those at the bottom, hidden from view. This idea was first popularized by Clayton Christensen in his book *The Innovator's Dilemma*. Nokia, Ericson, BlackBerry, and Sony kept an eye on each other but could not imagine a start-up phone without a keyboard from a computer company called Apple—and how this would change the rules of the game. In industry after industry, upstarts leveraging new platforms help them compete with large companies. The ones lacking a legacy mindset and without huge investment dollars are the ones that are growing.

According to the *Economist*:

> Companies such as Casper, which sells mattresses, Warby Parker, a spectacles brand, and Glossier, a cosmetics firm, were once seen as interesting curiosities. Touting their products online, luring customers with digital advertising and eschewing conventional retailers and marketers, they were anomalies shaking up small segments of retail. In fact, the growth of microbrands—or direct-to-consumer (DTC) brands—represents a profound shift in the consumer-goods sector.[10]

Per Nielsen, the biggest twenty-five food-and-beverage companies generated 45 percent of sales in the category in America but drove only 3 percent of the total growth in the industry between 2011 and 2015. A long tail of twenty thousand companies below the top one hundred produced half of all growth.[11]

These small companies that emerge from the slime use technology to get their stories heard. Their cultures are more transparent and agile than their bigger brethren. Employees are encouraged to take risks, to beta-test ideas, to speak honestly and authentically. They listen harder and more continuously to what their customers are saying; they use technology astutely to obtain customer stories, setting up online forums for idea exchanges and tracking customer behaviors in innovative ways.

The start-ups and upstarts are poised to take over their respective industry worlds, armed with the best technology and using it to meet people's needs.

Limit Exposure to Screens
Like a Responsible Parent

Too much of anything can be a bad thing. New technology is like a big bowl of the best chocolate chip cookies fresh out of the oven—we want to eat every single one of them. Businesses are hungry for new and better technology. They are eager to consume whatever is hot, whatever is promising more delicious data.

Imagine the prototypical tech geek, spending ten hours daily in front of screens, stuffing his face with junk food and obsessively coding, texting, and responding to notifications. As brilliant as this techie might be, he is not someone who is leading a balanced work life. His story is lost to his myopic spreadsheet focus.

Let's switch analogies for a moment. You may be aware of the trend among Silicon Valley parents to restrict their children's use of digital devices. A recent *New York Times* article noted, "The people who are closest to a thing are often the most wary of it. Technologists know how phones really work, and many have decided they don't want their own children anywhere near them. A wariness that has been slowly brewing is turning into a region wide consensus: The benefits of screens as a learning tool are overblown, and the risks for addiction and stunting development seem high. The debate in Silicon Valley now is about how much exposure to phones is O.K."[12]

As much as I believe that the benefits of technology outweigh the negatives, too much screen time increases children's isolation and limits them socially. Similarly, organizations that are too enmeshed in their digital worlds fail to nurture qualities such as empathy, creativity, and agility.

For this reason, they need to limit their own version of screen time. Organizational leaders must continually ask themselves questions such as

- Are we becoming overreliant on the data to read the market and underreliant on people's perceptions and experiences?
- Are we spending too much time communicating via devices and too little time in face-to-face interactions?
- Are we measuring performance primarily based on if people or teams make their numbers—versus the relationships they establish, their ability to inspire others, their provocative and wide-ranging ideas?

These types of questions don't subvert or subordinate machines; they balance them with story. It's a mistake to think that in our increasingly technologically sophisticated future, it's a matter of machines versus people. Instead, we need companies where each maximizes its capabilities. If they do this, they will gain two significant advantages:

COMPETITIVENESS. Without modern technology, a company cannot be competitive. But with only technology most companies cannot differentiate and therefore garner market share. The differences in most companies will come from the layer they add to technology and how they integrate the human and data. These are skills of creativity, innovation, communication, design, and storytelling.

FULFILLMENT. People are happiest when they have a sense of autonomy, mastery, and purpose. While the world is increasingly digital, people at heart remain analog. All of us are stories filled with memories, feelings, and dreams intersecting with other stories, and in the intersection we connect, live, and learn. When technology serves as a boost to these innate expressions and allow us to connect and communicate, we feel like we're doing something meaningful. Identity, purpose, affiliation—these are the outcomes for employees who work in spreadsheet-story balanced companies. People who feel fulfilled work harder, longer, and more creatively—they care, and their caring drives them.

Companies of the Future

The challenge today, and even more so in the years to come, is finding the sweet spot between story and spreadsheet. It's a growing challenge because our technological capabilities continue to increase exponentially. Organizations are enticed by the possibilities of robotics, analytics, and the like. They are enticed because these advances promise greater speed and efficiency, more revenue, and more profit.

The danger for organizations is that they can become astonishingly productive and profitable, but they lose their soul in the process. And companies without soul are places where no one wants to work, and eventually their fabulous productivity and profit will exit along with their best people.

Business leaders need to strive to balance story and spreadsheet continuously and variously as new technology flows into the workplace. It's a significant challenge, but one that can be met. Two companies today provide models for how.

Pixar is a technology company pioneering at the cutting edge of computer animation. It is also known as one of the most compelling and emotional storytelling companies in the world. Almost every one of its dozen-plus movies has been a massive hit that left audiences in rapture about not only what they see on the screen but its emotional impact.[13]

It's not just that Pixar's product balances humanity and technology; its culture also strives for this balance. Cofounder Ed Catmull has noted that Pixar's culture focuses on caring for employees as people, ensures a purpose that people can be proud of, and encourages self-expression and diversity of thought.[14]

In an article in the *Irish Times*, Catmull was asked if technical challenges emerge from the artistic ideas for a film or if films emerge out of new technical capabilities. He said that both were true. "We say, the technology inspires the art, and the art challenges the technology."[15]

Like Pixar, Adobe's policies and culture reflect a blend of human and machine. Adobe began as a technology company selling creativity-related products like Photoshop. Over the past five years, it has transformed itself into a company that sells online subscriptions for a suite of creative, marketing, and document solutions, helping people change the world through digital experiences.[16]

From a product standpoint, Adobe balances data and software with humanity and storytelling. But they don't stop there. This balance is incorporated into every aspect of its culture and marketing. CEO Shantanu Narayen begins each week analyzing real-time data and results in granular data using their own powerful technology. Their depth of data detail on running the company is second to none; they rely on deep data to drive the sale of engaging experiences.[17]

But the company is also a pioneer in an inclusive, open, diverse, and human culture. Narayen has said, "At Adobe, we believe that when people feel respected and included they can be more creative, innovative, and successful. While we have more work to do to advance diversity and inclusion, we're investing to move our company and industry forward. We call this Adobe For All."[18]

Organizations Reflect Society

In the November 18, 2018, *New York Times Magazine*, the cover headline was, "What Will Become of Us? How Technology Is Changing What It Means to Be Human."[19] The articles in the magazine explore topics ranging from

AI to gene editing to data-driven medicine, but the overriding point is that developing technologies will have a huge impact on every aspect of our lives. Articles suggest that AI might serve as a sort of crystal ball enabling us to predict future events, that DNA analysis can determine our chances of being successful human beings.

Yes, technology will change humanity, and it will also change business. Like most change, there's a lot of good and a lot of bad accompanying the evolution. My refrain in this book about balancing the story and the spreadsheet is all about maximizing the good and minimizing the bad. Only by embracing the best of both worlds—the digital one of machines, the analog one of people—can we create and sustain great organizations.

We need to prepare for breakthrough technologies—for AI that allows us to see five years down the road and the new, emerging markets and changing customer preferences. In our enthusiasm to embrace these technologies, we also need to take a step back and think about how they will affect the human elements of our businesses. Then we need to implement programs and policies designed to preserve the human—the creativity, risk-taking, relationship-building, empathy, and so on—that defines us at our best.

If we can do that, the future is ours, and we have no limits on what we can accomplish.

KEY TAKEAWAYS

- Advances in science and technology will improve people's lives, as long as we recognize and manage the accompanying risks and downsides.
- Success in the future will require integrating the story and the spreadsheet, the math and the magic, the analog and the digital.
- In the end, it's people and dreams that matter, and companies must never forget the soul that drives them.

ACKNOWLEDGMENTS

Growing up in India, I was surrounded by books. My parents loved to read, and we always had books everywhere. Once every few weeks on weekends they would take me to the local bookstores and for every book they selected for me (mostly a Penguin Classic in softcover), I would get to choose a more recent bestseller. I still have many of those classics or have bought newer copies of them, but have long forgotten my own selections.

I soon began to write short stories and poems of a sort and my favorite subject was literature. I wanted to be a writer and take courses in doing so but my father dissuaded me, saying I should pursue mathematics. If you love writing, you can always do it, he said, but you will never learn math yourself. The math will help you be more employable, and it will teach you to think. After much drama about me not being allowed to pursue my dreams, I agreed to pursue an advanced degree in math.

My mother consoled me by saying I could keep writing and reading, and one day, who knows?—you may end up writing a book. My younger sister Moeena, who used to listen to my storytelling and to this day bears my yarns and storytelling with a smile, reminds me of this these days as my book gets ready for publication.

This book wouldn't have existed if not for my parents, not only because without them I wouldn't have existed, but because their love of books made me appreciate the power of words, and their insight on the importance of analytic thinking made me appreciate the rigor of math.

While this book is not about advertising or marketing, it is deeply informed by my thirty-seven-year business career in these fields, which aim to achieve business results through the alchemy of data and hard business decisions, fused with storytelling informed by people's desires and dreams.

After graduating from business school, a single company took a chance on an immigrant with a student visa. It was the Leo Burnett Company in Chicago. Thirty-seven years later, as I prepare for a new career as writer, speaker, and advisor I am still in the Leo Burnett building, which has been part of the Publicis Groupe since 2002.

Over the past four decades, as communication technology has changed with the revolution of cable, search engines, social media, and mobile, and the world has become more globalized and people's expectations and behaviors have changed, I've been fortunate to have a front-row seat on how businesses and people adapt to and align with such changes, because of Leo Burnett and Publicis Groupe.

The clients, our partners, and most importantly the talent and management at these companies, have not only provided a career and friendship, but the experience and learning that is contained in this book. Just a few stories of these people made it into the book, but the spirit and generosity of all of them informs every page.

While this book wouldn't have existed without the family I was born into and my Publicis Groupe family, it finds its inspiration in my immediate family. My wife Rekha, who has known me since I was twelve, and our daughters Ria and Rohini, who wondered, when seeing photographs of my younger days, why their astonishingly smart and beautiful mother decided to give me a chance. In fact, they even wonder these days!

For many years I have written a blog and have been encouraged to write a book, but the intensity of work and family didn't allow me to do so. A few years ago, as my long-time bosses retired or evolved their roles, and I completed thirty-five years at Publicis and was getting close to sixty years old, I decided it was time to plan career 2.0.

It was time to attempt to write a book.

I shared my thoughts about future plans with my outgoing boss, Maurice Lévy, and my incoming boss, Arthur Sadoun, and after some discussion they enabled the writing of this book by allowing me to evolve my role and significantly free up a large swath of time necessary to write. The exceptions they made and support and understanding they provided over the past two years has made all the difference.

Bruce Wexler has been instrumental in making this book happen. He helped me write a proposal that got me an agent, who enabled me to get an advance from HarperCollins to write this book. Bruce not only helped with guiding me through the proposal process but then served as a coach and initial editor to help me craft the first draft.

Giles Anderson of Anderson Literary Agency immediately got the idea of the book and agreed to take me on as a client. As my agent he drummed up interest in the proposal from major American publishers for English rights and procured advances for global Mandarin rights from a leading Chinese publisher.

I had been a longtime fan of Ken Auletta, author and writer at *The New Yorker*, and finally got to meet with him three years ago, when he was writing a book about the advertising industry. Ken has been a great advisor and mentor in that he encouraged me to write this book and shared his techniques and volunteered to help me with my first draft. His great enthusiasm for it, as well as some clear advice on improving it, gave me a great deal of inspiration. Ken continued to help by agreeing to write the foreword to this book.

In addition to Ken I shared my first draft with folks who know me well and would not be shrinking violets in giving me critical feedback.

Thanks to Courtney Acuff, Valerie Beauchamp, Jeannie Caggiano, Alok Choudhary, Rebecca Clarkson, Susan Giannino, Tim Harris, Jack Klues, Laura Krajecki, Christian Kugel, Maurice Lévy, Helen Lin, Jeff Marshall, Saneel Radia, Angela Steele, Alex von Plato, and Michael Wiley, who took time to provide detailed notes and feedback that have significantly enhanced and informed this book.

Emmanuel Andre, in addition to his role as the chief talent officer of Publicis Groupe, is an accomplished professional photographer who volunteered his time and talent to take the cover photo.

This book has been sculpted into its final form and birthed into the world by the terrific team at HarperCollins. My two amazing editors, Tim Burgard and Amanda Bauch, who not only are very talented but awfully funny and great to work with. Jeff James, my publisher, who bet on the book and then gave me an opportunity to present it at the company sales conference, and

ACKNOWLEDGMENTS

Hiram Centeno and Sicily Axton, a dynamic duo whose expertise in marketing and publicity I lean on.

I grew up believing books are amazing and magical things. Getting to write one and see how it comes to form has added and not detracted from the magic.

Thank you to all the magicians who made it possible.

NOTES

Chapter 1: Too Much Math, Too Little Meaning

1. Katie Thomas and Charles Ornstein, "Memorial Sloan Kettering's Season of Turmoil," ProPublica, December 31, 2018, https://www.propublica.org/article /memorial-sloan-kettering-season-of-turmoil; Walt Bogdanich and Michael Forsythe, "How McKinsey Lost Its Way in South Africa," *New York Times*, June 26, 2018, https://www.nytimes.com/2018/06/26/world/africa/mckinsey -south-africa-eskom.html; Michael Forsythe and Walt Bogdanich, "McKinsey Advised Purdue Pharma How to 'Turbocharge' Opioid Sales, Lawsuit Says," *New York Times*, February 1, 2019, https://www.nytimes.com/2019/02/01 /business/purdue-pharma-mckinsey-oxycontin-opiods.html.

2. Bernard Marr, "How Much Data Do We Create Every Day? The Mind-Blowing Stats Everyone Should Read," *Forbes*, May 21, 2018, https://www .forbes.com/sites/bernardmarr/2018/05/21/how-much-data-do-we-create-every -day-the-mind-blowing-stats-everyone-should-read/#6d11a7d760ba.

3. Tom Hale, "How Much Data Does the World Generate Every Minute?" IFLScience!, July 26, 2017, https://www.iflscience.com/technology/how-much -data-does-the-world-generate-every-minute/; Mikhal Khoso, "How Much Data Is Produced Every Day?," Northeastern University, May 13, 2016, http://www .northeastern.edu/levelblog/2016/05/13/how-much-data-produced-every-day/.

4. Rani Molla, "2017 Is Already the Biggest Year Ever for Data Center Investment in the U.S.," Vox, September 28, 2017, https://www.recode.net/2017/9/28 /16374640/2017-biggest-year-data-center-investment-energy-cloud-streaming -internet-traffic.

5. Gil Press, "6 Predictions for the $203 Billion Big Data Analytics Market," *Forbes*, January 20, 2017, https://www.forbes.com/sites/gilpress/2017/01/20/6 -predictions-for-the-203-billion-big-data-analytics-market/#7c0229932083.

6. Venus Tamturk, "The ROI of Recommendation Engines," CMSC Media, April 10, 2018, https://www.cms-connected.com/News-Archive/April-2018/The-ROI -of-Recommendation-Engines.

7. Elvis Picardo, "10 of the World's Top Companies Are American," Investopedia, May 30, 2019, https://www.investopedia.com/articles/active-trading/111115/why -all-worlds-top-10-companies-are-american.asp.

8. Mark Twain, *Chapters from My Autobiography* (n.p.: CreateSpace, 2017), 122.

9. Jack Makhlouf, "Your Annual Performance Reviews Are Hurting You (Just Ask Adobe)," ELM Learning, September 21, 2016, https://elmlearning.com /annual-performance-reviews/.

10. Bob Nease, "How Too Much Data Can Hurt Our Productivity and Decision-Making," *Fast Company*, June 16, 2016, https://www.fastcompany.com/3060945 /how-too-much-data-can-hurt-our-productivity-and-decision-making.

11. "How Companies Are Using Big Data and Analytics," McKinsey & Company, April 2016, https://www.mckinsey.com/business-functions/mckinsey-analytics /our-insights/how-companies-are-using-big-data-and-analytics.

12. Thomas Hobbs, "Pepsi's Ad Failure Shows the Importance of Diversity and Market Research," *Marketing Week*, April 7, 2017, https://www.marketingweek .com/2017/04/07/pepsi-scandal-prove-lack-diversity-house-work-flawed/?ct _5ce866d3b5495=5ce866d3b5496.

13. André Burton, "MBUX Voice Assistant: It Understands You Perfectly," *The Daimler-Blog*, December 28, 2018, https://blog.daimler.com/en/2018/12/28 /mbux-voice-assistant-hey-mercedes/.

14. Abhijeet Pratap, "An Analysis of Costco's Organizational Culture and Human Resource Management," Notesmatic, October 8, 2018, https://notesmatic.com /2017/08/an-analysis-of-costcos-organizational-culture-and-human-resource -management/.

15. Patty McCord, "How Netflix Reinvented HR," *Harvard Business Review*, January–February 2014, https://hbr.org/2014/01/how-netflix-reinvented-hr.

16. McCord, "How Netflix Reinvented HR."

17. Ali, "Starbucks—Grinding Data," Digital Initiative, April 5, 2017, https://digit .hbs.org/submission/starbucks-grinding-data/; Michael Boezi, "Starbucks Rewards: An Evolution in Data-Driven Marketing," Control Mouse Media, March 22, 2018, https://controlmousemedia.com/starbucks-rewards-data -driven-marketing/.

18. Larry Fink, "Larry Fink's Chairman's Letter to Shareholders from BlackRock's 2018 Annual Report," BlackRock, January 12, 2018, https://www.blackrock.com

/corporate/investor-relations/larry-fink-chairmans-letter; Andrew Ross Sorkin, "BlackRock's Message: Contibute to Society, or Risk Losing Our Support," *New York Times*, January 15, 2018, https://www.nytimes.com/2018/01/15/business/dealbook/blackrock-laurence-fink-letter.html.

19. Julian Lin, "JPMorgan Chase Cornered the Millennial Credit Card Market," Seeking Alpha, October 20, 2017, https://seekingalpha.com/article/4112664-jpmorgan-chase-cornered-millennial-credit-card-market.

Chapter 2: Managing the Dark Side of Bright Screens

1. William Shakespeare, "There is nothing either good or bad, but thinking makes it so," *Hamlet* 2.2. References are to act and scene.

2. Naveen Narayanan, "The New Workplace Reality Out of the Office," *Wired*, June 2013, https://www.wircd.com/insights/2013/06/the-new-workplace-reality-out-of-the-office/.

3. Cal Newport, "Deep Work," on Newport's website, accessed May 12, 2019, http://calnewport.com/books/deep-work/.

4. Nancy B. Schess, "Then and Now: How Technology Has Changed the Workplace," *Hofstra Labor and Employment Law Journal* 30, no. 2 (2013), https://scholarlycommons.law.hofstra.edu/cgi/viewcontent.cgi?article=1550&context=hlelj.

5. Michael J. Maher, "7L: United American Commercial 1990 'Speech,'" YouTube video, 1:00, posted by Get Referrals, August 16, 2010, https://www.youtube.com/watch?v=mU2rpcAABbA.

6. Jillian D'Onfro, "Steve Jobs Had a Crazy Idea for Pixar's Office to Force People to Talk More," *Business Insider*, March 20, 2015, https://www.businessinsider.com/steve-jobs-designing-pixar-office-2015-3.

7. Debra Bradley Ruder, "The 'Water Cooler' Effect," *Harvard Magazine*, May–June 2011, https://harvardmagazine.com/2011/05/water-cooler-effect.

Chapter 3: The Quest for Meaning in the Modern Workplace

1. Joan Didion, *The White Album* (New York: Farrar, Straus and Giroux, 1990), 11.

2. "The Top 8 Methods for Accurately Measuring Employee Productivity," Universal Class, accessed May 12, 2019, https://www.universalclass.com/articles/business/the-top-8-methods-for-accurately-measuring-employee-productivity.htm.

3. Lauren Sausser, "Most Hospitals Tie Doctor Pay to Productivity; New Research Examines How That Impacts Academic Medicine," *Post and Courier*, October 7, 2017, https://www.postandcourier.com/health/most-hospitals-tie-doctor-pay

-to-productivity-new-research-examines/article_81d2f232-a930-11e7-94c6-fbe
5e3985c3a.html.

4. Kartikay Mehrotra, Laura J. Keller, and Margaret Cronin Fisk, "How Wells
Fargo's Troubles Went from Bad to Worse," *Bloomberg Businessweek*, August 6,
2017, https://www.bloomberg.com/news/articles/2017-08-07/how-wells-fargo-s
-troubles-went-from-bad-to-worse-quicktake-q-a.

5. Jared Diamond, "How the Cubs Mastered the Free-Agent Sales Pitch," *Wall
Street Journal*, March 1, 2018, https://www.wsj.com/articles/how-the-cubs
-mastered-the-free-agent-sales-pitch-1519922402?mod=searchresults&page=1&
pos=1.

6. Rishad Tobaccowala, "8 Management Lessons from a Great Boss," *Re-Inventing
by @Rishad* (blog), July 6, 2013, https://rishadt.wordpress.com/2013/07/06/8
-management-lessons-from-a-great-boss/.

7. *2017 State of the Industry* (Alexandria, VA: ATD Research, 2017), https://www
.td.org/research-reports/2017-state-of-the-industry; David Wentworth, "Top
Spending Trends for Training, 2016–2017," *Training*, November 30, 2016,
https://trainingmag.com/top-spending-trends-training-2016-2017.

8. Andrew Likierman, "The Five Traps of Performance Measurement," *Harvard
Business Review*, October 2009, https://hbr.org/2009/10/the-five-traps-of
-performance-measurement.

9. "Don't Just Survive, *Thrive*! How to Become the Best Possible Version of
Yourself," Gala Darling, accessed May 12, 2019, http://galadarling.com/article
/dont-just-survive-thrive-how-to-become-the-best-possible-version-of-yourself/.

10. Mihaly Csikszentmihalyi, *Flow: The Psychology of Optimal Experience* (New
York: Harper Perennial Modern Classics, 2008), 4.

11. "Why Corporate Social Responsibility Is Important," Double the Donation,
accessed May 13, 2019, https://doublethedonation.com/why-corporate-social
-responsibility-is-important/; Olivia Vande Griek, "6 Ways Corporate Social
Responsibility Benefits Your Employees," Conscious Company Media, August
24, 2017, https://consciouscompanymedia.com/workplace-culture/hr
-innovations/6-ways-corporate-social-responsibility-benefits-employees/.

Chapter 4: Talk about the Turd on the Table

1. Rishad Tobaccowala, "The Turd on the Table," *Re-Inventing by @Rishad* (blog),
August 7, 2012, https://rishadt.wordpress.com/2012/08/07/the-turd-on-the-table/.

2. Sue Shellenbarger, "The Best Ways to Tell the Hard Truth at Work," *Wall Street*

Journal, October 10, 2017, https://www.wsj.com/articles/the-best-ways-to-tell
-the-hard-truth-at-work-1507647758.

3. Lena Roland, "The Renaissance of Marketing and the Decline of Interruptions:
Publicis' Rishad Tobaccowala in Conversation," WARC, March 21, 2018, https://
www.warc.com/newsandopinion/opinion/the_renaissance_of_marketing_and
_the_decline_of_interruptions_publicis_rishad_tobaccowala_in_conversation/2654.

4. Joe Mandese, "Publicis' Tobaccowala: Advertising Will Decline 30% in Next 5
Years," MediaPost, February 2, 2018, https://www.mediapost.com/publications
/article/313938/publicis-tobaccowala-advertising-will-decline-30.html.

5. "Drinking the Kool-Aid," Wikipedia, last updated April 23, 2019, https://en.m
.wikipedia.org/wiki/Drinking_the_Kool-Aid.

6. Rishad Tobaccowala, "The 4, 5 and 6 Letter Words," *Re-Inventing by @Rishad*
(blog), accessed June 22, 2019, https://rishadt.wordpress.com/2018/04/06/the
-4-5-and-6-letter-words/.

7. Kevin Daum, "5 Reasons You Should Speak Up (Even If You Think You
Shouldn't)," *Inc.*, February 28, 2014, https://www.inc.com/kevin-daum/5-reasons
-you-should-speak-up-even-when-you-think-you-shouldnt.html.

8. "Non-Tech Businesses Are Beginning to Use Artificial Intelligence at Scale,"
Economist, March 28, 2018, https://www.economist.com/news/special-report
/21739431-artificial-intelligence-spreading-beyond-technology-sector-big
-consequences; "The Workplace of the Future," *Economist*, March 28, 2018,
https://www.economist.com/leaders/2018/03/28/the-workplace-of-the-future.

9. Plato, *Laches, or Courage, in The Dialogues of Plato*, trans. Benjamin Jowett, 2nd
ed. (Oxford, UK: Clarendon Press, 1875), 1:85.

Chapter 5: Address the Reality That Change Sucks

1. "Transform (verb): 1a: to change in composition or structure; b: to change
the outward form or appearance of; c: to change in character or condition:
convert." "Definition of Transform," Merriam-Webster, accessed May 14, 2019,
https://www.merriam-webster.com/dictionary/transform.

2. John Jones, DeAnne Aquirre, and Matthew Calderone, "10 Principles of Change
Management," *Strategy + Business*, April 15, 2004, https://www.strategy-business
.com/article/rr00006?gko=643d0.

3. Wikipedia, s.v., "Change Management," last updated April 24, 2019, https://en
.wikipedia.org/wiki/Change_management.

4. John L. Bennett and Mary Wayne Bush, *Coaching for Change* (New York:
Routledge, 2013), 8.

5. Mikl Em, "Pace Layers Thinking: Paul Saffo and Stewart Brand @ the Interval," *The Long Now Foundation* (blog), January 27, 2015, http://blog.longnow.org /02015/01/27/stewart-brand-pace-layers-thinking-at-the-interval/.

6. Thomas B. Edsall, "Industrial Revolutions Are Political Wrecking Balls," *New York Times*, May 3, 2018, https://www.nytimes.com/2018/05/03/opinion/trump -industrial-revolutions.html.

7. Peter Miskell, "How Crest Made Business History," Harvard Business School, January 17, 2005, https://hbswk.hbs.edu/archive/how-crest-made-business-history.

8. "Toothpaste Pump Battle Near," *New York Times*, October 11, 1984, https://www .nytimes.com/1984/10/11/business/toothpaste-pump-battle-near.html.

9. Steven Levitt, *Freakonomics: A Rogue Economist Explores the Hidden Side of Everything* (New York: Harper Perennial, 2009).

Chapter 6: Unleash Creativity by Inserting Poetry into the PowerPoint

1. Linda Naiman, "The Intersection of Art and Business," Catalyst Ranch, accessed May 15, 2019, https://www.catalystranchmeetings.com/Thinking-Docs /The-Intersection-of-Art-and-Business.pdf, 2.

2. Daniel Pink, *A Whole New Mind* (New York: Penguin, 2006).

3. Douglas K. Smith and Robert C. Alexander, *Fumbling the Future: How Xerox Invented, Then Ignored, the First Personal Computer* (Lincoln, NE: toExcel, 1999).

4. Quy Huy, "Who Killed Nokia? Nokia Did," Insead Knowledge, September 22, 2015, https://knowledge.insead.edu/strategy/who-killed-nokia-nokia-did-4268.

5. DSchlaegel, "Why Apple Resorts to Self-Cannibalization," Marketing Hog, November 4, 2016, https://marketinghog.com/why-apple-resorts-to-self -cannibalization/; Dan Ostrower, "Netflix Applies Disruptive Innovation to Itself," Altitude, accessed June 22, 2019, https://www.altitudeinc.com/netflix -applies-disruptive-innovation-to-itself/; Kara Sprague, "Reborn in the Cloud," McKinsey Digital, July 2015, https://www.mckinsey.com/business-functions /digital-mckinsey/our-insights/reborn-in-the-cloud.

6. "5 Rules of Storytelling by Jeff Bezos," 234 Finance, August 23, 2017, https:// www.234finance.com/5-rules-of-storytelling-by-jeff-bezos/.

7. Julie Bort, "Amazon CEO Jeff Bezos Explains His Famous One-Character Emails, Known to Strike Fear in Managers' Hearts," *Business Insider*, April 21, 2018, http:// www.businessinsider.com/bezos-explains-his-dreaded-one-character-emails-2018-4.

8. Bradley Gauthier, "Connecting the Dots: How Steve Jobs Changed My Life," *Bradley Gauthier* (blog), accessed May 15, 2019, http://blog.bradleygauthier.com /connecting-the-dots/.

9. Luke Smilie and Anna Antinori, "People with Creative Personalities Really Do See the World Differently," The Conversation, May 28, 2017, http://the conversation.com/people-with-creative-personalities-really-do-see-the-world -differently-77083.

10. Pablo Picasso, *Pablo Picasso: Metamorphoses of the Human Form: Graphic Works, 1895–1972* (New York: Prestel, 2000), quoted on Goodreads, https://www .goodreads.com/quotes/1611-others-have-seen-what-is-and-asked-why-i-have.

11. Sarah L. Kaufman et al., "This Is Your Brain on Art," *Washington Post*, September 18, 2017, https://www.washingtonpost.com/graphics/2017/lifestyle /your-brain-on-art/?utm_term=.96eb569a0d6f.

12. *The 400 Blows*, directed by François Truffuat (Paris: Les Films du Carrosse, 1959).

13. Rebecca Rolfes, "Class, Behave!," *Chicago Booth Magazine*, Spring 2018, https:// www.chicagobooth.edu/magazine/spring-2018/features/class-behave-richard-thaler.

Chapter 7: Recognize That Talent Does Not Work for Companies but Rather Companies Work for Talent

1. Véronique Weill and Rishad Tobaccowala, "The Marcel Mindset: Why Companies Need to Work for Talent," LinkedIn, May 24, 2018, https://www .linkedin.com/pulse/marcel-mindset-why-companies-need-work-talent-rishad -tobaccowala/.

2. Daisuke Wakabayashi, "Google's Shadow Work Force: Temps Who Outnumber Full-Time Employees," *New York Times*, May 28, 2019, https://www.nytimes.com /2019/05/28/technology/google-temp-workers.html.

3. Michael Sheetz, "Technology Killing Off Corporate America: Average Lifespan of Companies Under 20 Years," CNBC, August 24, 2017, https://www.cnbc.com /2017/08/24/technology-killing-off-corporations-average-lifespan-of-company -under-20-years.html.

4. Erin Duffin, "Distribution of Gross Domestic Product (GDP) across Economic Sectors in the United States from 2000 to 2016," Statista, last updated April 29, 2019, https://www.statista.com/statistics/270001/distribution-of-gross-domestic -product-gdp-across-economic-sectors-in-the-us/.

5. Daniel H. Pink, *Drive: The Surprising Truth About What Motivates Us* (New York: Riverhead, 2011), 64.

6. Staff, "Netflix Updates Its Famous Culture Document with Focus on Inclusion and Respect," Gartner *Talent Daily*, June 22, 2017, https://www.cebglobal.com /talentdaily/netflix-updates-its-famous-culture-document-with-focus-on-inclusion -and-respect/.

Chapter 8: Diversify and Deepen Time Usage

1. Peter F. Drucker, "How to Be an Effective Executive," *Nations' Business*, April 1961, 34–35.
2. Wikipedia, s.v., "Time and Motion Study," accessed April 13, 2019, https://en .wikipedia.org/wiki/Time_and_motion_study.
3. Steven Levy, "Jeff Bezos Owns the Web in More Ways Than You Think," *Wired*, November 13, 2011, https://www.wired.com/2011/11/ff_bezos/.
4. Chip Bayers, "The Inner Bezos," *Wired*, March 1, 1999, https://www.wired.com /1999/03/bezos-3/.
5. Robert A. Guth, "In Secret Hideaway, Bill Gates Ponders Microsoft's Future," *Wall Street Journal*, March 28, 2005, https://www.wsj.com/articles/SB11119 6625830690477.
6. "The Eisenhower Box," James Clear, https://jamesclear.com/wp-content/uploads /2014/04/eisenhower-box.jpg.
7. Frankki Bevins and Aaron De Smet, "Making Time Management the Organization's Priority," *McKinsey Quarterly* (January 2013), https://www .mckinsey.com/business-functions/organization/our-insights/making-time -management-the-organizations-priority.
8. Maria Popova, "How We Spend Our Days Is How We Spend Our Lives: Annie Dillard on Choosing Presence over Productivity," Brain Pickings, June 7, 2013, https://www.brainpickings.org/2013/06/07/annie-dillard-the-writing-life-1/.
9. Kat Boogaard, "Take It from Someone Who Hates Productivity Hacks—the Pomodoro Technique Actually Works," The Muse, accessed May 15, 2019, https://www.themuse.com/advice/take-it-from-someone-who-hates-productivity -hacksthe-pomodoro-technique-actually-works.
10. Alan Henry, "Productivity 101: A Primer to the Pomodoro Technique," Life Hacker, July 2, 2014, https://lifehacker.com/productivity-101-a-primer-to-the -pomodoro-technique-1598992730.

Chapter 9: Schedule More Meetings

1. Maya Angelou, "I've Learned That People Will Forget What You Said," quoted on Goodreads, accessed July 30, 2019, https://www.goodreads.com/quotes/5934 -i-ve-learned-that-people-will-forget-what-you-said-people.

Chapter 10: Upgrade Your Mental Operating System

1. Evelyn Lamb, "Review: *Weapons of Math Destruction*," *Scientific American*, August 31, 2016, https://blogs.scientificamerican.com/roots-of-unity/review -weapons-of-math-destruction.

2. Jacob Brogan, "What's the Deal with Algorithms?," *Slate*, February 2, 2016, http://www.slate.com/articles/technology/future_tense/2016/02/what_is_an _algorithm_an_explainer.html.

3. Lee Rainie and Janna Anderson, "Code-Dependent: Pros and Cons of the Algorithm Age," Pew Research Center, February 8, 2017, https://www.pew internet.org/2017/02/08/code-dependent-pros-and-cons-of-the-algorithm-age/.

4. Tristan Harris, "How Technology Hijacks People's Minds: From a Magician and Google's Design Ethicist," Observer, June 1, 2016, https://observer.com /2016/06/how-technology-hijacks-peoples-minds%E2%80%8A-%E2%80%8 Afrom-a-magician-and-googles-design-ethicist/.

5. Wikipedia, s.v., "Architecture," last updated May 4, 2019, https://en.wikipedia.org /wiki/Architecture.

6. Johann Wolfgang von Goethe, *Goethe's Literary Essays* (New York: Harcourt, Brace, 1921), 267.

7. C. Custer, "Jack Ma: 'What I Told My Son About Education," Tech in Asia, May 13, 2015, https://www.techinasia.com/jack-ma-what-told-son-education.

8. Jennifer Mueller, "Most People Are Secretly Threatened by Creativity," *Quartz*, March 13, 2017, https://qz.com/929328/most-people-are-secretly-threatened -by-creativity/. Studies referenced are Markus Baer, "Putting Creativity to Work: The Implementation of Creative Ideas in Organizations," *Academy of Management Journal* 55, no. 5 (2012): 1102–1119, http://apps.olin.wustl.edu/workingpapers /pdf/2012-08-001.pdf; Paola Criscuolo et al., "Evaluating Novelty: The Role of Panels in the Selection of R&D Projects," *Academy of Management Journal* 60, no. 2 (2016), https://doi.org/10.5465/amj.2014.0861; Jennifer Mueller, "Managers Reject Ideas Customers Want," *Harvard Business Review* (July–August 2014), https://hbr.org/2014/07/managers-reject-ideas-customers-want.

9. James Altucher, "Do You Make Fear Decisions or Growth Decisions?," JA, May 12, 2015, https://jamesaltucher.com/2015/12/make-fear-decisions-growth-decision/.

10. Maria Popova, "Fixed vs. Growth: The Two Basic Mindsets That Shape Our Lives," Brain Pickings, January 29, 2014, https://www.brainpickings.org/2014 /01/29/carol-dweck-mindset/.

11. "A Journey of a Thousand Miles Begins with a Single Step," Wikipedia, last updated November 29, 2018, https://en.wikipedia.org/wiki/A_journey_of_a _thousand_miles_begins_with_a_single_step.

12. John Terry, "What Is Continuous Improvement?," Planview, accessed May 16, 2019, https://www.planview.com/resources/articles/what-is-continuous-improvement/.

13. Eric Ries, *The Lean Startup: How Today's Entrepreneurs Use Continuous Innovation to Create Radically Successful Businesses* (New York: Crow Business, 2011).

14. Jason Shen, "Why Practice Actually Makes Perfect: How to Rewire Your Brain for Better Performance," *Life Hacking* (blog), last updated October 15, 2014, https://blog.bufferapp.com/why-practice-actually-makes-perfect-how-to-rewire -your-brain-for-better-performance.

15. Kevin J. Delaney, "Filter Bubbles Are a Serious Problem with News, Says Bill Gates," *Quartz*, February 21, 2017, https://qz.com/913114/bill-gates-says-filter -bubbles-are-a-serious-problem-with-news/.

16. Isabel Thottam, "10 Companies with Awesome Training and Development Programs," Monster, accessed May 17, 2019, https://www.monster.com/career -advice/article/companies-with-awesome-training-development-programs.

Chapter 11: Robots Compute. People Dream.

1. Mohamed Zairi and Yaser Jarrar, *Impact of Organisational Values on Business Performance* (Bradford, UK: European Center for Total Quality Management, 2000), http://yasarjarrar.com/wp-content/uploads/2012/07/Impact-of -Organisational-Values-on-Business-Performance_Report_2000.pdf.

2. Michael F. Steger, Bryan J. Dik, and Ryan D. Duffy, "Measuring Meaningful Work: The Work and Meaning Inventory (WAMI)," *Journal of Career Assessment* (2012), http://www.michaelfsteger.com/wp-content/uploads/2012/08/Steger-Dik -Duffy-JCA-in-press.pdf; Michael F. Steger, "The Work and Meaning Inventory," Laboratory for the Study of Meaning and Quality of Life, accessed May 17, 2019, http://www.michaelfsteger.com/wp-content/uploads/2012/08/WAMI.pdf.

3. Tony Schwartz, "The Twelve Attributes of a Truly Great Place to Work," *Harvard Business Review*, September 19, 2011, https://hbr.org/2011/09/the-twelve -attributes-of-a-tru.html.

4. "Most U.S. Workers Not Fully Engaged, Struggling to Cope with Tough Workplace Situations, Towers Watson's Global Workforce Study Finds," Willis Towers Watson, July 11, 2012, https://www.towerswatson.com/en/Press/2012 /07/Most-US-Workers-Not-Fully-Engaged-Struggling-to-Cope-with-Tough -Workplace-Situations-Towers-Watson.

5. Janice Deringer, "Business Culture: Why Core Values Matter," *OneBite* (blog), November 3, 2016, https://onebiteblog.com/business-culture-why-core-values-matter/.

6. "There Will Be Little Privacy in the Workplace of the Future," *Economist*, March 28, 2018, https://www.economist.com/special-report/2018/03/28/there -will-be-little-privacy-in-the-workplace-of-the-future.

7. Paul Zak, "Measurement Myopia," Drucker Institute, July 4, 2013, https://www .drucker.institute/thedx/measurement-myopia/.

8. "Not Everything That Counts Can Be Counted," Quote Investigator, May 26, 2010, https://quoteinvestigator.com/2010/05/26/everything-counts-einstein/.

9. William Bruce Cameron, *Informal Sociology: A Casual Introduction to Sociological Thinking* (New York: Random House, 1963), 13.

10. Taylor Sober, "Starbucks Is a Tech Company: Why the Coffee Giant Is Heavily Investing in Digital Innovation," GeekWire, July 31, 2017, https://www.geekwire.com/2017/starbucks-tech-company-coffee-giant-investing-heavily-digital-innovation/; Bernard Marr, "Starbucks: Using Big Data, Analytics and Artificial Intelligence to Boost Performance," *Forbes*, May 28, 2018, https://www.forbes.com/sites/bernardmarr/2018/05/28/starbucks-using-big-data-analytics-and-artificial-intelligence-to-boost-performance/.

11. Alex Eule, "Starbucks Teaches Silicon Valley a Lesson in Tech," *Barron's*, August 19, 2017, https://www.barrons.com/articles/starbucks-teaches-silicon-valley-a-lesson-in-tech-1503115292.

12. Alex Horton, "Starbucks CEO Apologizes after Employee Calls Police on Black Men Waiting at a Table," *Washington Post*, April 15, 2018, https://www.washingtonpost.com/news/business/wp/2018/04/14/starbucks-apologizes-after-employee-calls-police-on-black-men-waiting-at-a-table/.

13. Taylor Soper, "Business Advice from Howard Schultz: The 'Humanity' of a Company Will Create Long-Term Value," GeekWire, September 14, 2018, https://www.geekwire.com/2018/business-advice-howard-schultz-humanity-company-will-create-long-term-value/.

14. Denise Lee Yohn, "How to Fix the United Airlines' Culture Problem," *Forbes*, March 28, 2018, https://www.forbes.com/sites/deniselyohn/2018/03/28/how-to-fix-united-airlines-culture-problem/.

15. Kirstin Robertson, "Southwest Airlines Reveals 5 Culture Lessons," *Culture University* (blog), May 29, 2018, https://www.humansynergistics.com/blog/culture-university/details/culture-university/2018/05/29/southwest-airlines-reveals-5-culture-lessons.

16. Samuel Stebbins et al., "Bad Reputation: America's Top 20 Most-Hated Companies," *USA Today*, February 1, 2018, https://www.usatoday.com/story/money/business/2018/02/01/bad-reputation-americas-top-20-most-hated-companies/1058718001/.

17. Michelle Pannor Silver, *Retirement and Its Discontents* (New York: Columbia University Press, 2018), https://cup.columbia.edu/book/retirement-and-its-discontents/9780231188562.

18. Lori Goler et al., "The 3 Things Employees Really Want: Career, Community,

and Cause," *Harvard Business Review*, February 20, 2018, https://hbr.org/2018
/02/people-want-3-things-from-work-but-most-companies-are-built-around
-only-one.

19. Goler et al., "3 Things Employees Really Want."

20. Don DeLillo, *Underworld* (New York: Simon & Schuster, 2007), 63.

21. Craig Smith, "25 Amazing WeWork Statistics and Facts (2019)," DMR, May
11, 2019, https://expandedramblings.com/index.php/wework-statistics/;
"Newsroom," WeWork, accessed May 17, 2019, https://www.wework.com
/newsroom; "3 Benefits of Freelancing at a Co-Working Hub," Invoice Ninja,
accessed May 15, 2019, https://www.invoiceninja.com/3-benefits-of-freelancing
-at-a-co-working-hub/.

22. Isobel Asher Hamilton, "Jeff Bezos Explains Why His Best Decisions Were
Based Off Intuition, Not Analysis," *Inc.*, September 14, 2018, https://www.inc
.com/business-insider/amazon-ceo-jeff-bezos-says-his-best-decision-were-made
-when-he-followed-his-gut.html.

23. Carmine Gallo, "Jeff Bezos Banned PowerPoint in Meetings. His Replacement
Is Brilliant," *Inc.*, April 25, 2018, https://www.inc.com/carmine-gallo/jeff-bezos
-bans-powerpoint-in-meetings-his-replacement-is-brilliant.html.

24. Claire Cain Miller and Catherine Rampell, "Yahoo Orders Home Workers
Back to the Office," *New York Times*, February 25, 2013, https://www.nytimes
.com/2013/02/26/technology/yahoo-orders-home-workers-back-to-the-office
.html.

25. Agustin Chevez and DJ Huppatz, "The Rise of the Corporate Campus," The
Conversation, September 25, 2017, http://theconversation.com/the-rise-of-the
-corporate-campus-84370.

26. Charles Ornstein and Katie Thomas, "Sloan Kettering's Cozy Deal with
Start-Up Ignites a New Uproar," *New York Times*, September 20, 2018, https://
www.nytimes.com/2018/09/20/health/memorial-sloan-kettering-cancer-paige
-ai.html.

27. Adrian Swinscoe, "The Implosion of Trust and What to Do About It," *Forbes*,
January 28, 2017, https://www.forbes.com/sites/adrianswinscoe/2017/01/28
/the-implosion-of-trust-and-what-to-do-about-it/#73b45f7b7851.

Chapter 12: How to Lead with Soul

1. Carol Stephenson, "How Leadership Has Changed," *Ivey Business Journal* (July–
August 2011), https://iveybusinessjournal.com/publication/how-leadership-has
-changed/; Bill George, "The New 21st Century Leaders," *Harvard Business*

Review, April 30, 2010, https://hbr.org/2010/04/the-new-21st-century-leaders-1 .html.

2. Janet Adamy, "Gen Z Is Coming to Your Office. Get Ready to Adapt," *Wall Street Journal*, September 6, 2018, https://www.wsj.com/graphics/genz-is -coming-to-your-office/.

3. Brené Brown, *The Power of Vulnerability: Teachings on Authenticity, Connection, and Courage* (Louisville, CO: Sounds True, 2013).

4. Leo Tolstoy, *Anna Karenina* (n.p.: Xist, 2016), pt. 1, chap. 1.

5. "Top 10 Signs of a Bad Boss and How to Avoid Them," *6Q Blog*, accessed May 17, 2019, https://inside.6q.io/top-10-signs-of-a-bad-boss/.

6. "Jeff Bezos' Decision-Making Secrets (and How They Impact Your Time Management)," Club of United Business, February 21, 2018, https://cub.club /blog/jeff-bezos-decision-making-secrets-and-how-they-impact-your-time -management/.

7. Suzanne Kapner, Rachael Levy, and Juliet Chung, "Edward Lampert, the Hedge-Fund Star Who Bet on Sears, Is Unrepentant," *Wall Street Journal*, October 17, 2018, https://www.wsj.com/articles/edward-lampert-the-hedge -fund-star-who-bet-on-sears-is-unrepentant-1539796363.

8. James B. Stewart, "Sears's Edward Lampert Was a Wizard. Now He's Coming to Terms with Failure," *New York Times*, October 18, 2018, https://www .nytimes.com/2018/10/18/business/sears-edward-lampert-bankruptcy.html.

Conclusion: Thriving in the Third Connected Age

1. Rishad Tobaccowala, "CES 2017: The Dawn of the Third Connected Era, Media Post, January 11, 2017, https://www.mediapost.com/publications/article /292678/ces-2017-the-dawn-of-the-third-connected-era.html; Rishad Tobaccowala, "CES 2018: A SEA of Change in the Third Connected Era," *Re-Inventing by @Rishad* (blog), January 15, 2018, https://rishadt.wordpress.com /2018/01/15/ces-2018-sea-of-change-in-the-third-connected-era/.

2. James Manyika et al., "Jobs Lost, Jobs Gained: What the Future of Work Will Mean for Jobs, Skills, and Wages," McKinsey & Company, November 2017, https://www.mckinsey.com/featured-insights/future-of-work/jobs-lost-jobs -gained-what-the-future-of-work-will-mean-for-jobs-skills-and-wages.

3. Joshua Bateman, "Why China Is Spending Billions to Develop an Army of Robots to Turbocharge Its Economy," CNBC News, June 29, 2018, https://www .cnbc.com/2018/06/22/chinas-developing-an-army-of-robots-to-reboot-its -economy.html.

4. Erin Winick, "Amazon's Automation Goes White Collar," *MIT Technology Review,* June 13, 2018, https://www.technologyreview.com/the-download/611461 /amazons-automation-goes-white-collar/.

5. Atul Gawande, "Why Doctors Hate Their Computers," *New Yorker,* November 8, 2018, https://www.newyorker.com/magazine/2018/11/12/why-doctors-hate -their-computers.

6. Steve Levitt, *Freakonomics: A Rogue Economist Explores the Hidden Side of Everything* (New York: Harper Perennial, 2009).

7. Nellie Bowles, "Tech C.E.O.s Are in Love with Their Principal Doomsayer," *New York Times,* November 9, 2018, https://www.nytimes.com/2018/11/09 /business/yuval-noah-harari-silicon-valley.html.

8. Yuval Noah Harari, *21 Lessons for the 21st Century* (New York: Sipgel & Grau, 2018), 318.

9. Chris Perry, "Mary Meeker's 2012 Trends Take-Away: Get Ready to Re-Imagine Business," *Forbes,* June 1, 2012, https://www.forbes.com/sites/chrisperry/2012 /06/01/mary-meekers-2012-trends-take-away-get-ready-to-re-imagine-business /#36f0d1845d0b.

10. "The Growth of Microbrands Threatens Consumer-Goods Giants," *Economist,* November 8, 2018, https://www.economist.com/business/2018/11/08/the-growth -of-microbrands-threatens-consumer-goods-giants.

11. Elaine Watson, "Nielsen Unveils 2016 Breakthrough Innovation Winners: There Will Be More Change in CPG in the Next Five Years Than There Was in the Last 50," Food Navigator, June 29, 2016, https://www.foodnavigator-usa.com/Article /2016/06/29/Nielsen-unveils-2016-CPG-breakthrough-innovation-report#.

12. Nellie Bowles, "A Dark Consensus About Screens and Kids Begins to Emerge in Silicon Valley," *New York Times,* October 26, 2018, https://www.nytimes.com /2018/10/26/style/phones-children-silicon-valley.html.

13. Bria G. Peters, "6 Rules of Great Storytelling (as Told by Pixar)," *Medium,* May 21, 2018, https://medium.com/@Brian_G_Peters/6-rules-of-great-storytelling -as-told-by-pixar-fcc6ae225f50.

14. Michael Lee Stallard, "3 Ways Pixar Gains Competitive Advantage from Its Culture," *Michael Lee Stallard* (blog), May 23, 2014, http://www.michael leestallard.com/3-ways-pixar-gains-competitive-advantage-culture.

15. Karlin Lillington, "Marriage of Artists and Technologists Drives Pixar's Success," *Irish Times,* December 3, 2015, https://www.irishtimes.com/business /marriage-of-artists-and-technologists-drives-pixar-s-success-1.2451955.

16. Rachel Metz, "Adobe Bets That AI Tools Can Foster Real Creativity," *MIT*

Technology Review, March 26, 2018, https://www.technologyreview.com/s/610625/adobe-bets-that-ai-tools-can-foster-real-creativity/.

17. "Why Adobe?" Adobe, accessed May 18, 2019, https://www.adobe.com/careers/why-adobe.html.

18. Adobe, "Diversity and Inclusion," Adobe website, accessed May 18, 2019, https://www.adobe.com/diversity.html.

19. *New York Times Magazine* (@NYTmag), "THIS WEEK'S COVER: Technology is changing what it means to be human. What will become of us?," Twitter, November 14, 2018, 7:52 a.m., https://twitter.com/nytmag/status/1062735017422532609.

INDEX

INDEX

ABOUT THE AUTHOR

Rishad Tobaccowala most recently was the chief growth officer at Publicis Groupe, an advertising and communications firm whose 80,000 employees worldwide are dedicated to delivering marketing and business transformation. For his pioneering innovation, *Businessweek* named Tobaccowala as a top business leader. He regularly presents keynotes at industry conferences and speaks at well-known global organizations, including Bank of America, Walmart, Google, and Facebook.